Beginning LEGO
MINDSTORMS EV3

Mark Rollins

Apress®

Beginning LEGO MINDSTORMS EV3

ISBN-13 (pbk): 978-1-4302-6436-1

ISBN-13 (electronic): 978-1-4302-6437-8

President and Publisher: Paul Manning
Lead Editor: Michelle Lowman
Developmental Editor: Matthew Moodie
Technical Reviewer: Mannie Lowe and Christopher Smith
Editorial Board: Steve Anglin, Mark Beckner, Ewan Buckingham, Gary Cornell, Louise Corrigan, Jim DeWolf, Jonathan Gennick, Jonathan Hassell, Robert Hutchinson, Michelle Lowman, James Markham, Matthew Moodie, Jeff Olson, Jeffrey Pepper, Douglas Pundick, Ben Renow-Clarke, Dominic Shakeshaft, Gwenan Spearing, Matt Wade, Steve Weiss
Coordinating Editor: Jill Balzano
Copy Editor: Lori Cavanaugh
Compositor: SPi Global
Indexer: SPi Global
Artist: SPi Global
Cover Designer: Anna Ishchenko

Distributed to the book trade worldwide by Springer Science+Business Media New York, 233 Spring Street, 6th Floor, New York, NY 10013. Phone 1-800-SPRINGER, fax (201) 348-4505, e-mail orders-ny@springer-sbm.com, or visit www.springeronline.com. Apress Media, LLC is a California LLC and the sole member (owner) is Springer Science + Business Media Finance Inc (SSBM Finance Inc). SSBM Finance Inc is a Delaware corporation.

For information on translations, please e-mail rights@apress.com, or visit www.apress.com.

Apress and friends of ED books may be purchased in bulk for academic, corporate, or promotional use. eBook versions and licenses are also available for most titles. For more information, reference our Special Bulk Sales–eBook Licensing web page at www.apress.com/bulk-sales.

Any source code or other supplementary material referenced by the author in this text is available to readers at www.apress.com. For detailed information about how to locate your book's source code, go to www.apress.com/source-code/.

Contents at a Glance

Contents

About the Author

Mark Rollins was born in Seattle in 1971, and attended Washington State University in Pullman, Washington. After four years, he graduated in 1994 with a degree in English. After college, he began to write skits for college-age groups.

After four years working for Wal-Mart, and another five years working for Schweitzer Engineering Laboratories (SEL), Mark decided to pursue a full-time career in writing, beginning in 2005.

Since then, he has written for many tech and gadget blogs including screenhead.com, image-acquire.com, cybertheater.com, mobilewhack.com, carbuyersnotebook.com, gearlive.com, zmogo.com, gadgetell.com, gadgets-weblog.com, androidedge.com, and coolest-gadgets.com. He has also written for video game blogs such as gamertell.com and digitalbattle.com.

In 2009, Mark decided to create his own tech and gadget blog known as www.TheGeekChurch.com. The purpose of the blog was to report on the latest in technology, as well as inform the church-going crowd (who are often not very technically adept) on the benefits of using more technology in the ministry. Since 2012, Mark has completely devoted his time to this blog, and considers it his ministry and mission.

Recently, Mark has become a Tech consultant, offering his years of experience in technology to Consumer Electronics companies.

Mark currently resides in Pullman, Washington with his wife and three children.

About the Technical Reviewer

Mannie Lowe is currently the *FIRST* Program Manager for the Center for Mathematics and Science Education at the University of Mississippi. He is responsible for the *FIRST* Tech Challenge (FTC) program for Mississippi after doing the same thing in Georgia previously. Mannie has helped grow FTC in Mississippi from four teams to more than 40 in just two years. Mannie is a firm believer in the mission of *FIRST* and how it can impact students to achieve a better way of life. He has coached and mentored several FTC, *FIRST* Robotics Competition (FRC), and FIRST LEGO League (FLL) teams to award-winning seasons as well as serving as a resource to many other coaches and mentors throughout the country.

Mannie is co-author of *Winning LEGO MINDSTORMS Programming* with James Trobaugh and is currently working on a book about the *FIRST* Tech Challenge.

Acknowledgments

I would like to thank Jill Balzano and Mark Powers, who helped with the editing of this book.

I also want to thank Trisha McDonell, who was able to provide the EV3 kits and programming kits that I needed to write this book.

Introduction

Have you ever looked at some new toy and thought: "I wish this had been around when I was a kid?" LEGO MINDSTORMS are that to me, and much more. As someone who has been playing with LEGO since the first grade, I would have gladly made programmable LEGO blocks my new favorite toy if they had come out in the early 1980s.

In case you haven't figured it out, I am one of those guys that never really stopped playing with LEGO. I realize that there are a lot like me out there, but hopefully you understand that I don't greet someone I have never met before with this fact about myself right away. If you think that adults that play with LEGO are people who need to grow up, then you should take a look at what they can create.

That's all I will say about that. I believe that the motivation to play with LEGO at any age comes from a desire to create. Considering most of us don't have the budget or materials to build an automobile in our backyard, it is comforting to know that LEGO has given us the capacity to construct a mechanical marvel in our own living room, on a smaller scale.

Why a book on LEGO MINDSTORMS EV3

The LEGO MINDSTORMS collection, first introduced in 1998, is one of LEGO's top best-selling sets/series. The reason for its success is the same as the reason for LEGO's success before its release: the chance to kick your creativity up a notch.

If you are like most avid LEGO enthusiasts, you don't just purchase a LEGO set, build what is on the instructions, and consider yourself done. If anything, you see the set as something to add to your collection. I'm not talking about a room with shelves full of completed LEGO sets/models; I am talking about several boxes of LEGO pieces, with a creator who is waiting for a brand new idea.

LEGO used to advertise in its catalog that just one set was capable of building all kinds of toys. Merging sets creates infinite possibilities of creations. LEGO began offering special types of bricks so that creators could make their creations automated, but even the later types of automated bricks (such as the Technic Power Functions) were still rather limited with what you could do.

The problem is that LEGO Power Functions are all stop or go. For example, you can make a LEGO car that could ride across the floor, but it could only go at one speed and then stop. You could even take control of it and make it steer, but this also has limitations. Depending on what method of steering you use, you sometimes have to deliberately jam the motors in order to make it work.

LEGO MINDSTORMS takes automation a step further by making these programmable parts. With MINDSTORMS, you can make a model car go at different speeds, stop where you want it to, and turn where you want, all with a simple program. In short, the MINDSTORMS series turned what was once a mere electronic toy for amusement and turned them into programmable machines.

In this book, you will learn how to make many machines. As someone who has written two books about LEGO Technic, *Practical LEGO Technics* and *LEGO Technic Robotics*, I can teach you how to build vehicles like cars as well as other robotic machines. I will also teach you how to program these creations.

The History of LEGO MINDSTORMS

In order to understand LEGO MINDSTORMS, one should know the history of these technical LEGO creations.

By 1984, LEGO was already a household name, thanks to its unique blocks whose success can be seen by their number of imitators. In October of 1984, then president and CEO of LEGO, Kjeld Kirk Kristiansen, saw a television broadcast of children using Seymour Papert's LOGO programming language to make robot turtles. Fascinated with the idea of programmable LEGO toys, Kristiansen sent a team to the MIT Media Lab in Boston.

Two years later, in 1986, both LEGO Education and MIT produces LEGO TC LOGO, which allows users to control models built from LEGO pieces. They create a special version of the LOGO computer language to program the software. As for the hardware, it uses an interface box to send signals to LEGO motors and receive information from sensors. In that same year, the product development department, LEGO Futura Boston Branch, works with the MIT Media Lab to create the first working prototype of a programmable brick.

The first MINDSTORMS kit did not arrive to the market until 1998. You might be wondering why it took so long (12 years) from the concept of a programmable brick to an actual product. This was because fewer homes had PCs back in 1986, and the price of the electrical components was high. With the advent of the Internet and computers being a requirement for most homes, the time was finally at hand for the first MINDSTORMS kit to hit the market.

The 1998 Kit introduced LEGO users to the RCX, a LEGO microcomputer that was the heart of the first MINDSTORMS system.

The RCX code ran on Microsoft Windows (and eventually on Mac) and had ROBOLAB, LEGO MINDSTORMS for schools, based on software from National Instruments LabVIEW, developed by Professor Chris Rogers of Tufts University.

One year later, in 1999, the LEGO Group partners with FIRST (For Inspiration and Recognition of Science and Technology) in order to create on the LEGO League. The LEGO League still goes strong until this day, and maintains its goals of inspiring young people's interests in science and technology through engaging, hands-on, and minds-on experiences. Every year there are tournaments with different challenges, and LEGO MINDSTORMS are used to overcome those challenges.

The success of the first generation of LEGO MINDSTORMS eventually leads to version 2, released in 2006. This LEGO MINDSTORMS: NXT has new and improved software, wireless Bluetooth technology, expanded sensor capabilities, and more challenges to encourage its users, especially the young ones, to create original ideas.

The software with NXT is also powered by National Instruments LabVIEW, but this program is very visual, with icons representing different commands that a robot can perform.

The NXT 2.0 sets are also a hit, and Carnegie Mellon creates 18-week curriculums for it, with an emphasis on programming basics as well as STEM (Science, Technology, Engineering, and Math).

In 2013, LEGO MINDSTORMS unveils the EV3, or third generation (the EV3 stands for "evolution"). With the new version comes a more intelligent brick, new motors and sensors, and an improved icon-based programming.

Books from Apress about LEGO MINDSTORMS

Since LEGO MINDSTORMS was such a hit, there is no shortage of books from this publishing house. I wanted to take some time to point them out, as I believe they will come in handy to the LEGO MINDSTORMS creator who is in need of a few new innovations, or simply to compare the older versions of the programming language with the new.

- *Extreme MINDSTORMS An Advanced Guide to LEGO MINDSTORMS* By Michael Gasperi, Ralph Hempel, Luis Villa, Dave Baum (Apress 2000). This is a book on how to build projects for MINDSTORMS version 1. I have no idea how well it will work with EV3 models.

- *Dave Baum's Definitive Guide To LEGO MINDSTORMS 2nd Edition* By Dave Baum (Apress 2002). This is another book that deals with the first version of MINDSTORMS, but it might give you ideas for future MINDSTORMS EV3 projects.

- *Competitive MINDSTORMS A Complete Guide to Robotic Sumo using LEGO MINDSTORMS* By David J. Perdue (Apress 2004). This book was written back when BattleBots was popular, and it shows how to build robots with LEGO MINDSTORMS version 1.

- *Advanced NXT The Da Vinci Inventions Book* By Matthias Paul Scholz (Apress 2007). Even though this book is made for NXT era, it is quite creative as it shows how to make some of Leonardo Da Vinci's greatest inventions with MINDSTORMS pieces.

- *Creating Cool MINDSTORMS NXT Robots* By Daniele Benedettelli (Apress 2008). The world's most respected NXT robot builders shows how to build and program robots from scratch.

- *LEGO MINDSTORMS NXT The Mayan Adventure* By James Floyd Kelly (Apress 2009). This is another book with some serious robotics NXT 2.0 challenges as well as an engaging adventure. You'll learn how to program robotics to solve adventures, and it might be able to use EV3 products.

- *Extreme NXT: Extending the LEGO MINDSTORMS NXT to the Next Level, Second Edition* By Michael Gasperi and Philippe Hurbain (Apress 2009). This book really breaks MINDSTORMS out of the box with about 45 projects with easy-to-follow, step-by-step directions. These might be able to be ported to EV3.

- *LEGO MINDSTORMS NXT 2.0 The King's Treasure* By James Floyd Kelly (Apress 2009). This is another book with some serious robotics NXT 2.0 challenges as well as an engaging adventure. You'll learn how to program robotics to solve adventures, and it might be able to be used on EV3 products.

- *Winning Design: LEGO MINDSTORMS NXT Design Patterns for Fun and Competition* by James Jeffrey Trobaugh (Apress 2010) This book is written by an experienced coach and leader for the FIRST LEGO League, and he uses his experience in design techniques to show how to create some excellent models with LEGO MINDSTORMS. He also shows how to make the model run and how to navigate it using NXT sensors. There are a lot of things in this book that can easily apply to EV3.

- *Winning LEGO MINDSTORMS Programming* by James J. Trobaugh and Mannie Lowe (Apress 2010)This book focuses on NXT-G, the programming language of MINDSTORMS 2.0. Even though EV3 uses an entirely different programming language, you should not ignore the basic concepts laid down in this book as it deals with programming tips and tricks, code management, and other relevant programming information.

- *LEGO MINDSTORMS NXT-G Programming Guide 2nd Edition* By James Floyd Kelly (Apress 2010) This is another guide to LEGO MINDSTORMS NXT 2.0, intended to cover all of the features and parts.

- *LEGO MINDSTORMS NXT: Mars Base Command* By James Floyd Kelly (Apress 2011) There is a lot of creativity in James Floyd Kelly's book, including eight challenges for MINDSTORMS teams to complete. It reads like a science-fiction novel at the beginning, and they might work for EV3 projects.

How to Use this Book

This book is constructed in such a way so that it is pretty step-by-step structure. You will note that I begin with a basic assumption that you may not know anything about EV3, or LEGO MINDSTORMS at all. The models in this book range from basic to advanced, so you might not want to skim over sections too much.

1. What's New with MINDSTORMS EV3. Before we start building, I will discuss the new bricks added to the EV3 collection, as well as the basic Technic pieces you will need to create advanced models.

2. Programming with the EV3 Language. Programming the EV3 Brick, the microcomputer for the LEGO MINDSTORMS EV3, is as important as building a LEGO MINDSTORMS creation. This chapter lays the foundation for programming in EV3, and will continue in later chapters.

3. Creating a LEGO MINDSTORMS Vehicle. This chapter is about creating a vehicle that you can move and can steer, and will follow exactly what you want it to. It will detail how to program the motors and sensors to operate as your programming commands.

4. Creating Sight, Sound, and other Data on the EV3 Brick. In addition to being able to take controlling motors and sensors, the EV3 Brick allows for creating graphics on the display, making sounds, and even controlling the status light.

5. Data Logging and Advanced Programming Bricks. In addition to being able to program the EV3 Brick, you can also analyze data captured by the motors and sensors, and graph the results. This chapter shows how to set up the EV3 Brick for this.

6. Special Construction Projects and Macros. This chapter will show you how to create vehicles like forklifts, cranes, scissorlifts, and other types of vehicles found on a construction site.

7. The LEGO MINDSTORMS EV3 Robot Arm. This chapter describes how to create a robotic arm that will flex, grip, and work like a real arm.

8. Thinking like a LEGO MINDSTORMS Creator and the Walking Robot. This is the answer to a problem that baffled me for years: how to make a creation walk. I also give some advice on how to build further LEGO MINDSTORMS projects.

■ ■ ■

CHAPTER 1

What's New with LEGO MINDSTORMS EV3

It is always difficult to determine what audience this book will find its hands in, and I am going to assume that most readers have at least heard of LEGO MINDSTORMS. LEGO offers many instructions with their LEGO MINDSTORMS kits, but this book is really about how to get the most out of LEGO MINDSTORMS. In short, my desire is that you use the concepts and precepts in this book to make just about anything with LEGO MINDSTORMS EV3 parts.

Since EV3 is the new version, I'm going to structure this book as if EV3 was the first, and not even address aspects of versions 1 and 2, such as programming, parts, and so forth unless it becomes absolutely necessary. Yes, we are wiping the slate clean, which means that those new to LEGO MINDSTORMS and those who built with previous versions are now on an equal playing field. Of course, this means that you will need to get started in some manner.

Getting Started with LEGO MINDSTORMS EV3

I'm going to assume that you probably have purchased some kind of LEGO MINDSTORMS EV3 set. If you go to the LEGO main website and click on "Products", you will find Set 31313, a set that was made for the holiday season of 2013. This set is good for an introductory user, and contains many of the sensors and motors that will be discussed in this section.

Much of what I discuss in this book can be constructed from the EV3 Core Set (45544), the EV3 Expansion Set (45560), and the EV3 Software. The Core Set comes with several Lego pieces as well as the EV3 Brick and all the sensors and motors that I will list below. The Expansion Set comes with a lot more Lego pieces, but assumes that you already have the intelligent EV3 pieces. The EV3 Software package is excellent for programming Lego EV3 projects, and we will go into more detail on it in Chapter 2.

The New Sensors and Motors of EV3

The previously mentioned sets contain numerous Technic LEGO pieces. I will discuss the non-motorized ones later. For now, I want to address the sensors and motors that you will discover while working with EV3. The number that you see after the heading in parenthesis is the Element Number, which is a system that LEGO uses to catalog their pieces.

The EV3 Brick (6009996)

This particular brick is the computerized and interactive brick. There is an iteration of it in every LEGO MINDSTORMS version, and this is what the LEGO team spent years of research to attain: the programmable brick. Think of this brick as the "brain" of your creation. You will tell this brick what to do through the programming language of EV3, and it will carry out its specific functions, provided you programmed it correctly. Note the clause at the end of that last sentence, as you will discover that many of your LEGO MINDSTORMS creations will not work because you didn't get the programming right.

I will cover how to program this EV3 Brick in Chapter 2. For now, I want you to get to know it. Figure 1-1 shows various views of the EV3 Brick, and there are several things worth noting.

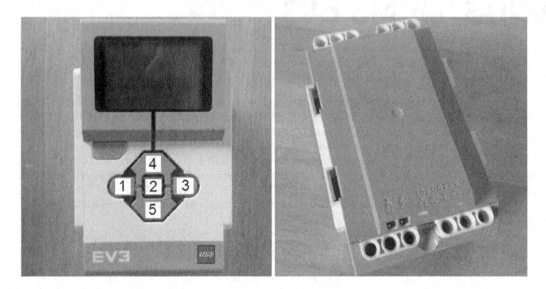

Figure 1-1. *Front and back views of the EV3 Brick. The back is the 10V battery*

You can see on the front is the screen. If it were turned on, you will see a basic menu screen with four tabs. I will discuss what these tabs do in the next chapter on programming. Sadly, this screen is not a touchscreen (maybe next version), but control is possible with the buttons below it.

As you will soon discover, the buttons in the north, west, south, and east positions are the controls for up, left, down, and right, respectively. The key in the center works as an "enter" key, and the key directly under the left side of the screen is the "back" button. If you have the EV3 Brick, then you have noticed that the buttons are not numbered as shown in Figure 1-1. These numbers will become more important in later chapters, such as Chapters 2 and 3.

I'll go ahead and say something quickly about the rechargeable battery pack (6012820), shown on the right side of Figure 1-1. It comes with the Core Set and takes the place of 6 AA batteries, which have been known to lose their juice in a hurry. The battery pack is very easy to install and can charge via AC outlet with the included cord.

You will notice on the "north" and "south" sides of this brick are four ports on each side. These will become very useful in creations as you will use cables of various lengths to connect to other special bricks that we will discuss later (see Figure 1-2).

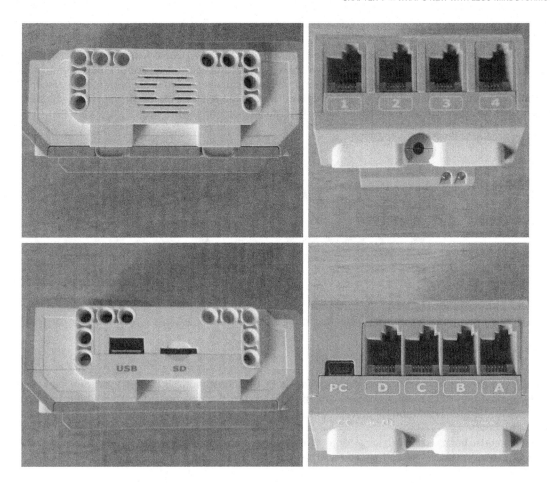

Figure 1-2. *The other sides of the EV3 Brick*

These ports have specific purposes which I will describe in the next chapter. For now, I'll summarize it by saying that input ports 1-4, located on the north side, are used to connect the sensors, while the output ports labeled A-D, located on the south side, are made for the motors. You will notice that every motor and sensor has a port on it, and you are meant to use connector cables to attach it to these inputs.

You will also notice that there is a (micro) USB port labeled "PC". In the Core Set, you will get a USB cable that you can connect to this. The USB Cable then attaches to your computer, which allows you to program the EV3 Brick from your PC or Mac. Unfortunately, the set-up kit does not include the software, which must be purchased separately. I will discuss this more in Chapter 2.

As for the east and west sides, you will see a speaker on one, and a USB Host Port labeled "USB" and SD Card Port labeled "SD" on the other. The USB port can be used as a USB Wi-Fi dongle for connecting to a wireless network, or daisy chaining three other EV3 bricks to it. The SD card port increases the available memory for the EV3 Brick with an SD card with a maximum of 32 GB. This comes in handy for when you want to program something on an SD card and then put it on your EV3 Brick.

Large Motor (6009430)

I wrote a lot about motors in my LEGO Technic books, and the LEGO MINDSTORMS Large Motors operate on the same basic principle. That is, you insert an Axle or cross-shaped part into one end, and power the motor up to make it spin. However, the user can stick the axle all the way through the circular area on the Large Motor (see Figure 1-3), and it will spin when prompted by the EV3 brick; this is different to the Technics motor which has one axle hole or cross-shaped hole at one end like the Medium Motor (see separate description).

Figure 1-3. *Two views of the Large Motor*

Another difference between the Large Motor and a LEGO Technic motor is that EV3 software allows you much more precision. LEGO Technic motors can only go and stop, but the Large Motor has a built-in rotation sensor with one-degree resolution for precise control. This means that you can tell the Large Motor how fast to spin, and for how long.

Another added bonus is that two Large Motors can be programmed to be completely in sync with each other. This is really good for vehicles. I will discuss how to put them in sync in Chapter 2.

Medium Motor (6008577)

This particular motor is also made for spinning, but in a different way. It works more like a LEGO Technic motor, in that the axle part is stuck in the middle instead of through the side like the Large Motor (See Figure 1-4 for a view of the Medium Motor).

Figure 1-4. *Front and back views of the LEGO MINDSTORMS EV3 Medium Motor*

The Medium Motor contains the built-in rotation sensor with the one-degree resolution, but it is much lighter and can respond faster than the Large Motor.

Ultrasonic Sensor (6008924)

This particular part looks like a pair of eyes, and it works like a bat "sees". A bat sends out high-frequency sound waves that reflect or echo off objects, and they process that information to discover how far an object is away (see Figure 1-5).

Figure 1-5. *Two views of the Ultrasonic Sensor*

In the same manner, this LEGO MINDSTORMS piece allows for seeing that there is an obstruction directly ahead of it. This comes in handy when you create a LEGO MINDSTORMS creation that must stop at a wall or other obstacles.

You will notice that there is a steady light around the Ultrasonic Sensor's eyes, which means that it is in measure mode. If the light is blinking, this is when it is in Presence Mode. Presence mode allows the Ultrasonic Sensor to detect another Ultrasonic Sensor operating nearby. This means it is detecting other sound signals, but it is not sending them.

Gyro Sensor (6008916)

This part can often be confused with the other sensors at first glance, except for the telltale arrows on the top of it. These arrows mark its rotational motion on a single axis, and it can, when properly powered, know when it is moving, how fast it is moving, and what angle it is facing (see Figure 1-6).

Figure 1-6. *Front and back view of the Gyro Sensor*

This sensor can measure a maximum rate of spin of 440 degrees per second, and can even keep track of the total rotation angle in degrees. This means that it can keep track of steering, and it also knows what rate it is travelling at as well. We will definitely come back to this helpful brick in Chapter 3.

Color Sensor (6008919)

The Color Sensor (see Figure 1-7) is an interesting brick that can not only recognize seven colors, but it can also detect the amount of reflected light as well as the intensity of ambient light. What does that mean? I'll have programming examples in later chapters, but let me briefly go over each of its separate features individually.

Figure 1-7. *Front and back views of the Color Sensor*

Color mode gives the Color Sensor the ability to scan seven colors that include the three primary (red, blue, and yellow), one secondary of green, plus black, white, and brown. It can also detect no color, which means it can be programmed to act (or not act) when none of the seven colors are scanned. With the proper use of the Color Sensor, your LEGO MINDSTORMS creation can actually "see" what color an object is. You can even program the robot to perform a certain action when it scans a certain color. We will discuss this much more in separate chapters.

The Color Sensor can also measure reflected light on a scale of 0–100, with 0 representing very dark and 100 representing very light. How will this help you? The Color Sensor can be taught to stop at a black line on a white floor. There is an example of this in the instructions of The Core Set.

As for the ambient light detector, it can be programmed to know the difference between the brightest day and the darkest night. This is useful in situations where a LEGO MINDSTORMS creation must do something different in the dark than when in the light.

Touch Sensor (6008472)

This part has a red button on it that knows when it is pressed and released. It can be programmed to do something when pressed, which comes in handy for stopping or starting actions (see Figure 1-8).

Figure 1-8. *The front and back view of a Touch Sensor*

This button can also be set up for doing actions when the button is released as well as pressed. Another set-up can include something on when the action is "bumped". That is, quickly pressed and released. I will discuss the particulars in later chapters like Chapter 3.

Infrared Sensor (6009811) and Infrared Beacon (6014051)

The sensor and beacon are designed to work together, and they can do many things. The Infrared Beacon (IR Beacon) sends out a signal of infrared light, the same kind of signals that most TV remote controls use. Pressing the button marked "9" in Figure 1-9 allows this signal to be sent out, and there is an indicator light showing that the signal is being broadcast. The other buttons are labeled 1–4, and I will explain the numbering in the next chapter. The IR Beacon has four channels, which allow its Infrared Sensor to detect four kinds of signal.

Figure 1-9. *The EV3 Infrared Sensor (left) and Infrared Beacon (right). (Photo credit: The LEGO Group)*

The Infrared Sensor detects the beacon, and it can sense its proximity of its beacon. It also allows the IR Beacon to be used as a wireless remote, which comes in handy for taking control of projects. The Infrared Sensor can also sense when some object is in front of it, but is less sensitive than the Ultrasonic Sensor.

Connector Cables

In order to get the sensors or motors to work, they need to be properly powered. You need to use the connector cables for that, and they connect like landline telephone cords; you can see some in Figure 1-10.

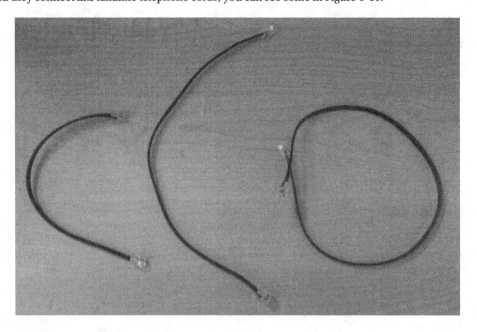

Figure 1-10. *The three sizes of connector cables*

As you can see, the connector cables come in three sizes. The small (6024581) measures in at 10 inches/25 centimeters, the medium (6024583) measures at 14 inches/35 centimeters, and the large (6024585) measures at 20 inches/50 centimeters.

A Basic Introduction to LEGO Technic Pieces

You will notice that LEGO MINDSTORMS sets come with LEGO pieces. If you are not familiar with sets like LEGO in general you might find that these pieces look different than the traditional set with bricks and plates (the flat LEGO pieces). The pieces in a MINDSTORMS set are more associated with a series of LEGO sets known as LEGO Technic.

If you aren't familiar with LEGO Technic, it is a specific type of LEGO set which is made for older children in the tween age range. I have written two books for Apress on the subject with *Practical LEGO Technics* and *LEGO Technic Robotics*. These are books that talk about what you can do with LEGO Technic pieces, as well as the Power Functions motors. Believe me, you can do a lot with LEGO Technic, but LEGO MINDSTORMS really kicks it up a notch, maybe even a few notches.

I would have to say that pieces provided with the LEGO MINDSTORMS kits are a good example of what is available in the Technic series, but you might find that you want more of them to make bigger or more elaborate models. I wish I could say that there is an "ultimate set" of Technic. The current selection on their catalog is for individual models, and you may have many of one piece but not so many of another piece. As someone who isn't interested in spending too much of their budget on LEGO pieces, you sort of learn to adapt to the pieces that you have.

Most LEGO enthusiasts simply build from whatever pieces they have based on the particular sets they have bought in the past. I highly suggest that you find a way to keep your pieces organized, as you will lose a lot of time rummaging through a pile looking for that piece that you need so you can move on to the next step.

As much as I like to hear the sound of LEGO bricks being scraped together, to keep your pieces in order, I recommend buying some kind of tackle box, as the little drawers and storage containers are good at keeping pieces separate from each other. Another way to organize is to purchase some kind of tool box in your hardware store that has drawers or other compartments for storing individual pieces. Of course, you may not want this type of organization, and that is fine. The important thing is that you are having fun with this.

Much of this next section may seem elementary to most LEGO builders. I already covered this in my first book on LEGO Technic, but I felt it necessary to really distinguish one LEGO Technic piece from another, as I will constantly refer to them in this book. Please keep in mind that the numbers within the illustration are for the figure only, made for labeling purposes in this book and are not an official LEGO number.

I put the official Element number in parentheses so you can find it on Pick a Brick or Brickfactory, online sites that help you purchase specific LEGO pieces. I will go more into detail on those types of sites later in this chapter. In my past LEGO Technic books, I have used the Design number, but the Element number is longer and actually designates the color of the piece.

This next section is not meant to be an exhaustive list of what LEGO Technic parts are available to LEGO builders. LEGO creates new parts every year, and there are some parts that I didn't list here, as they were not used on models in this book. What you will see here are the parts that come with the Core Set and the Expansion Set.

Beams

When LEGO introduced the "Expert Sets" back in the late 1970s (they changed the name to Technic in the mid-1980s), they introduced a new kind of brick. In addition to having the traditional studs (the round shaped things on the top), these bricks had holes or through-holes on the sides for connector pegs and axles (see individual descriptions below). Sometime around 2000, LEGO Technic began to emphasize beams rather than traditional studded pieces. Most LEGO Technic sets shun these old-style Technic brick pieces now, and generally are completely studless.

In other words, recent LEGO Technic sets have been less about traditional LEGO pieces like bricks and are now about studless beams. As you can see in Figure 1-10, organizing them is simple by length. The number of through-holes on the beam is equal to the length. All beams tend to have an odd number of holes except for the ones that are 2M length.

You will note the beams on the left side of Figure 1-11 have bends in them. Some of them are at a right angle (90 degrees), while others are at a 53.13 degree angle, with the exception of the double angular beam.

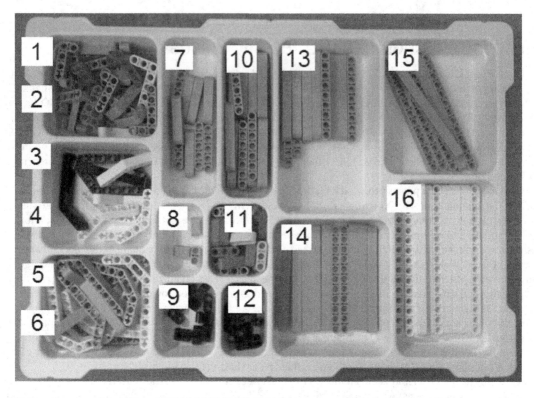

Figure 1-11. *A sectioned area from the LEGO MINDSTORMS Expansion set, filled with LEGO beams*

Referring to Figure 1-11, the numbered beams are as follows:

1. Technic Angular Beam 4 x 2 (Red 4141270, Gray 4211610). This is the merging of two Technic beams to form a 4 x 2 beam at a perfect right angle. This works well when creating square or rectangular creations. You will notice that one of the holes is cross-shaped, perfect for an axle.

2. Technic Angular Beam 5 x 3 (Gray 4211651, White 4585040). Like the 4 x 2 angular beam, this is another 90-degree angular beam that is slightly larger at 5 x 3. Unlike the 4 x 2 angular beam, there is no cross-shaped hole on one end.

3. Technic Angular Beam 4 x 4 (4509912). This angular beam is at an angle of 53.1 degrees. Note the cross holes at each end.

4. Technic Angular Beam 4 x 6 (4112282). This angular beam is like the 4 x 4 as it is at the same angle at 53.1 degrees, but it measures at 4 x 6.

5. Technic Angular Beam 3 x 7 (4211624). This angular beam has the same angle at 53.1 degrees, but measures at 3 x 7.

6. Technic Double Angular Beam 3 x 7 (White 4495412, Gray 4234240). This particular beam has two 45-degree angles, so it is essentially a 90-degree angle with a good curve to it.

7. Technic 5M Beam (4211651).

8. Technic 2M Beam (4211655). As I have stated before, most beams are odd-numbered in their measurement. This 2M one is the only exception, save for the cross and hole beam in the next compartment.

9. Technic Beam 1 x 2 Beam with Cross and Hole (Black 6006140). Also known as a cross and hole beam, this has the unique ability to have a hole for a connector peg or axle, and a cross-shaped one made specifically for an axle.

10. Technic 7M Beam (4495930).

11. Technic 3M Beam (Red 4153718, Black 4142822, Blue 4509376, Yellow 4153707, Green 6007973, Gray 4211655). This is the lowest in number of the odd-numbered beams.

12. Technic T-Beam 3 x 3 (4552347). This is essentially two 3M beams fused together into a T shape, and you will find that angled beam pieces help on a lot of creations.

13. Technic 9M Beam (4211866).

14. Technic 11M Beam (4611705).

15. Technic 13M Beam (4522934).

16. Technic 15M Beam (4542578). This is the longest length of beam in the LEGO Technic and/or LEGO MINDSTORMS sets.

Axles

Like the beams, the axles can be easily organized by length (see Figure 1-12). Axles are like screws in the LEGO Technic world. You can use them to link just about anything, and their cross shape ensures that they fit on cross holes securely.

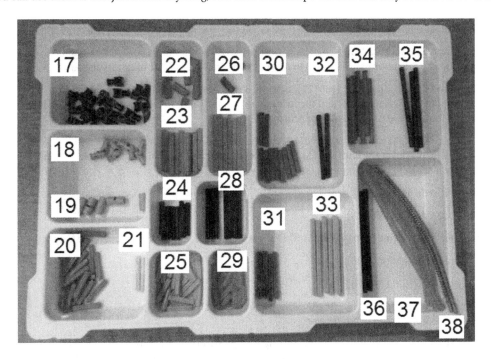

Figure 1-12. A collection of LEGO axles

Referring to Figure 1-11, the numbered axles are as follows:

17. Technic Catch with Cross Hole (4107081). This is essentially two cross holes, put at 90 degrees to each other.

18. Universal Joint (4525904). This allows an axle to go at any angle provided it is below 90 degrees. This is especially helpful when creating vehicles with spinning axles that need to bend.

19. Technic Tube 2M (4526985). This is a way to put a hard plastic tube over 2M of an axle for increased stability, and you can also join a connector peg to each of its sides.

20. Technic Axle 3M with Knob (6031821). Unlike ordinary 3M axles, these have a bump on the end that can serve as a perfectly good LEGO stud.

21. Axle with Positioning Stop (4666999). This particular axle has a "stop" in the middle that is not cross-shaped in any way. This allows for some interesting creations.

22. Technic Cross Axle Extension (4513174). This is a type of cross axle extension, which allows you to join two axles together.

23. Technic Axle 5M (4211639). Like the 3M axles, there are a few black 5M axles, but these are usually gray.

24. Technic Axle 4M (370526). This is the beginning of the axles that are usually black.

25. Technic Axle 3M (4211815). Generally, most axles with an odd-numbered measurement are gray, and this one is the lowest odd number.

26. Technic Cross Axle Extension, Ribbed (4207456). This is another way to join two axles together, and these are ribbed on the side, making them easy to pull off.

27. Technic Axle 7M (4211805).

28. Technic Axle 6M (370626).

29. Technic Axle 2M (4142865). Usually 2M axles are red, and they are also notched. I'm not certain why that is, but perhaps it is to make it easier for the LEGO builder to pry out.

30. Technic Axle 4M with Stop (4560177). Like the 3M axle with knob, the 4M with Stop has something that will make certain the axle can only go so far. While the stop is not a LEGO stud, I found these useful in a lot of projects.

31. Technic Axle 5.5M with 1M Stop (4508553). This piece is really 5.5 M in length, and the stop is not placed at the end, but 1M from the end on one point. This is good for situations with wheel axles and other projects.

32. Technic Axle 8M (370726).

33. Technic Axle 9M (4535768).

34. Technic Axle 8M with Stop (4499858). This is just like the 4M axle with stop, but twice as long.

35. Technic Axle 10M (373726).

36. Technic Axle 12M (370826).

37. Corrugated Pipe 152mm (4631648). This is another part that can be placed over an axle, but this is longer than a regular axle.

38. Flex Hose 19M (6044636). This is a very long flexible part that can be bent in all kinds of directions, and its small ends can fit into a cross hole.

Connector Pegs and Bushes

The connector pegs (sometimes called pins) are the rivets of the LEGO Technic world. You can use them to link beams and levers together, and they come in many forms. As for the bushes, this is a very common part in LEGO Technic, and they slide very easily on an axle and are made for holding them in place. Like the other aforementioned parts, you will accrue a lot of these.

Some of the connector pegs have "friction" which means that they do not spin as easily as the ones that do not. You will discover that there are some times when you want a piece to spin freely and easily, so you will want the pieces that do not have friction. Then there are times where you want a construction to lock securely in place, so using a piece with friction is your best course of action. Figure 1-13 shows how these pieces can be organized.

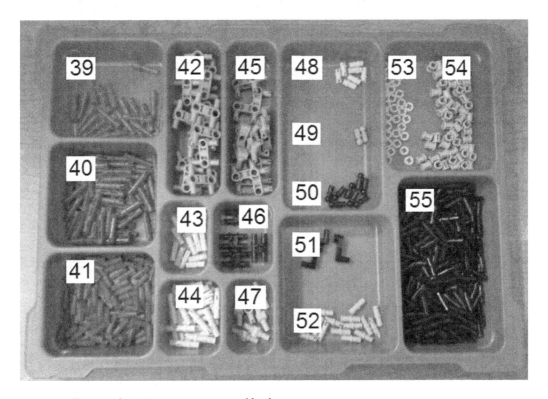

Figure 1-13. *A collection of LEGO connector pegs and bushes*

Referring to Figure 1-13, the numbered pieces are as follows:

39. Technic Friction Snap with Cross Hole (4140806). The connector peg that you see here has some friction on it so you can lock two things together securely, and they will not spin very freely. The cross hole section on the end forms an interesting peg-like appendage.

40. Technic Connector Peg 3M with Friction (4514553). This connector peg can hold two 1M pieces on one side, so it can join 3 beams together so they cannot freely spin. You will notice the ring that divides it with 2M of peg on one side and 1M on the other.

41. Technic Connector Peg with Friction and Cross-Axle (4206482). This is the connector peg/cross axle with some friction, so it spins somewhat freely.

13

42. Technic Beam 3M with Four Snaps (4225033). Sometimes this can be called a wide H due to its shape. It is probably the best way to describe this piece, but it has four connector pegs, with round holes on another, and a hole in between the connector pegs.

43. Technic Connector Peg with Cross-Axle (4666579). One side is a connector peg, the other side a 1M axle. This piece can link up a part with a round hole and a part with a cross hole very securely, and still allow for some spinning.

44. Technic Connector Peg 3M (4514554). This connector peg can hold two 1M pieces on one side, so it can join 3 beams together so they can freely spin.

45. Angular Beam 90 Degrees with 4 Snaps (4296059). Also known as a wide L, this particular connector allows for snapping in place with a beam or other piece at a 90-degree angle from it.

46. Technic Module Bush (4119589). Also known as a narrow H, this is similar to the 3M beam with four snaps. It has two connector pegs on each side, and you can insert an axle in the middle.

47. Double Bush 3M (4560175). This is essentially a 3M connector peg with a round hole in the middle.

48. Technic 1 1/2 Connecting Bush (6013938). This piece is 3/4 the size of a connector peg, with a bump half the size on one side.

49. Ball with Cross Axle (4211375). This is a ball with 1M of an axle on one end for attaching to cross-holes. This ball fits into a lot of handy pieces.

50. Ball with Friction Snap (4184169). Sometimes referred to as a trailer hitch, this is similar to the ball with cross axle, this piece has a connector peg on one side with a ball on the other.

51. Technic Steering Knuckle Arm 2 x 1 x 3 (4563044). Also known as a lift arm, this is like a lever with half a connector peg on one side and a cross hole notch on the other. I believe it is called a steering knuckle arm because it comes in handy for steering.

52. Technic Connector Peg (4211807). This piece is designed to snap into a round hole, and the other will snap into another hole. It allows for a lot of free spinning on each side.

53. Technic Half Bush (4239601). The half bush is only 1/2 M in length, and does the same function as the Technic bush.

54. Technic Bush (4211622). This piece is about 1 M in length, and fits snug on an axle. It is made to hold an axle in place, and many other uses described within this book.

55. Technic Connector Peg with Friction (4121715). Like the other type of connector peg, this has some friction. I would have to say that I use this part, along with the bushes, the most with LEGO Technic and MINDSTORMS creations, as it is the easiest way to link two parts with round holes together.

Cross Blocks and Angle Elements

As you are building, you are going to find it necessary to link beams together in a perpendicular manner. In other words, you are going to have a part with holes facing one direction, but you want to make it so holes also face 90 degrees in the other direction. You can shift angles in many creative ways using the nine types of cross blocks that you can see here in Figure 1-13. As for the angle elements, you can see six examples of them in Figure 1-14, and these pieces are designed to link axles together so they fit at certain angles.

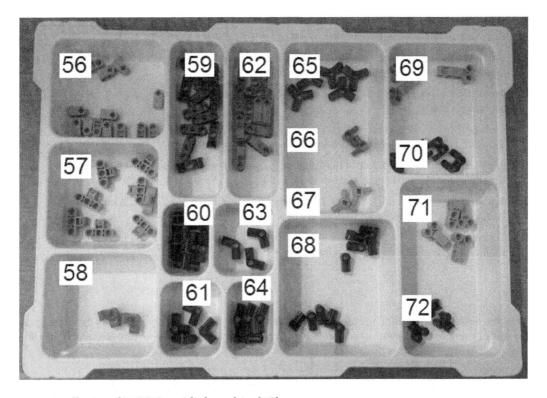

Figure 1-14. *A collection of LEGO Cross Blocks and Angle Elements*

Referring to Figure 1-14, the numbered pieces are as follows:

56. Technic Cross Block 90 Degrees (4211775). This is a part with a round hole in one direction and a cross hole facing 90 degrees the other way.

57. Technic Cross Block 3 x 2 (4538007). This is like having a 3M beam, and then gluing a bush on the top, and turning it 90 degrees.

58. Angular Block with axles, 90 Degrees (6008527). This part is two 1M axles that intersect at a round hole.

59. Technic Double Cross Block (4121667). I found this piece to be very useful to join together some pieces. It has two cross holes on each side, with a round hole on the other side.

60. Technic 180 Degree Angle Element #2 (4107783). Used for joining two axles together in a straight line, with a hole in the middle that can also be used for other uses.

61. Technic 90 Degree Angle Element #6 (4107767). Used for joining two axles together at a 90 degree angle, with a through-hole in the middle.

62. Technic Cross Block 3M (4210857). This is a 3M beam with two round holes and a cross hole on 90 degrees on the other side.

63. Technic 112.5 Degree Angle Element #5 (4107084).

64. Technic 157.5 Degree Angle Element #3 (4107082). This angle element and the three others here are made to join two axles together, with the hole in the middle for more uses.

65. Three-Spoke Angular Block, 3x120 Female (6005755). This is a lot like the other three-spoke angular block, but with "female" axle ends.

66.   Beam 1M W. 2 Cross Axles 90°(6005331). Take two 1M axles, join them together on a ring that is a through-hole, and you have this part.

67.   Three-Spoke Angular Block, 3x120 (4502595). This is a part with three axles pointing 120 degrees from the center, which also has an axle hole.

68.   Technic Zero Degree Angle Element #1 (4107085). Used for capping off an axle with a round hole at 90 degrees.

69.   Technic Cross Block 2 x 3 (4652234). This piece is interesting with two round holes in one direction and three round holes below it at 90 degrees and centered.

70.   Technic Cross Block/Fork 2 x 2 (4162857). This part is two round holes and then a cross hole on each side, at 90 degrees below it.

71.   Technic Cross Block 2 x 2 (4211714). This piece is a lot like the cross block 2 x 3, but it has two holes at a 90-degree angle instead of three.

72.   Technic Cross Block 1 x 2 (4162857). This is a lot like the cross block 3 x 2, but it is a bush mounted 90 degrees on a 2M beam instead of a 3M beam.

Gears

These pieces are designed to spin, and the teeth are designed to mesh together so one spins and the other spins in turn. They come in various sizes, and they can often turn in perpendicular fashion with one gear placed at a 90-degree angle to the other. Figure 1-15 shows them in storage.

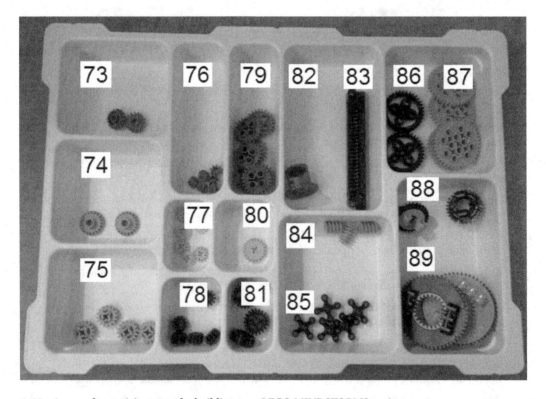

Figure 1-15. *A way of organizing gears for building your LEGO MINDSTORMS projects*

Referring to Figure 1-15, the numbered gears are as follows:

73. Technic Gear Wheel (16 Teeth) Special (4237267). Instead of having a cross hole in the center, this has a round hole. It is helpful for situations where you need another gear, such as shifting gears on a LEGO Technic vehicle.

74. Technic Cone Wheel (4558690). I think this gear gets its name from being slightly conical in shape as the area about its round hole (not a cross hole) extends a bit.

75. Technic Gear Wheel 16 Teeth (4640536). This gear is slightly similar to the other 16-tooth gear that I just mentioned, with a single cross hole in the middle.

76. Technic Gear Wheel 8 Teeth (6012451). This is one of the smallest gear pieces, and has a cross hole in the middle.

77. Technic Conical Wheel Z12 (4565452). This gear is flat with 12 teeth, and it can spin in a perpendicular fashion with another Wheel.

78. Technic Double Conical Wheel 12 Teeth (4177431). Like the conical wheels, these can spin in a perpendicular fashion, but they are also thicker.

79. Technic Gear Wheel 24 Teeth (4514558). This is similar to the other gears, but it has three cross holes and four round holes.

80. Technic Double Conical Wheel 20 Teeth (6031962). This is like the previously mentioned double conical wheel, but slightly bigger.

81. Technic Bevel Gear Z20 (4177430). Similar to the conical wheel Z12, this gear is slightly larger at 20 teeth and can also spin in a perpendicular fashion.

82. Technic Differential 3M (4525184). This is similar to the other differential gear casing, with an extra gear on it.

83. Technic Rack 13M (4540906). Like the 7M rack, it has the round holes for connector pegs and the axle holes on the side.

84. Technic Worm Gear (4211510). This gear is designed to mesh with another round gear above it. By turning this worm gear, the gear connected to it will turn.

85. Technic Angular Wheel (4248204). I found that these angular wheels mesh together and spin well in a perpendicular fashion.

86. Double Conical Wheel Z36. (4255563). This is a double beveled gear that is quite thick.

87. Technic Gear Wheel 40 Teeth (4285634). This is quite a huge LEGO piece, and it has twelve round holes and five cross holes.

88. Turntable Z28 (Gray 4652235 and Black 4542236). These are two pieces that fit perfectly together and are designed to mount something. Another gear beside it can turn it perfectly.

89. Large Turntable 4.85 (4624645). This is like the Z28 turntable, but larger.

Levers

Levers are essentially half the width of a beam, and stacking two of them equals one beam. Like the beams, they often have axle holes on the ends of them. Figure 1-16 shows levers in storage.

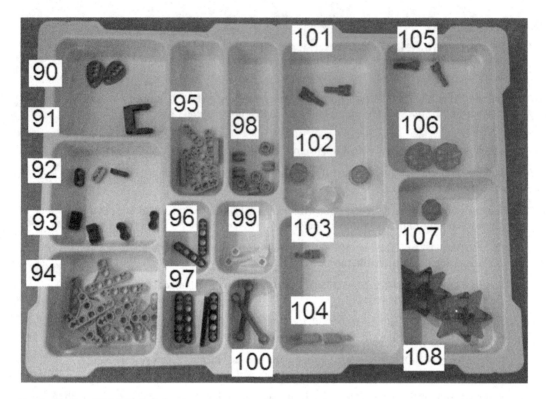

Figure 1-16. *Various LEGO Technic levers*

Referring to Figure 1-16, the numbered levers are as follows:

90. Technic Comb Wheel (4210759). This is not really a wheel in shape, but this lever is slightly round. I am guessing that it is called a comb wheel because it looks slightly like a comb, and it is good for securing bricks with axle holes.

91. Beam 3M W. Fork (4558692). Picture a 3M beam with levers on the end, and you have the basic idea of this piece.

92. Technic 2M Lever (Black 4164133, Gray 4211741). This lever has two cross shaped holes and is 2M in length, very helpful for securing axles in place.

93. Damper 2M (4198367). This piece is essentially 2M levers stacked together, with two axle holes. It is completely made of rubber.

94. Technic Triangle (6009019). This piece has an odd shape with five round holes and two cross-shaped holes.

95. Technic 3M Lever (4211566). This type of lever has two cross-shaped holes on each end, and a round hole in the middle.

96. Technic 4M Lever (4142236). This type of lever is larger than the 3M, with two round holes in its middle.

97. Technic 5M Lever (6030286). This type of lever is larger than the 4M, with three round holes in its middle.

98. Hub (4211758). This is a round piece that has a round hole in the middle.

99. Pointer (White 417941, Red 4185661). This part allows for connecting to an axle, and it good for all kinds of things, particularly showing direction.

100. Steering Wheel Axle (4629920). Many Lego sets use this piece for steering, and the ends fit perfectly over pieces with that have the ball shape on them.

101. Technic Catch (4210665). This is essentially an axle with a bush placed 90 degrees of it.

102. Brick 2 x 2 Round (Blue Transparent 4178398, Yellow Transparent 611649) This is one brick that I consider a part of "mainstream" Lego. This is round instead of square, and has a center of a cross-hole.

103. Technic Change-over Catch (4270473). This is a way to perfect shifting on a Technic creation, and it has other uses as well.

104. CVC Ball Joint (4268659). This piece is has a through-hole on one end, and a ball joint that fits into the cup joint.

105. CVC Cup Joint (4610374). This piece fits in perfectly with the previous piece.

106. Weapon Barrel (4654432). I am assuming that this piece is named because it looks like a Gatling-gun barrel, and it is full of round-holes and cross-holes.

107. Driving Ring (4278957). Like the change-over catch, it is also helpful in situations with shifting of gears and such.

108. Half Spike Ball (6027626). This is a very unusual piece whose shape I cannot really describe in simple words. It does have a cross-hole in the middle.

Wings and Panels

Most of these pieces have a wing shape, which is where their name derives. You will notice that each of the wings has a designated left side and right side. As for the panels, they are more rectangular and good for structure. Figure 1-17 shows them in storage.

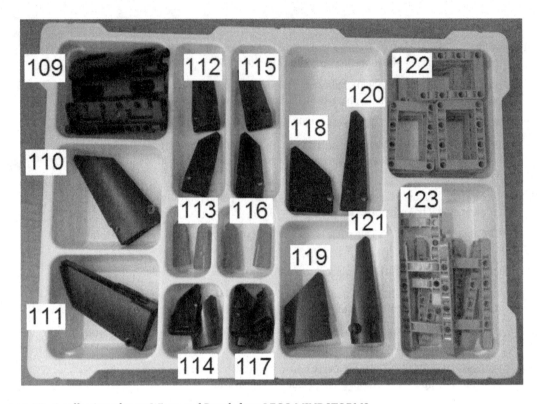

Figure 1-17. *A collection of some Wings and Panels from LEGO MINDSTORMS*

Referring to Figure 1-17, the numbered wings and panels are as follows:

109. Bowed Panel 3 x 11 x 2 (6031916). This piece is full of through-holes and can fit in many places.

110. Right Panel 5 x 11 (4543490). One of the larger wing pieces.

111. Left Panel 5 x 11 (4541326). Also one of the larger wing pieces, made for the left.

112. Left Panel 3 x 7 (4541924).

113. Left Panel 2 x 5 (6022752).

114. Left Panel 3 x 5 (4566251).

115. Right Panel 3 x 7 (4541325).

116. Right Panel 2 x 5 (6022750).

117. Right Panel 3 x 5 (4566249).

118. Left Panel 5 x 7 (4558775).

119. Right Panel 5 x 7 (4558740).

120. Left Panel 3 x 11 (4558774).

121. Right Panel 3 x 11 (4558731).

122.   Beam Frame 5 x 7 (4539880). This particular frame is terrific for when you need to fit things at right angles with each other. It has a lot of through holes.

123.   Beam Frame 5 x 11 (4540797). Similar to the 5 x 7, it also has a bunch of through-holes.

Wheels and Treads

I will discuss a lot of wheeled creations in this book, so I will briefly introduce the wheels here (see Figure 1-18). I also include tank treads, rubberbands, and various other pieces associated with wheels.

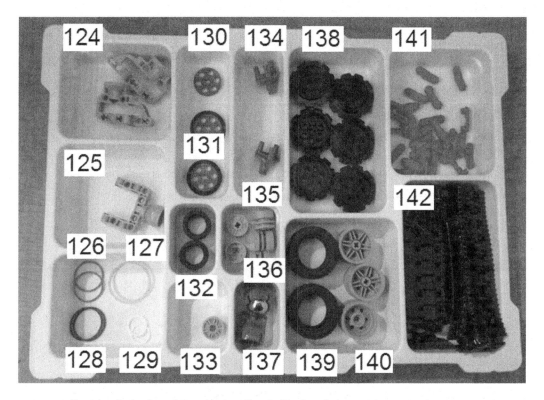

Figure 1-18. *A collection of Wheels and Treads, as well as Rubberbands for LEGO creations*

Referring to Figure 1-18, the numbered wheels and treads are as follows:

124.   Gear Block 3.5 x 6.5 x 3 (4610377). This is a very good joint section for a wheel.

125.   Power Joint Ballpart (4610379). Also another good joint for a wheel.

126.   V-Belt 24 Red Rubberband (4544143). Rubberbands are often used in Lego creations, and their size does matter depending on what you would like to do with them.

127.   V-Belt 33 Yellow Rubberband (4544151).

128.   V-Belt 26 Blue Rubberband (4544147).

129.   V-Belt 15 White Rubberband (4544140).

130.   Wedge-Belt Wheel (4587275). This piece has six through holes that are ½ M thick.

131.   Tire for Wedge-Belt Wheel (6028041). This piece goes right on the wedge-belt wheel and turns it into something like a bike tire.

132.   Tire Low Wide 24 x 14 (4639695).

133.   Rim Narrow 18 x 7 W Hole (6044729).

134.   3 Snap Gearblock (4610378). This is very good for mounting a wheel, especially with the rims in this set.

135.   Rim Wide 18/14 W. Cross (4490127).

136.   Ball, Metal (6023956). This ball forms a kind of spherical wheel for a Lego MINDSTORMS creation. More about this later.

137.   Power Joint (4610380). This is made to mount the metal ball.

138.   Sprocket (4582792). These are good for holding the tank tread.

139.   Tire, Normal Wide 43, 2 x 22 (4184286).

140.   Rim Wide W. Cross 30/20 (4297210).

141.   Rubber Attachment for Track Element (6036424). This is an excellent cushion for the tank tread.

142.   Track Element, 5 x 1, 5 (6014648). If you want to make a tank tread, this is what you will use.

Figure 1-19 shows some more samples of rims and tires you might want to use.

Figure 1-19. *Other types of wheels for LEGO creations*

Referring to Figure 1-19, the numbered wheels are as follows:

143.   Tire, Low Wide 56 x 28 (6035364).

144.   Rim Wide 43, 2 x 25 w/6 Hol. (4634091).

145.   Tire Low Wide 8 x 36 (4614801).

146.   Rim 56 x 34 (4211845).

Where to Begin with your LEGO MINDSTORMS Kit

Now that I got all that out of the way, I'm sure that you are anxious to get your hands on some LEGO Technic pieces and start building some robots. If you have been working with LEGO for a while, then you have a collection of all kinds of pieces from various sets. I am going to assume that is the case, but perhaps you are the reader who wants to start a LEGO Technic collection. If you flipped through this book before purchase, you will see a lot of instructions. If you want to try to build them yourself, you will need to get some of the pieces. There are several places online to do that.

LEGO Pick a Brick

First of all, you could go to the official LEGO site and head to their Pick a Brick section at http://shop.lego.com/PAB. The Pick a Brick website has a place for "Category", and you can search for the LEGO piece that you are looking for under "Technic".

I know that some of you LEGO builders are sticklers for color, and demand that your creation conform to a certain color scheme. You don't have that freedom if your LEGO collection is an amalgamation of many LEGO Technic sets over the years. You can also search by color or its item number, which is specific number that LEGO gives its part. If you are ever looking for a specific brick, you can do an Advanced Search in the column on the left using the brick name, which is the formal name for the brick. I will have to admit that this will produce mixed results, unless you know exactly what you are looking for.

When you are ready to purchase the part that you are looking for, you can hit the "Add To Bag" link and your individual pieces will appear at "Brick Bag" column. When you have selected all the parts you need, just hit the "Update Bag" and add the part to your personal Shopping Cart. Yes, you will need an account with LEGO to have your items sent to you.

BrickLink

If you are looking for another place to find LEGO Technic pieces, then I also suggest looking at BrickLink (http://www.bricklink.com). BrickLink is an unofficial LEGO marketplace, and it is often referred to as the "eBay of LEGO." If you want to buy or sell LEGO sets, new and used, this is the online place to shop (see Figure 1-20).

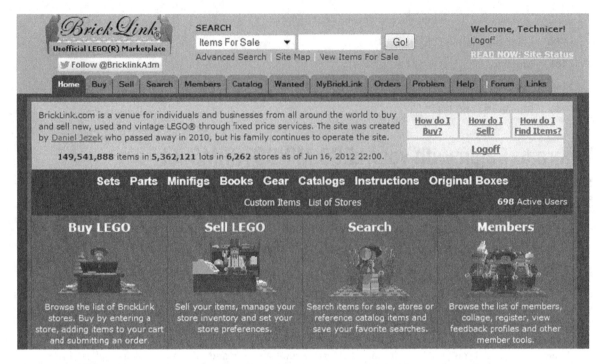

Figure 1-20. *The BrickLink site, a place to find LEGO bricks, both new and used*

If you click on "Buy", you will have the option of purchasing several items including sets, books, gear, catalogs, and parts. As of this writing, there are over 116 million parts available for purchase. Selecting "Parts" will result in a category tree that branches out into several types of pieces, and there are 16 sub-categories for Technic including:

- Axle: Anything that is an axle or has an axle attachment (see Figure 1-12).

- Brick: I did not show some of the Technic bricks, but they do exist.

- Connector: This is an umbrella term that refers to angle elements and cross blocks (see Figure 1-14).

- Disk: These are disk-shaped pieces that I did not describe above. I don't really have them on any of the models in this book, and I don't really see them on more recent sets.

- Figure Accessory: At one point in time, Technic had figures that were to the scale of the Technic vehicles. They don't make them anymore, but here is a place where you can find the accessories like helmets and feet.

- Flex Cable: Some Technic sets have flexible cable that helps to create a more curvaceous shape. If that is what you are interested in, here is a place to find it.

- Gear: Parts as we listed in Figure 1-15.

- Liftarm: This refers to pieces like beams and levers, and all of their variations in Figures 1-11 and 1-16.

- Liftarm Decorated: This refers to pieces that have stickers or printed graphics on them.

- Link: A good example of a piece for steering.

- Panel: These are very big pieces that take up a lot of space.

- Panel, Decorated. Also like the pieces in Figure 1-17, but these often have stickers or some type of graphics on them.

- Pin: This is where you would find various types of connector pegs.

- Plate: These are flat bricks with Technic holes in them. I didn't discuss them at all and don't really have any models in this book that use them.

- Shock Absorber: These are some LEGO Technic pieces that I discuss in my LEGO Technic Robotics book.

- Steering: This is various parts used for steering, which will includes many previously mentioned categories.

Please note that the descriptions of parts that BrickLink uses might not be exactly the same names that I have given to the parts above. I used the official names that LEGO designates their parts, which can be different than what BrickLink calls them.

If you are looking for buying many LEGO Technic pieces, BrickLink is very similar to Pick a Brick in that you can assemble your parts in a shopping cart and then checkout when you are ready. I found that their catalog is a little more extensive and easier to search through if you are looking for a specific piece, and you might be able to get a deal on pieces if you buy them in bulk. If you are looking to build one of the models in this book, and want to purchase every piece for it, this is one place to go.

In addition to having parts, some of you might be interested in purchasing the actual sets.

Websites for LEGO Instructions

Some of you might want to build a LEGO Technic set that you may remember being made several years ago, but LEGO changes their models every year. You might be able to find the actual set with instructions on BrickLink, and the more recent ones on LEGO.com, but if you have all the pieces, all you really need are the instructions. I highly recommend looking at these sites below, just to generate ideas for LEGO Technic robots.

The LEGO Official Site

Oddly enough, every model that is available on the official LEGO Technic site has a place where you can click and download instructions, as a PDF file that can be saved on your computer. I have noticed that more recent LEGO instructions have a parts list in them, and this is a good place where you can order them on Pick a Brick or BrickLink. Keep in mind that LEGO likes to introduce new pieces as often as it produces new models. You may find that some of the newer pieces are harder to find, and you might have to figure out how to build it in some simple or complex workaround.

Peeron

If you are interested in building Technic LEGO sets from over the years, then I highly recommend that you go to a site that contains both LEGO catalogs and instructions. Peeron (www.peeron.com) is especially helpful with its database of LEGO sets and catalogs (see Figure 1-21). Peeron's inventory only goes up to the 2008 collections (as of this writing), and they often take very long to load.

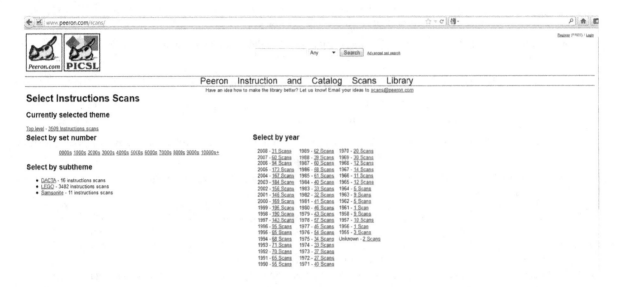

Figure 1-21. *A shot of Peeron website, a place to find out instructions for LEGO sets*

Brickfactory

I also found Brickfactory (`www.brickfactory.com`) to be helpful, and it does have some of the more recent collections; Figure 1-22 shows the main page. Generally, LEGO Technic sets are given a number that is in the 8000 range or higher, with the exception of the 900 series when it first began in 1977. You will notice that several model series like Bionicle are filed under the same umbrella with advanced Technic sets.

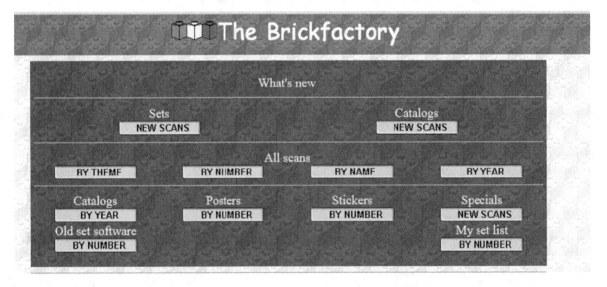

Figure 1-22. *The* `Brickfactory.com`*, a place to find all kinds of LEGO instructions*

You may discover that a lot of the models in Peeron and BrickFactory have most of their pieces available on Pick a Brick. Peeron is especially good at cataloging the individual pieces of a set, and you will find that a search for any set will reveal the individual pieces, including their individual Element ID. For example, you can see Technic set 8002 from the year 2000 with a complete list of all of its parts. Unfortunately, you might discover that the Element ID on Peeron, BrickLink, or whatever site is a perfect match for the Element ID on Pick a Brick.

Summary

The LEGO MINDSTORMS EV3 series uses all new pieces including the EV3 Brick, Large Motor, Medium Motor, Ultrasonic Sensor, Gyro Sensor, Color Sensor, and the Touch Sensor. In addition to these pieces, a LEGO MINDSTORMS builder should equip him or herself with a haul of Technic pieces. You can purchase bricks that you may not own from BrickLink, and you can find instructions for older models on Peeron, Brickfactory, and the LEGO site itself.

■ ■ ■

CHAPTER 2

Programming with the EV3 Language

Now that you have been introduced to the pieces that you will need for building excellent LEGO MINDSTORMS EV3 models, let's talk about how to do one of the most important things: programming the EV3 Brick. One of the challenges in building with LEGO MINDSTORMS is that "building is only half the battle." Once you get your motors and sensors properly constructed on your MINDSTORMS machine, you are going to have to tell it what to do. This will require programming skills, and the EV3 Brick is your microcomputer of choice.

Just to let you know, it is entirely possible to program your EV3 Brick using the six buttons on the EV3 Brick, which I only briefly introduced you to in Chapter 1. I'm not going to show you how to specifically program the EV3 Brick for every program that you will see in this book. For me, I found it was easier for me to create EV3 programs with the use of my computer. I did this for three reasons: 1) It is a lot easier for me to get a screenshot from my computer than the EV3 Brick, 2) it is easier for me to upload the code that you can download off the Apress website, and 3) you will probably be programming from your computer rather than directly on the EV3 Brick anyway.

The Four Basic Screens of the EV3 Brick

If you hold down the center key, the EV3 Brick will come on. You will then see a screen with four tabs, and the following explains what each tag signifies after Figure 2-1.

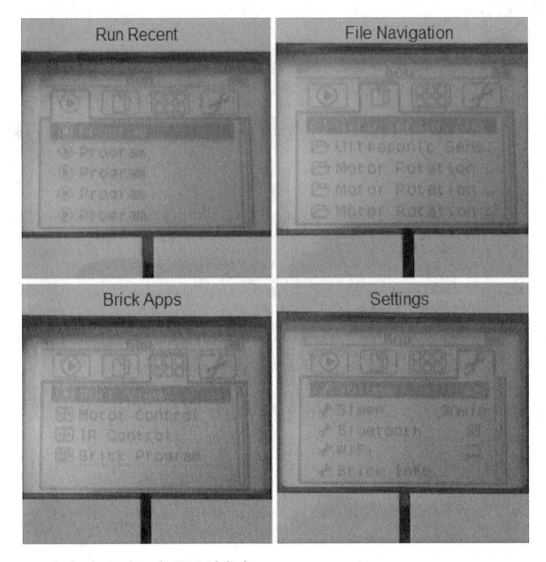

Figure 2-1. *The four basic tabs on the EV3 Brick display*

Run Recent

You will find that this screen is blank unless you downloaded and ran specific programs. Those programs that you have most recently ran will be on this screen, the one at the top being the most recently run program. I'll discuss how to download programs at a later time, but when the programs are visible, you can select one with the buttons and press center to execute.

File Navigation

Here is where you can access and manage all files on the EV3 Brick. This includes any files stored on an SD card. You will note that all these files are located in project folders and they include the sounds and/or images used in each project. You can use sounds and/or images on the EV3 Brick display for your LEGO MINDSTORMS project, and I will detail how to do that in the chapter on Sight and Sound in Chapter 4.

Brick Apps

If I may steal a phrase from Apple, "there's an app for that." In working with EV3, you will find many apps which will be helpful when working with EV3 programs. The EV3 Brick comes with four apps pre-installed (three of which are shown in Figure 2-2).

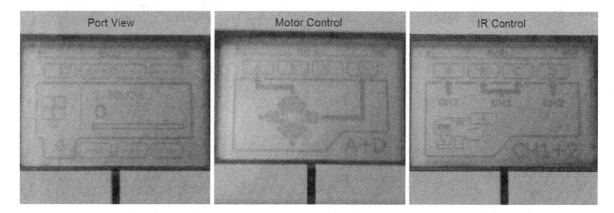

Figure 2-2. Three of the four pre-installed programs for the Brick apps

It is possible to make apps of your own. For now, I will discuss each app from left to right.

Port View

As I stated in Chapter 1, the sensors and/or motors must be attached to the EV3 Brick via connector cables in order to function. You will discover that certain projects occupy many ports, and it is often difficult to keep track of what sensors and motors go with what ports. Port View will give you a quick view about what is attached, as well as their specific ports.

Motor Control

In this app, you can control the movement of the motors at a touch of an EV3 Brick button. You can control motors connected to Port A using the up and down buttons and to Port D using the Left and Right buttons. You can also toggle into a different mode by hitting the center key, which will allow you to control a motor at Port B with the Up and Down keys and a motor at Port C using the left and right buttons.

IR Control

This particular app requires that the Remote Infrared Beacon acts as the remote control and the Infrared Sensor is the receiver. This allows for all types of wireless motor controls, and you should consult the User Guide for more information.

Brick Program

This is the place where you can create programs on the EV3 Brick (no computer required). I'm not going to spend a lot of time talking about this section, but I wanted to let all those new to LEGO MINDSTORMS EV3 know that it exists.

You can see in Figure 2-3 that you can set up a program. All that is required is to click the middle button in the middle of the two posts that you can see in the Brick Button main screen.

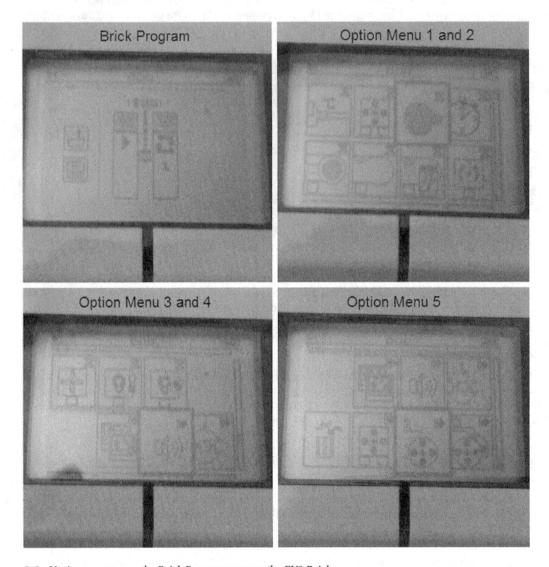

Figure 2-3. *Various screens on the Brick Program app on the EV3 Brick*

From there, you can take command of the motors, sensors, displays, and sounds. You can open an individual program and adjust the speed of a motor and other such parameters that I will explain later.

The Brick Program app is where you can look at programming blocks, and the Instruction Manual for the basic set has a few activities that you can try out to show how they work. I recommend spending some time playing around here just to get used to how these work, but I will go more into detail about the programming blocks when I discuss the software later in this chapter. In fact, you might find it easier to program from your computer and then just download it straight to the EV3 Brick itself.

Settings

As the name of the fourth tab implies, this screen will enable you to adjust some general settings on the EV3 Brick, such as:

- Volume, adjusting the sound levels of the EV3 speaker.

- Sleep, changing the amount of inactive time occurring before the EV3 Brick goes into its Sleep mode.

- Bluetooth, adjusting privacy settings as well as connecting Bluetooth devices wirelessly. It comes with four options:

  - Bluetooth: To enable standard Bluetooth on the EV3 Brick.

  - iPhone/iPad/iPod: To wirelessly connect the EV3 Brick with Apple iOS devices.

  - Connections: To discover and choose other available Bluetooth devices.

  - Visibility: To select when you need to discover and connect with other Bluetooth devices not seen in Connections, such as another EV3 Brick.

- Wi-Fi, enabling Wi-Fi communication on the EV3 Brick in order to connect to a wireless network. As I briefly explained in Chapter 1, a Wi-Fi dongle is required to get this function to work.

- Brick Info, receiving current information on the EV3 Brick such as technical specifications as well as current hardware and software versions.

The EV3 Software

It is possible to program your LEGO MINDSTORMS creations from the EV3 Brick alone. I would recommend connecting the EV3 Brick to your computer, and performing all of your programming from your desktop or laptop. Unfortunately, this EV3 MINDSTORMS program does not come with the basic kit. The program is available online at `http://education.LEGO.com/en-us/LEGO-education-product-database/MINDSTORMS-ev3/2000045-LEGO-MINDSTORMS-education-ev3-software-single-user`, where you can find the specs to see if it will work with your computer.

Once it is downloaded to your computer, the first thing that you will see when you open the EV3 Software is a Lobby (see Figure 2-4), and I highly recommend exploring it as much as you can.

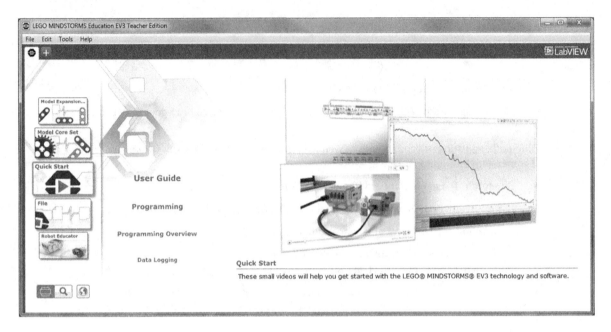

Figure 2-4. *The Lobby of the EV3 Software*

Once you open the Lobby, you can explore the section known as the Activity Tab (the column all the way to the left in Figure 2-4) which gives you access to all the programs with the EV3 Software. The software used for this book has about five tabs with several sub-categories:

- Model Expansion: The Instructions for six models of the Expansion kit, as well as its LEGO Element Survey (that's a parts list of what pieces come with the set). In addition to the instructions, these models come with the program that you will need to download into the EV3 Brick to make them come to life. The model instructions are as follows, and they require a Core Set and an Expansion set, with the exception of the Spinner Factor, which requires two Core sets.

  - Tank Bot: A vehicle with two tank treads that uses the Gyro Sensor to control its movements.

  - Znap: A robot monster that also has two tank treads as well as a set of snapping jaws.

  - Stair Climber: A vehicle that uses a Gyro Sensor and Touch Sensor to traverse a staircase.

  - Elephant: A model of a robot elephant that can walk, roar, raise its trunk, and even pick up objects. It can be controlled with the buttons on the EV3 Brick.

  - Spinner Factory: A machine that makes and launches spinning tops.

  - Remote Control: A multifunctional hand controller that can control other EV3 projects via Bluetooth.

- Model Core Set: This contains the instructions for four models that can be built with the Core Set, including:

  - Gyro Boy: A Robot that can stand on only two wheels and can be manipulated using the Color Sensor.

  - Color Sorter: A machine that uses the Color Sensor to sort four types of bricks on an interesting conveyor belt mechanism.

  - Puppy: A robot puppy that can bark, whine, and even lift its leg.

  - Robot Arm H25: A robot arm that can pick up objects and put them in other places.

- Quick Start: This has a variety of resources to help you out. With the exception of the User Guide (a PDF file), most of them are videos, including:

  - User Guide: An overview of the LEGO MINDSTORMS technology, which I highly recommend going over. It is available as a PDF file which is about 69 pages in length.

  - Programming: A video showing how to use a program for a simple function on the Large Motor.

  - Programming Overview: A video showing the EV3 Software programming environment, which I will explain in more detail later in this chapter.

  - Data Logging: An introductory video showing how to get data from the Gyro Sensor. I will discussing Data Logging in Chapter 5.

  - Data Logging Overview: A more detailed introduction of the data logging environment for EV3.

  - Content Editor: An introduction to the EV3 Software Content Editor.

  - Content Editor-Teacher: This is a short video introducing the EV3 Content Creator, in Teacher Mode.

- File Menu: This is where you can begin a new program or experiment, or open a program or experiment that you have saved in the past.

- Robot Educator: These are groups of videos, building instructions, and programs to help you get very familiar with EV3. For example:

  - Basics: In the Core Set, there are some instructions for a Driving Base, and some of the instructions and programs in this section can help the user take control of it by learning the basics of programming here.

  - Beyond Basics: This section shows how to do more advanced programming topics like Loops, Switches, Multiple Switches, Arrays, and Data Wires, which I will discuss in this chapter and others.

  - Hardware: This allows the user to familiarize himself/herself with the EV3 Brick and other motors/sensors. Much of this is discussed in Chapter 1.

  - Data-Logging: This shows how to use data logging concepts.

  - Tools: Shows how to use the various software tools, like the sound editor, My Blocks, and Image Editor.

  - Building Instructions: Some models of basic driving robots that you can use to help learn more about EV3 MINDSTORMS.

  - Teacher's Guide: These are some PDF files for teachers to help to familiarize oneself with a complete list of LEGO elements.

I highly recommend looking over each of these programs, and learn as much as you can. There are a few other icons worth noting on the Lobby main page with the three buttons (see bottom of Figure 2-5). The one with a box is the View button, to take you back to the Activity Overview page.

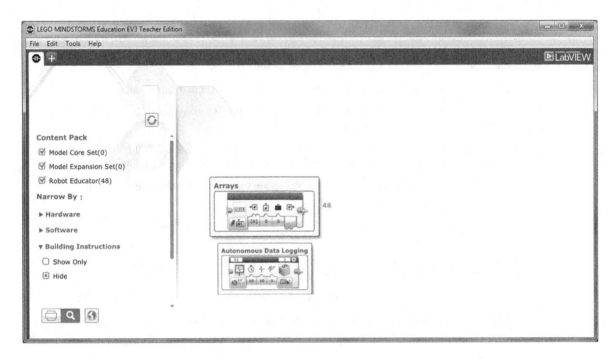

Figure 2-5. *The helpful Search Page for the EV3 Software program*

The Magnifying Glass is the Search Page, which allows you to search for particular topics from Arrays to Variables, and you can even narrow it by Hardware or Software subject (see Figure 2-5).

Finally, there is the button with the planet Earth on it, which will take you to the LEGO MINDSTORMS Education site at www.LEGOeducation.com/MINDSTORMS.

Creating a LEGO MINDSTORMS Program with the EV3 Software

As you can see from the Lobby, there is a lot that you can read and watch. If you are the type who learns by doing, then go into the open New Project by clicking the button as you can see in Figure 2-6.

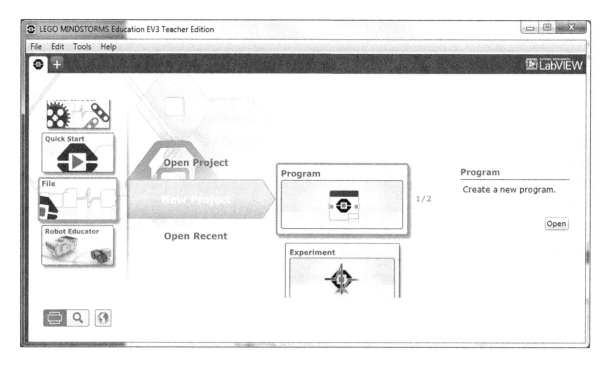

Figure 2-6. *The opening page for the EV3 Software, also known as the "Lobby"*

You can see that when you open a project, you will be taken to a screen with two tab bars that you can see atop Figure 2-6. The top bar has a tab that will take you to the Lobby if you click the EV3 symbol. Your new Project will be simply known as "Project" until you change it.

As for the area below this bar, it has sections simply known as "Program" that you can add on as you see fit. So if you want to work on part of a program in one section, you can do that.

In the white area over to the left in Figure 2-7 is the Programming Canvas, where you can lay out your program, in a very linear and visual format. Like building with LEGO, the programming is done with interconnecting blocks. It defaults to the programming block of Start, which is the green arrow that you see in Figure 2-7.

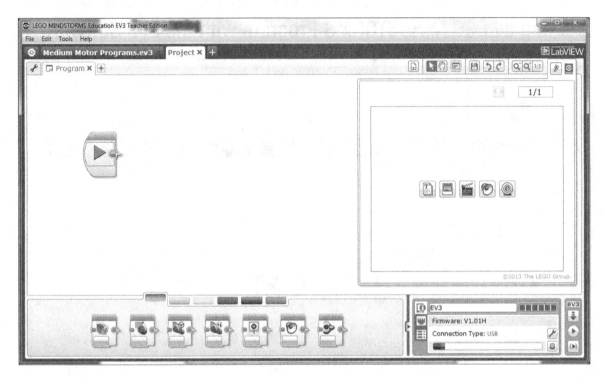

Figure 2-7. *The Programming Page for the EV3 Software*

Below the Programming Canvas is the Programming Palette, which organizes the programming blocks in six different categories:

- Green (Action): Programming blocks to control the motors, display, sounds, and Brick Status Lights.

- Orange (Flow Control): In addition to the Start programming block, this allows for some interesting programming moves like Wait, Loop, Switch, and Loop Interrupt. I will explain them all in more detail later in this chapter, but know that these are the blocks that wait on the sensors.

- Yellow (Sensor): This allows the user to read the sensors to do all sorts of interesting things as a result.

- Red (Data Operations): As you create LEGO MINDSTORMS EV3 programs, you will have to deal with data as much as you will deal with the motors and sensors. This is how to create variables, constants, random numbers, and other mathematical functions within an EV3 program. We will cover these in Chapter 4.

- Blue (Advanced): I will cover most of this in chapter 5 on Data Logging, but these programs will help you out when you want your LEGO MINDSTORMS creation to do something advanced.

- Turquoise (My Blocks): As your programs get longer and longer, you may find it easier just to drop in a My Block, which is a smaller program designed to work within a larger program. You can go to Chapter 6 if you want to learn how to program with this.

You will note the Toolbar in the upper-right corner which you can experiment with. This is what the symbols mean, from left to right:

- Program/Experiment List: A list of programs that are currently in use on the tab bar.

- Select: What you use when you are selecting programming blocks, or altering information within them (parameters).

- Pan: You may be working on a program that is so large that you might have to go outside the boundaries of the Programming Canvas. The Hand icon will help you get there.

- Comment: It is very helpful to write text on your programming, just so you know where you are going with it. You will notice on several figures below that I used it to write a sentence just so I know what a program will do.

- Save Project: Allows you to save a program to your computer.

- Undo: In case you make a change to a program, and then want it to go back to the way it was, this is what to press. There are five undo levels.

- Redo: In case you make a change to the program, hit Undo, and then decide that you want to keep that change, here is the button to push.

- Zoom Out: Allows you to see the entire program in case it is larger than the Programming Canvas.

- Zoom In: Allows for a narrower focus on areas of the program.

- Reset Zoom: Cancels any Zoom In or Zoom Out feature and brings the view to a 1:1 view.

Also in the upper-right corner is the content editor, which is a digital workbook for projects. You can see instructions there with texts, images, and videos. I will go into more detail on how to use this with the Data Logging Chapter (Chapter 5).

In the lower-right hand corner is the hardware page, where you can see whether or not the EV3 is connected to your computer. If you hit the Download and play button, the program will begin. Also listed here is the Brick Information, Port View, and Available Bricks.

Before I get into talking about the programming palettes, let me explain the basics of a programming block. Here are the basic ingredients:

- Picture. You can see the icon that represents the Programming Block.

- Block Mode. This is a changeable button located directly below the icon, and establishes what the Block will do in its given step.

- Parameters. These are numeric values that you can set by clicking and manually typing them in, or using a bar that you can just click and drag. You can also use Data Operations blocks to set these values, which will be discussed later.

- Ports. Located in the upper-right corner, this is what connector port the commands are being processed to, and they can be set manually. The ports for the sensors and motors will default, and it is important that you know which ones are made for controlling what. I briefly mentioned this in Chapter 1, but here is what you will need to know. By the way, if you don't want a motor or sensor at a certain port, you can always change it.

  - Port A: Medium Motor

  - Port B: Large Motor

  - Port C: Large Motor

  - Port D: Large Motor

- Port 1: Touch Sensor

- Port 2: Gyro Sensor or Temperature Sensor

- Port 3: Color Sensor

- Port 4: Ultrasonic Sensor or Infrared Sensor

In Chapter 1, I mentioned how EV3 Bricks can be daisy chained together, which will result in a Layer Selector on the EV3 programming blocks, and you will see more than one Port is available.

You may notice that sometimes there will be an exclamation point in a yellow sign at the Port indicator. This means that the port that you have set up does not have that particular sensor or motor. You can see in an example in Figure 2-23, which is the Temperature Sensor.

Using the Programming Palette

When you want to create a program, you simply click and drag the blocks from each section and put them into place. You will notice that all programs default with the Start block, and you join the programming block there like railroad cars. When you run a program, your computer will read your blocks one at a time, and will not start the next block until it is finished with the task of the previous one, unless otherwise notified.

If you like, you can place a block in another area, and stretch the tab out until it joins. This can be helpful for cases of multi-tasking, when you want two things to be running at once. See the examples in Figure 2-8. Note the two programs in the lower right is highlighted (as seen by the thin border around the Programming Blocks). These are more examples of multitasking, and if I were to click on the "Download and Play", then these programs would begin simultaneously.

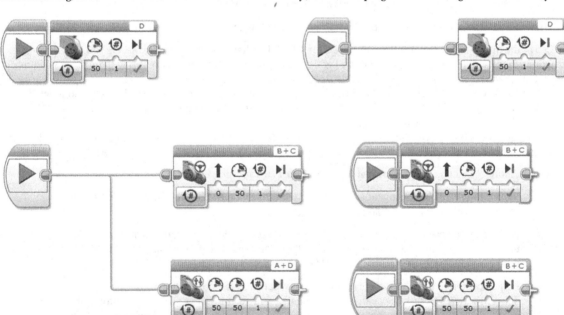

Figure 2-8. *Examples of programs*

If you want to remove a specific programming block, it is as simple as clicking the block and dragging it down below to the Palette like you are throwing it away. You can also highlight the programming bricks you want to remove and hit "Delete".

The Palette is organized by color, which I explained above, and now I will go into detail about the Green and Orange Programming blocks, along with examples.

Action (Green Area) Programming Blocks

The way I remember that the Action pieces are green is that green means go, and therefore these pieces are the ones that go (produce action). In this chapter, I will cover the Programming blocks for Medium Motor, Large Motor, Move Steering and Move Tank. I will cover the remaining three programming blocks (Display, Sound, and Brick Status Light) in Chapter 4.

Medium Motor

This program will operate the Medium Motor, and you can choose to operate on Ports A-D. From there, you can select five Block Modes iterations. You can see in Figure 2-9, the five Modes as well as the parameters and Port values of each.

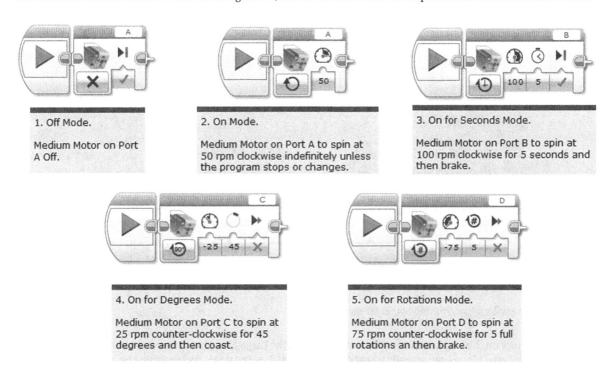

1. Off Mode.

Medium Motor on Port A Off.

2. On Mode.

Medium Motor on Port A to spin at 50 rpm clockwise indefinitely unless the program stops or changes.

3. On for Seconds Mode.

Medium Motor on Port B to spin at 100 rpm clockwise for 5 seconds and then brake.

4. On for Degrees Mode.

Medium Motor on Port C to spin at 25 rpm counter-clockwise for 45 degrees and then coast.

5. On for Rotations Mode.

Medium Motor on Port D to spin at 75 rpm counter-clockwise for 5 full rotations an then brake.

Figure 2-9. *The Five basic modes of the Medium Motor Block Function*

Off Mode is essentially that, and allows the motor to stop spinning. You might wonder why this is even here, but if you need a motor instantly off, this is the command to give it.

On Mode turns the motor on at whatever speed it is set for in the parameters, and it will continue to stay spinning until either the program ends or changed by another programming block.

On for Seconds allows you to pick the speed and time that it will go for. Note the negative speeds spin it counter-clockwise while the positive speeds spin it clockwise.

On for Degrees allows you to input the speed, and you can decide how many degrees it will spin. You can go more than 360, so 720 would be two complete turns, for example. Note that a negative value of degrees can be input, which will affect the direction of turning. Also note that two negatives make a positive, which I will show in later examples with the Large Motor.

On for Rotations will allow you figure out how many times around a circle that you want it to rotate. A parameter of 1 would be the same as an input of 360 for the On for Degrees Mode.

Large Motor

This is just like the Medium Motor, and you can set it up with the same modes and parameters. You can see some examples in Figure 2-10.

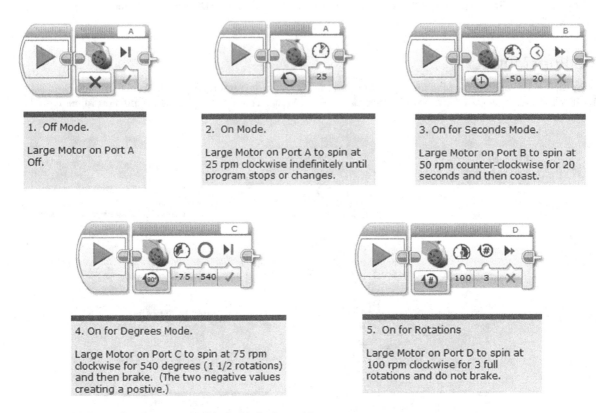

1. Off Mode.

Large Motor on Port A Off.

2. On Mode.

Large Motor on Port A to spin at 25 rpm clockwise indefinitely until program stops or changes.

3. On for Seconds Mode.

Large Motor on Port B to spin at 50 rpm counter-clockwise for 20 seconds and then coast.

4. On for Degrees Mode.

Large Motor on Port C to spin at 75 rpm clockwise for 540 degrees (1 1/2 rotations) and then brake. (The two negative values creating a postive.)

5. On for Rotations

Large Motor on Port D to spin at 100 rpm clockwise for 3 full rotations and do not brake.

Figure 2-10. *Examples of programing blocks for the Large Motor*

The same rules for the Medium Motor parameters apply to the Large Motor, such as two negatives equal a positive. The two Large Motors can actually be used together with these next two programming blocks.

Move Steering

LEGO MINDSTORMS allows you to work two Large Motors at once, which is helpful for creating vehicles with wheels. This particular setup allows for steering it, with interesting results. You can program to spin for seconds, degrees, or rotations.

Please understand that building a vehicle that can use a Move Steering function with two Large Motors is no guarantee that you will get it to steer with just a simple command like the ones in Figure 2-11. I will discuss how to use this to practically steer a vehicle in the next chapter, but some examples of the Modes are shown in Figure 2-11.

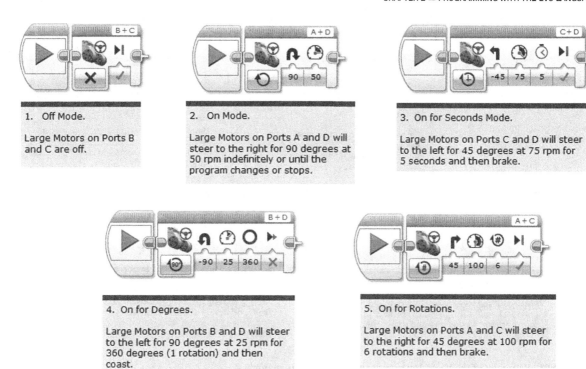

1. Off Mode.

Large Motors on Ports B and C are off.

2. On Mode.

Large Motors on Ports A and D will steer to the right for 90 degrees at 50 rpm indefinitely or until the program changes or stops.

3. On for Seconds Mode.

Large Motors on Ports C and D will steer to the left for 45 degrees at 75 rpm for 5 seconds and then brake.

4. On for Degrees.

Large Motors on Ports B and D will steer to the left for 90 degrees at 25 rpm for 360 degrees (1 rotation) and then coast.

5. On for Rotations.

Large Motors on Ports A and C will steer to the right for 45 degrees at 100 rpm for 6 rotations and then brake.

Figure 2-11. *Modes for Move Steering programming blocks*

Move Tank

As I mentioned before, you can program your Large Motors to work in sync, and if you want to arrange it so they start and stop spinning at the same time, this is the way to go. Note that you can have them spinning at different speeds, and even different directions. Like the Move Steering, you can produce some very interesting results with just two Large Motors. You can see some examples in Figure 2-12.

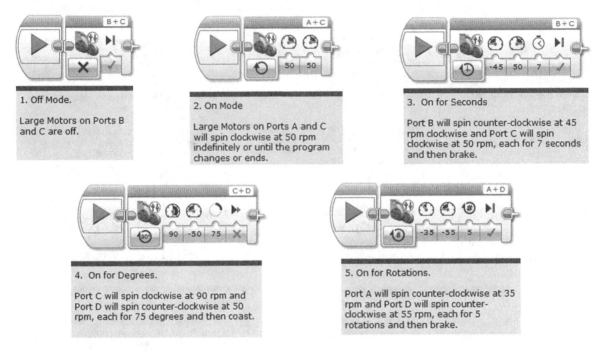

1. Off Mode.

Large Motors on Ports B and C are off.

2. On Mode

Large Motors on Ports A and C will spin clockwise at 50 rpm indefinitely or until the program changes or ends.

3. On for Seconds

Port B will spin counter-clockwise at 45 rpm clockwise and Port C will spin clockwise at 50 rpm, each for 7 seconds and then brake.

4. On for Degrees.

Port C will spin clockwise at 90 rpm and Port D will spin counter-clockwise at 50 rpm, each for 75 degrees and then coast.

5. On for Rotations.

Port A will spin counter-clockwise at 35 rpm and Port D will spin counter-clockwise at 55 rpm, each for 5 rotations and then brake.

Figure 2-12. Examples of the Move Tank programming blocks in action

Like the Move Steering, I will discuss how to use Move Tank practically with a vehicle in the next chapter. For now, let us discuss the last three green programming blocks.

Display, Sound, and Brick Status Light

The last three blocks also give you a lot of control over actions, and their potential is huge. I'm not going to cover these blocks in this chapter, as I have devoted an entire chapter to it in Chapter 4. If you want, you can skip to that chapter and learn about them, but I will briefly introduce these blocks here.

Display allows the screen to change what is shown on its display, and it can range from text to specific shapes. There is a way to even download your own shape, but this will be discussed in a later chapter.

In addition to the motion, the EV3 Brick allows the user to makes some good sound as well. The EV3 Sound Brick comes with a variety of sounds that give an impressive dimension of audio in your project.

Before I talk about the Brick Status Light programming block, I want to specifically talk about what the default of the Status light is on the EV3 Brick. If you haven't noticed, there is a light on the Brick Buttons that glows a certain color depending on these given situations:

- Red is for either Startup, Updating, or Shutdown. A pulsating red means that it is busy.

- Orange means to be alert or ready. A pulsating one means that something is running.

- Green, like on a traffic light, means you are ready to go. You will find that when it is flashing this color, it is running a program.

The programming block for the Brick Status Light allows you to manually change the color of the Status light on the programming block. I will explain this in Chapter 4. The rest of the chapter will be spent discussing the Orange Programming Blocks.

Orange Menu (Flow Control)

It isn't hard to see why these orange blocks are called Flow, as they do control the flow of programs. If programming was like the flow of water, then the Start programming block sets it in motion. The Wait program will stop the motion like a dam unless something specific is done. The Switch program is made to channel that water into separate areas, if need be. The Loop will insure that the water goes back to its source, and starts again. Loop Interrupt is made to stop that process.

Each of these bricks has many modes and parameters that I will explain below, and their use will affect the program. These orange programming blocks are essentially a "Wait for Sensor" while the yellow programming blocks (discussed in the next chapter) are "Use a Sensor" oriented.

Start

We already discussed this particular programming block, as it is the ramp that sets the ball in motion, metaphorically speaking. You will notice that any programming block that you move to the canvas will be near-transparent unless this Start is put on the front.

You will find that when you click on the green arrow or triangle of the Start programming block, whatever program you have after it will begin running. You can have two or more programs running at the same time, but it always starts with this one block.

Wait

The Wait or "Wait For" programming block is precisely what its name implies. This brick instructs the program to wait, and you can even shift its mode so it knows exactly what it is waiting for. You will see several examples of programs using this block, and you will note that they generally come in two forms: "Compare" and "Change".

With Compare, you are telling the program to wait for a very specific input, and not to proceed until this specific input is given. If you run any of the programs listed in the following figures, you will see that there is a highlight that appears on each block as it is running. For a Wait block in Compare mode, it will highlight until you tell it to do its specific task.

As for Change, this is a more general command that will cause something to happen provided you do just about anything in the mode. I realize this is unclear, but I'll let the Mode examples make it clear.

Brick Buttons

As I have stated before, the EV3 Brick comes complete with its own set of buttons. Not only can you use them to perform actions on the EV3 Brick itself, but you can program them to do things while a program is running. Go ahead and see the examples in Figure 2-13.

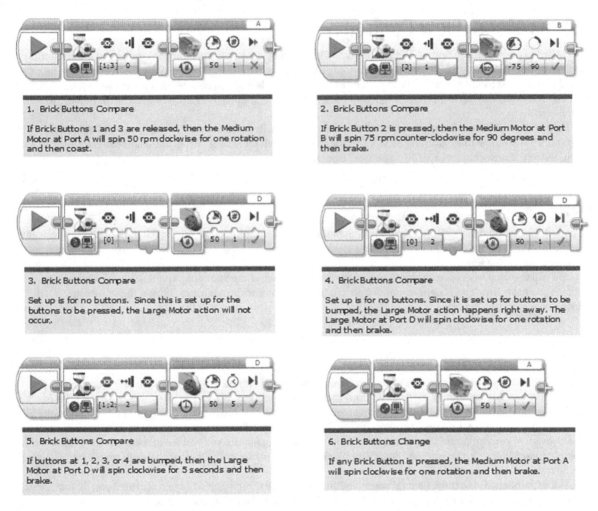

Figure 2-13. *Examples of Brick Buttons on the Wait programming block*

Note that it is possible to set the parameters for about six options: five of them are the individual buttons, and the zero option for no buttons. After the button is the state, and it comes in 0 for released (no contact to button whatsoever), 1 for pressed, and 2 for bumped (quickly pressed and released). Example 1 shows that multiple buttons can be pressed in order to end the wait, while Example 2 is only one particular button.

Example 3 shows a set-up for no buttons, and you will notice that it is set up to be pressed. If you attempt Example 3, you will not get any response, while you will receive an immediate response with Example 4. You will discover that you unintentionally create programs like this, and this is why it is important to know what the programming blocks do. This is also why I put captions under each example.

Example 5 shows how several buttons can be programmed to release the task after the Wait, and Example 6 is good for a Compare mode example where any button change will activate the waiting task.

Color Sensor

The Color Sensor Wait Modes work like the Brick Buttons in that you can ask it to accept many options. Note the examples in Figure 2-14.

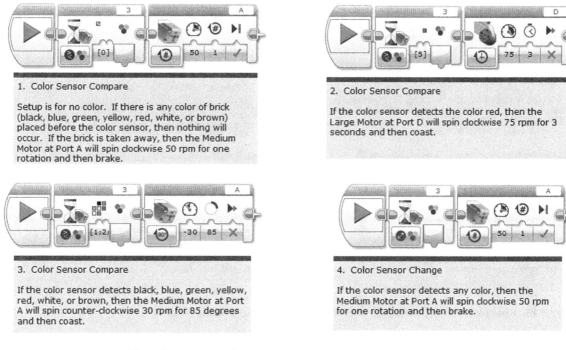

1. Color Sensor Compare

Setup is for no color. If there is any color of brick (black, blue, green, yellow, red, white, or brown) placed before the color sensor, then nothing will occur. If the brick is taken away, then the Medium Motor at Port A will spin clockwise 50 rpm for one rotation and then brake.

2. Color Sensor Compare

If the color sensor detects the color red, then the Large Motor at Port D will spin clockwise 75 rpm for 3 seconds and then coast.

3. Color Sensor Compare

If the color sensor detects black, blue, green, yellow, red, white, or brown, then the Medium Motor at Port A will spin counter-clockwise 30 rpm for 85 degrees and then coast.

4. Color Sensor Change

If the color sensor detects any color, then the Medium Motor at Port A will spin clockwise 50 rpm for one rotation and then brake.

Figure 2-14. *Examples of the Color Sensor on the Wait programming block*

Example 1 shows how a set up for no color (similar to the setup for No Buttons on the Brick Buttons mode) can create some interesting options. In this case, the wait task can occur provided none of the seven colored bricks are blocking the color scanner.

Example 2 is set up to scan just one specific color (red), while Example 3 is set up for all the colors of this Lego rainbow. The Compare Example 4 shows how any alteration of the color scanner starts the wait task.

Reflected Light Intensity

This mode is found under the Color Sensor, and allows for sensing white and black. I'll have a practical example of where to use this in the next chapter, but for now, I want to show you what it is capable of with Figure 2-15.

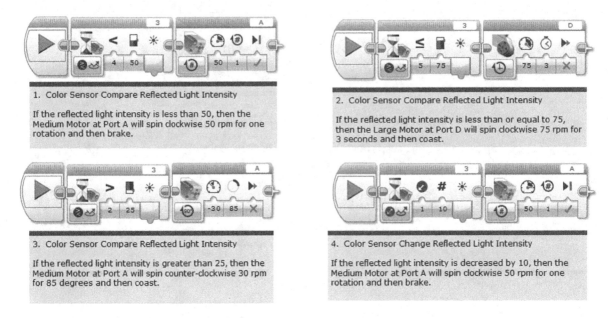

Figure 2-15. *Examples of the Reflected Light Intensity on the Wait programming block*

Note the use of inequality symbols as parameters in Examples 1 and 2. There are about six options including (not equal, less than, less than or equal to, equal to, greater than, and greater than or equal to). The other parameter is reflected light intensity, and a setting of 100 means completely dark while a setting of 0 equals very white. Generally, I use the extremes of these, but you can adjust it, as seen in Examples 1–3.

As for Example 4, this is a way of establishing a wait task based on an increase or decrease. Again, simply telling the computer that any change invokes a wait response.

Ambient Light Intensity

As I said before, the Color Sensor can detect if a room is dark and light, and the Wait Mode for this can create a response if the lights can be turned on or off. You will notice that the examples in Figure 2-16 look almost identical to Figure 2-15, and this is simply because they have identical parameters.

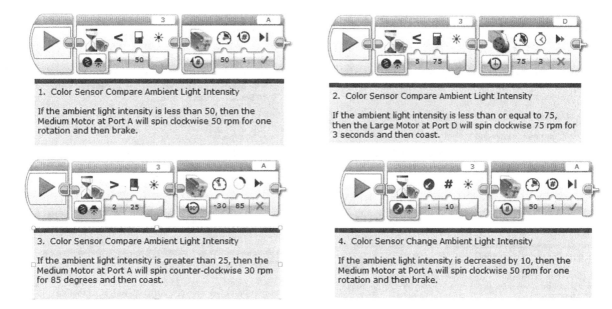

Figure 2-16. *Examples of the Ambient Light Intensity on the Wait programming block*

Generally, you might not have as good control of your lighting to create the distinct details, but I would suggest experimenting.

Gyro Sensor

This particular wait response will occur if the Gyro Sensor is at a certain angle. I'll show you where this comes in handy in the next chapter, and provide more detail on calibrating the Gyro Sensor as well. Figure 2-17 provides examples of this.

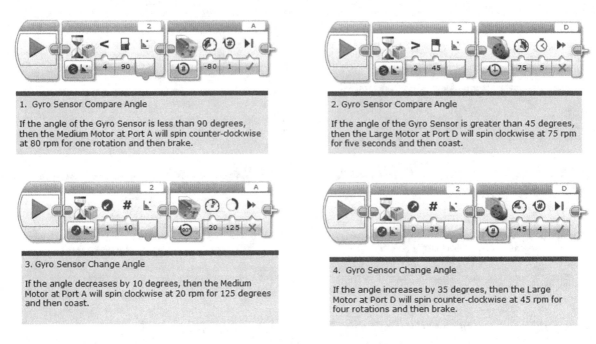

1. Gyro Sensor Compare Angle

If the angle of the Gyro Sensor is less than 90 degrees, then the Medium Motor at Port A will spin counter-clockwise at 80 rpm for one rotation and then brake.

2. Gyro Sensor Compare Angle

If the angle of the Gyro Sensor is greater than 45 degrees, then the Large Motor at Port D will spin clockwise at 75 rpm for five seconds and then coast.

3. Gyro Sensor Change Angle

If the angle decreases by 10 degrees, then the Medium Motor at Port A will spin clockwise at 20 rpm for 125 degrees and then coast.

4. Gyro Sensor Change Angle

If the angle increases by 35 degrees, then the Large Motor at Port D will spin counter-clockwise at 45 rpm for four rotations and then brake.

Figure 2-17. *Examples of the Gyro Sensor Angle on the Wait programming block*

In addition to detecting what angle it is facing, the Gyro Sensor can detect how fast it is going, and then have a proper Wait Response, as seen in the following examples (see Figure 2-18).

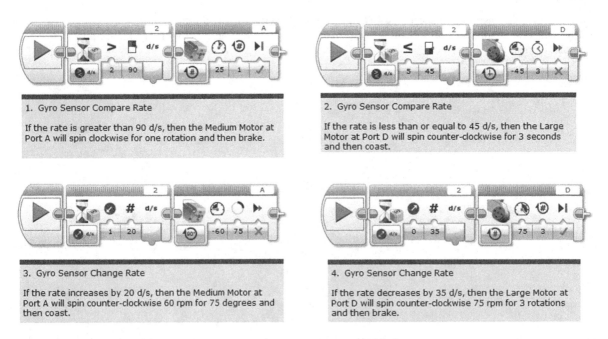

1. Gyro Sensor Compare Rate

If the rate is greater than 90 d/s, then the Medium Motor at Port A will spin clockwise for one rotation and then brake.

2. Gyro Sensor Compare Rate

If the rate is less than or equal to 45 d/s, then the Large Motor at Port D will spin counter-clockwise for 3 seconds and then coast.

3. Gyro Sensor Change Rate

If the rate increases by 20 d/s, then the Medium Motor at Port A will spin counter-clockwise 60 rpm for 75 degrees and then coast.

4. Gyro Sensor Change Rate

If the rate decreases by 35 d/s, then the Large Motor at Port D will spin counter-clockwise 75 rpm for 3 rotations and then brake.

Figure 2-18. *Examples of the Gyro Sensor Rate on the Wait programming block*

Infrared Sensor

The Infrared Sensor and Infrared Beacon have many uses in LEGO MINDSTORMS EV3. The first is Proximity, which means that the Infrared Sensor sends out an infrared signal and can in turn detect the reflection of this signal by some object in front of the sensor. This is very similar to the Ultrasonic Sensor, which I will discuss later. The Compare and Change modes allow you to set a specific number for proximity, that will range from 0 to 100. Unlike the Ultrasonic Sensor, this number is not in specific centimeters or inches, but 0 indicates very close while 100 means far away. I recommend playing around with it if you are looking at specific values, and you can use the examples in Figure 2-19.

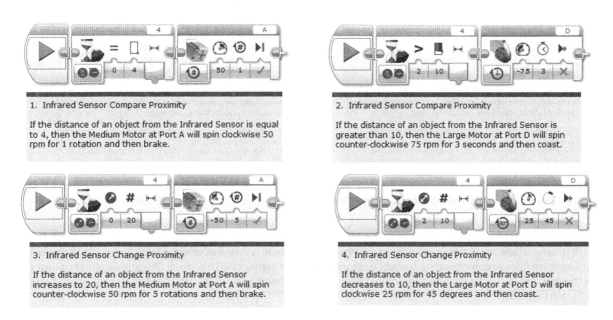

1. Infrared Sensor Compare Proximity

If the distance of an object from the Infrared Sensor is equal to 4, then the Medium Motor at Port A will spin clockwise 50 rpm for 1 rotation and then brake.

2. Infrared Sensor Compare Proximity

If the distance of an object from the Infrared Sensor is greater than 10, then the Large Motor at Port D will spin counter-clockwise 75 rpm for 3 seconds and then coast.

3. Infrared Sensor Change Proximity

If the distance of an object from the Infrared Sensor increases to 20, then the Medium Motor at Port A will spin counter-clockwise 50 rpm for 5 rotations and then brake.

4. Infrared Sensor Change Proximity

If the distance of an object from the Infrared Sensor decreases to 10, then the Large Motor at Port D will spin clockwise 25 rpm for 45 degrees and then coast.

Figure 2-19. *Examples of the Infrared Sensor's Proximity feature*

The two other modes are Beacon Heading and Beacon Proximity, which also work in Compare and Change variations. Heading is whether or not the Infrared Sensor can detect the IR beacon in front of it. Its parameters range from –25 to 25, with negative numbers signifying that the beacon is to the left, while positive values indicate the beacon is to the right. Proximity is like the previous examples in Figure 2-20, but this is the distance to the beacon. This is also used with parameters of 0–100, with 0 meaning very close and 100 meaning far away. Some examples are provided in Figure 2-20, and you will note that first parameter is the channel of the IR Beacon. In order for these programs to work, the IR Beacon has to be on and at the proper channel.

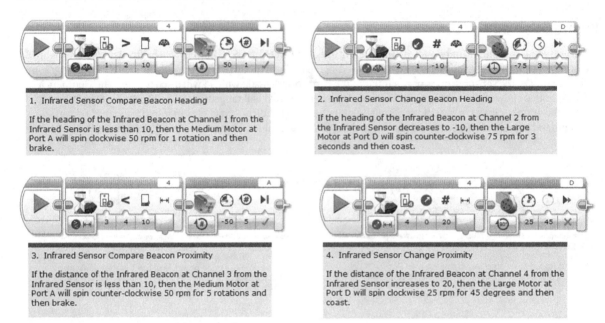

1. Infrared Sensor Compare Beacon Heading

If the heading of the Infrared Beacon at Channel 1 from the Infrared Sensor is less than 10, then the Medium Motor at Port A will spin clockwise 50 rpm for 1 rotation and then brake.

2. Infrared Sensor Change Beacon Heading

If the heading of the Infrared Beacon at Channel 2 from the Infrared Sensor decreases to -10, then the Large Motor at Port D will spin counter-clockwise 75 rpm for 3 seconds and then coast.

3. Infrared Sensor Compare Beacon Proximity

If the distance of the Infrared Beacon at Channel 3 from the Infrared Sensor is less than 10, then the Medium Motor at Port A will spin counter-clockwise 50 rpm for 5 rotations and then brake.

4. Infrared Sensor Change Proximity

If the distance of the Infrared Beacon at Channel 4 from the Infrared Sensor increases to 20, then the Large Motor at Port D will spin clockwise 25 rpm for 45 degrees and then coast.

Figure 2-20. Examples of the Beacon Heading and Beacon Proximity feature of the Infrared Sensor

The last mode for the Infrared Sensor in Wait Mode is the Remote, which tells the program to wait until a button on the IR Beacon is pressed, or simply change a state. Programming these is very similar to the Brick Buttons as I previously discussed, but this just corresponds to buttons and button combinations on the IR Beacon. The first parameter is again the channel, and the next is the button or combination of buttons, which range from 1 to 11 as follows (See Figure 1-9 for the button numbers.):

0. No button, with Beacon Mode off

1. Button 1

2. Button 2

3. Button 3

4. Button 4

5. Buttons 1 and 3 at the same time

6. Buttons 1 and 4 at the same time

7. Buttons 2 and 3 at the same time

8. Buttons 2 and 4 at the same time

9. Beacon Mode on

10. Buttons 1 and 2 at the same time

11. Buttons 3 and 4 at the same time

You can see some examples of the Compare and Change variations below in Figure 2-21.

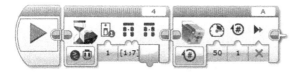

1. Infrared Sensor Compare Remote

If remote combinations 1 and 7 are pressed on the Infrared Beacon set at Channel 1, then the Medium Motor at Port A will spin 50 rpm clockwise for one rotation and then coast.

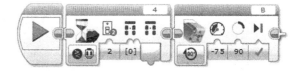

2. Infrared Sensor Compare Remote

If no button is pressed and the beacon mode is off on the Infrared Beacon set at Channel 2, then the Medium Motor at Port B will spin 75 rpm counter-clockwise for 90 degrees and then brake.

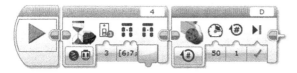

3. Infrared Sensor Compare Remote

If remote combinations 6-11 are pressed on the Infrared Beacon set at Channel 3, then the Large Motor at Port D will spin clockwise for one rotation and then brake.

4. Infrared Sensor Change Remote

If any of the buttons on the Infrared Beacon set on Channel 4 are pressed, then the Large Motor at Port D will spin 50 rpm clockwise for one rotation and then brake.

Figure 2-21. *Examples of the Infrared Sensor's Remote features*

Motor Rotation

In addition to the Sensor controls, it is possible to have a wait response after a motor does its work. It is possible to have a function wait until a motor has turned by degrees, rotations, or even when it gets to a certain speed. Some examples of it at work are provided in Figure 2-22.

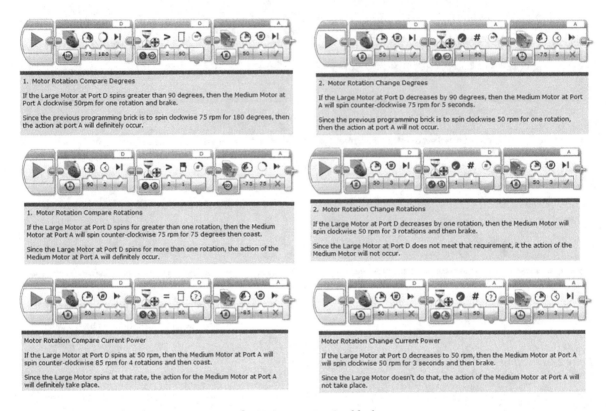

1. Motor Rotation Compare Degrees

If the Large Motor at Port D spins greater than 90 degrees, then the Medium Motor at Port A clockwise 50rpm for one rotation and brake.

Since the previous programming brick is to spin clockwise 75 rpm for 180 degrees, then the action at port A will definitely occur.

2. Motor Rotation Change Degrees

If the Large Motor at Port D decreases by 90 degrees, then the Medium Motor at Port A will spin counter-clockwise 75 rpm for 5 seconds.

Since the previous programming brick is to spin clockwise 50 rpm for one rotation, then the action at port A will not occur.

1. Motor Rotation Compare Rotations

If the Large Motor at Port D spins for greater than one rotation, then the Medium Motor at Port A will spin counter-clockwise 75 degrees then coast.

Since the Large Motor at Port D spins for more than one rotation, the action of the Medium Motor at Port A will definitely occur.

2. Motor Rotation Change Rotations

If the Large Motor at Port D decreases by one rotation, then the Medium Motor will spin clockwise 50 rpm for 3 rotations and then brake.

Since the Large Motor at Port D does not meet that requirement, it the action of the Medium Motor will not occur.

Motor Rotation Compare Current Power

If the Large Motor at Port D spins at 50 rpm, then the Medium Motor at Port A will spin counter-clockwise 85 rpm for 4 rotations and then coast.

Since the Large Motor spins at that rate, the action for the Medium Motor at Port A will definitely take place.

Motor Rotation Change Current Power

If the Large Motor at Port D decreases to 50 rpm, then the Medium Motor at Port A will spin clockwise 50 rpm for 3 seconds and then brake.

Since the Large Motor doesn't do that, the action of the Medium Motor at Port A will not take place.

Figure 2-22. *Examples of Motor Rotation on the Wait programming block*

Temperature Sensor

It is possible to sense the temperature, and create a wait response when something gets too hot or too cold. See Figure 2-23 for examples.

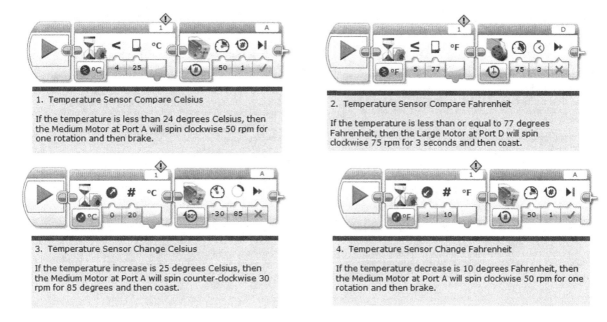

1. Temperature Sensor Compare Celsius

If the temperature is less than 24 degrees Celsius, then the Medium Motor at Port A will spin clockwise 50 rpm for one rotation and then brake.

2. Temperature Sensor Compare Fahrenheit

If the temperature is less than or equal to 77 degrees Fahrenheit, then the Large Motor at Port D will spin clockwise 75 rpm for 3 seconds and then coast.

3. Temperature Sensor Change Celsius

If the temperature increase is 25 degrees Celsius, then the Medium Motor at Port A will spin counter-clockwise 30 rpm for 85 degrees and then coast.

4. Temperature Sensor Change Fahrenheit

If the temperature decrease is 10 degrees Fahrenheit, then the Medium Motor at Port A will spin clockwise 50 rpm for one rotation and then brake.

Figure 2-23. Examples of the Temperature Sensor on the Wait programming block

Timer

It is possible to create a timer in order to simply wait a certain amount of time before the wait response. You will note you can select eight timers, and it is possible to export that amount of time for later in the program, but I will explain how to do that in later chapters. For now, enjoy the examples in Figure 2-24.

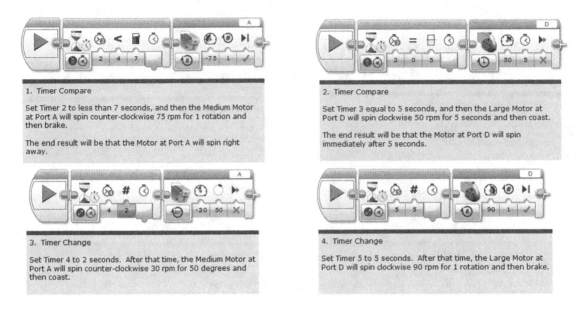

1. Timer Compare

Set Timer 2 to less than 7 seconds, and then the Medium Motor at Port A will spin counter-clockwise 75 rpm for 1 rotation and then brake.

The end result will be that the Motor at Port A will spin right away.

2. Timer Compare

Set Timer 3 equal to 5 seconds, and then the Large Motor at Port D will spin clockwise 50 rpm for 5 seconds and then coast.

The end result will be that the Motor at Port D will spin immediately after 5 seconds.

3. Timer Change

Set Timer 4 to 2 seconds. After that time, the Medium Motor at Port A will spin counter-clockwise 30 rpm for 50 degrees and then coast.

4. Timer Change

Set Timer 5 to 5 seconds. After that time, the Large Motor at Port D will spin clockwise 90 rpm for 1 rotation and then brake.

Figure 2-24. Examples of the Timer on the Wait programming block

Touch Sensor

Similar to the Brick Buttons Mode, the Touch Sensor Mode takes advantage of the Touch Sensor's button and allows you to create a wait response at the releasing, pressing, or bumping (a quick press and release) of the button. You can see examples of it in Figure 2-25, and there is very little difference between the Compare and Change Modes.

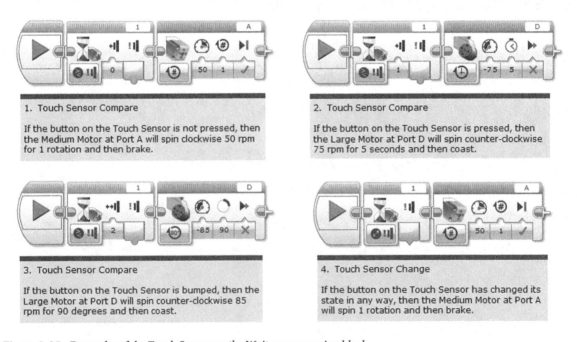

1. Touch Sensor Compare

If the button on the Touch Sensor is not pressed, then the Medium Motor at Port A will spin clockwise 50 rpm for 1 rotation and then brake.

2. Touch Sensor Compare

If the button on the Touch Sensor is pressed, then the Large Motor at Port D will spin counter-clockwise 75 rpm for 5 seconds and then coast.

3. Touch Sensor Compare

If the button on the Touch Sensor is bumped, then the Large Motor at Port D will spin counter-clockwise 85 rpm for 90 degrees and then coast.

4. Touch Sensor Change

If the button on the Touch Sensor has changed its state in any way, then the Medium Motor at Port A will spin 1 rotation and then brake.

Figure 2-25. Examples of the Touch Sensor on the Wait programming block

Ultrasonic Sensor

The Ultrasonic Sensor is that pair of electric eyes that just know what objects are put in front of it. You will notice that you can move the object closer or further away from the Ultrasonic Sensor in order to trigger the wait response, as seen in the examples in Figure 2-26. You should also notice that it is possible to set it for listening, and a loud sound will trigger the wait response.

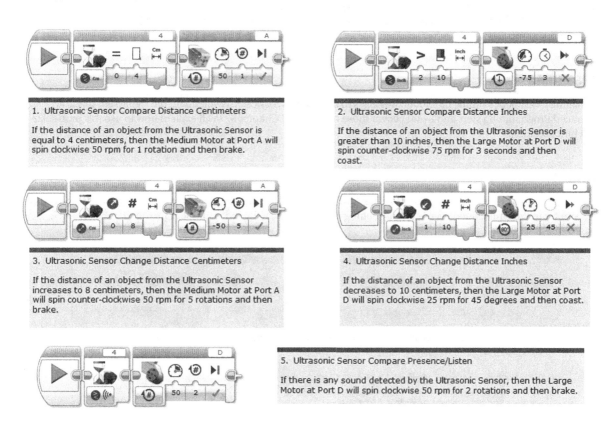

1. Ultrasonic Sensor Compare Distance Centimeters

If the distance of an object from the Ultrasonic Sensor is equal to 4 centimeters, then the Medium Motor at Port A will spin clockwise 50 rpm for 1 rotation and then brake.

2. Ultrasonic Sensor Compare Distance Inches

If the distance of an object from the Ultrasonic Sensor is greater than 10 inches, then the Large Motor at Port D will spin counter-clockwise 75 rpm for 3 seconds and then coast.

3. Ultrasonic Sensor Change Distance Centimeters

If the distance of an object from the Ultrasonic Sensor increases to 8 centimeters, then the Medium Motor at Port A will spin counter-clockwise 50 rpm for 5 rotations and then brake.

4. Ultrasonic Sensor Change Distance Inches

If the distance of an object from the Ultrasonic Sensor decreases to 10 centimeters, then the Large Motor at Port D will spin clockwise 25 rpm for 45 degrees and then coast.

5. Ultrasonic Sensor Compare Presence/Listen

If there is any sound detected by the Ultrasonic Sensor, then the Large Motor at Port D will spin clockwise 50 rpm for 2 rotations and then brake.

Figure 2-26. *Examples of the Ultrasonic Sensor on the Wait programming block*

Energy Meter

This Mode of the Wait programming block is referring to an Energy Meter that was part of a LEGO MINDSTORMS NXT kit known as the Renewable Energy Add-on Set (9688). The Energy Meter could be used for both data logging and programming, and it can be used as a sensor for Voltage, Current, Wattage, and Joules.

I'm not going to go into detail with this with examples, as the variations of Compare and Change are similar to that of the Temperature Sensor. I will say that if you have access to the NXT Energy Meter and you want to download the software to get it working with EV3 Brick, go to http://www.lego.com/en-us/mindstorms/downloads/ev3-blocks/energymeter/.

NXT Sound Sensor

Like the NXT Energy Meter, The NXT Sound Sensor is another NXT Brick that can also be programmed to work with the EV3 Brick. All you need to do is download the software to use it at http://www.lego.com/en-us/mindstorms/downloads/ev3-blocks/sound/.

The Sound Sensor is similar to the Ultrasonic Sensor when it is in Presence Mode, except it can measure very specific noise levels in dB (decibels) as well as dBA, which are frequencies around 3–6 kHz where the human ear is most sensitive. Again, I did not include any examples of Compare or Change for this Wait Mode, as it is quite similar to the Temperature Sensor and other programs.

Messaging

Messaging is all about sending Bluetooth Messages in between EV3 Bricks. As you might have guessed, this is an Advanced Programming step, and I won't cover those blocks until Chapter 5. I will explain how to use this particular Wait function then.

Time

You will notice that Time is the only Mode on the Wait block that doesn't have a Compare or Change sub-modes. It is very similar to the Timer, but does not require setting a specific timer. A good example is provided in Figure 2-27.

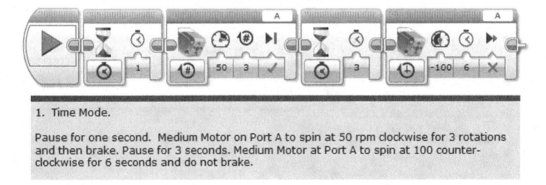

1. Time Mode.

Pause for one second. Medium Motor on Port A to spin at 50 rpm clockwise for 3 rotations and then brake. Pause for 3 seconds. Medium Motor at Port A to spin at 100 counterclockwise for 6 seconds and do not brake.

Figure 2-27. *Time Mode for the Wait block*

Loop

Occasionally, you will want to set up a program so that it does the same thing over and over again. Rather than put several similar programming blocks together, this can be accomplished with the Loop programming block. Not only can you use the Loop to do something over again, but you can program to stop at a certain response.

You will note in the many examples in this section that the user has the ability to name the loop with the descriptor up on top, which was possible on any of the green blocks. Unlike the Wait, the Loop has no "Change" mode, but it is all Compare.

Brick Buttons

You can see that the set up for the Brick Buttons is similar to the Wait. In this case, the action will repeat over and over again unless the proper Brick Button is released, pressed, or bumped, as seen in the examples in Figure 2-28.

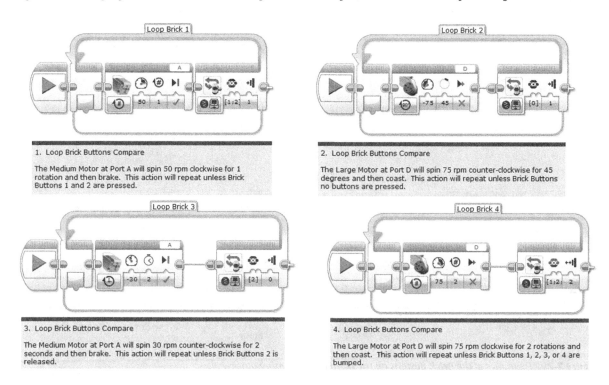

1. Loop Brick Buttons Compare

The Medium Motor at Port A will spin 50 rpm clockwise for 1 rotation and then brake. This action will repeat unless Brick Buttons 1 and 2 are pressed.

2. Loop Brick Buttons Compare

The Large Motor at Port D will spin 75 rpm counter-clockwise for 45 degrees and then coast. This action will repeat unless Brick Buttons no buttons are pressed.

3. Loop Brick Buttons Compare

The Medium Motor at Port A will spin 30 rpm counter-clockwise for 2 seconds and then brake. This action will repeat unless Brick Buttons 2 is released.

4. Loop Brick Buttons Compare

The Large Motor at Port D will spin 75 rpm clockwise for 2 rotations and then coast. This action will repeat unless Brick Buttons 1, 2, 3, or 4 are bumped.

Figure 2-28. *Examples of the Brick Buttons on the Loop programming block*

Color Sensor

You can see that the Color Sensor can be set up to accept several colors in order to close the loop. You will note that in Loop block 2 in Figure 2-29, the Color Scanner must scan no color to close that loop.

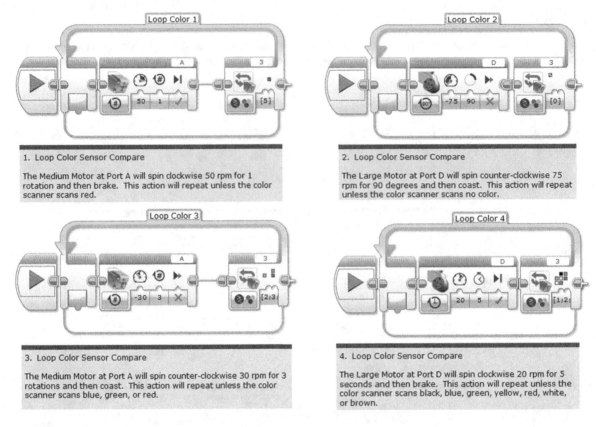

1. Loop Color Sensor Compare

The Medium Motor at Port A will spin clockwise 50 rpm for 1 rotation and then brake. This action will repeat unless the color scanner scans red.

2. Loop Color Sensor Compare

The Large Motor at Port D will spin counter-clockwise 75 rpm for 90 degrees and then coast. This action will repeat unless the color scanner scans no color.

3. Loop Color Sensor Compare

The Medium Motor at Port A will spin counter-clockwise 30 rpm for 3 rotations and then coast. This action will repeat unless the color scanner scans blue, green, or red.

4. Loop Color Sensor Compare

The Large Motor at Port D will spin clockwise 20 rpm for 5 seconds and then brake. This action will repeat unless the color scanner scans black, blue, green, yellow, red, white, or brown.

Figure 2-29. *Examples of the Brick Buttons on the Loop programming block*

Reflected Light Intensity

This is another function of the Color Sensor, and how it can detect the difference between very dark and very light. Again, I will discuss in the next chapter what to do with this, but I wanted to show you what can be done with it in Figure 2-30.

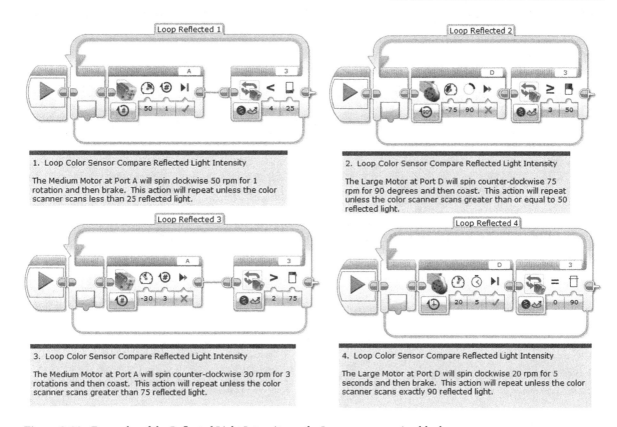

Figure 2-30. *Examples of the Reflected Light Intensity on the Loop programming block*

Ambient Light Intensity

This particular feature also works with the Color Sensor, and it is good for any model that you want to operate with some light and dark action. With this, you can create a model that will do actions over and over until the lights go on, or off. Some examples are provided in Figure 2-31.

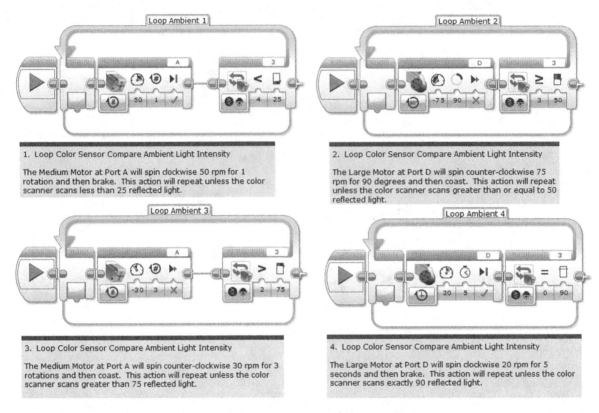

1. Loop Color Sensor Compare Ambient Light Intensity

The Medium Motor at Port A will spin clockwise 50 rpm for 1 rotation and then brake. This action will repeat unless the color scanner scans less than 25 reflected light.

2. Loop Color Sensor Compare Ambient Light Intensity

The Large Motor at Port D will spin counter-clockwise 75 rpm for 90 degrees and then coast. This action will repeat unless the color scanner scans greater than or equal to 50 reflected light.

3. Loop Color Sensor Compare Ambient Light Intensity

The Medium Motor at Port A will spin counter-clockwise 30 rpm for 3 rotations and then coast. This action will repeat unless the color scanner scans greater than 75 reflected light.

4. Loop Color Sensor Compare Ambient Light Intensity

The Large Motor at Port D will spin clockwise 20 rpm for 5 seconds and then brake. This action will repeat unless the color scanner scans exactly 90 reflected light.

Figure 2-31. *Examples of the Ambient Light Intensity on the Loop programming block*

Gyro Sensor

As explained before, you can arrange it so the Gyro Sensor can detect an angle, and the Loop Program can stop when that proper angle is reached. Figure 2-32 provides examples.

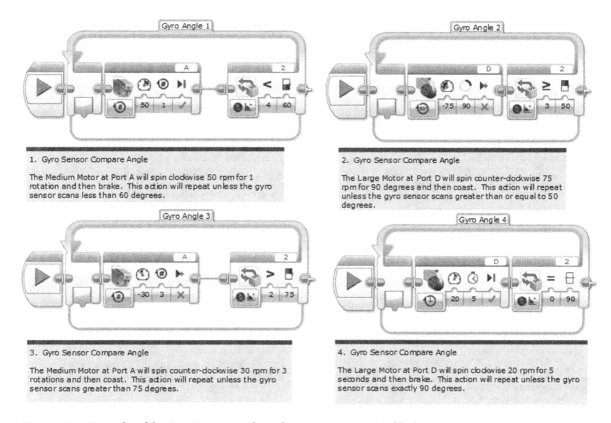

1. Gyro Sensor Compare Angle

The Medium Motor at Port A will spin clockwise 50 rpm for 1 rotation and then brake. This action will repeat unless the gyro sensor scans less than 60 degrees.

2. Gyro Sensor Compare Angle

The Large Motor at Port D will spin counter-clockwise 75 rpm for 90 degrees and then coast. This action will repeat unless the gyro sensor scans greater than or equal to 50 degrees.

3. Gyro Sensor Compare Angle

The Medium Motor at Port A will spin counter-clockwise 30 rpm for 3 rotations and then coast. This action will repeat unless the gyro sensor scans greater than 75 degrees.

4. Gyro Sensor Compare Angle

The Large Motor at Port D will spin clockwise 20 rpm for 5 seconds and then brake. This action will repeat unless the gyro sensor scans exactly 90 degrees.

Figure 2-32. *Examples of the Gyro Buttons Angle on the Loop programming block*

In addition to programming the loop at an angle, it is also possible to program it with a rate, such as the examples in Figure 2-33.

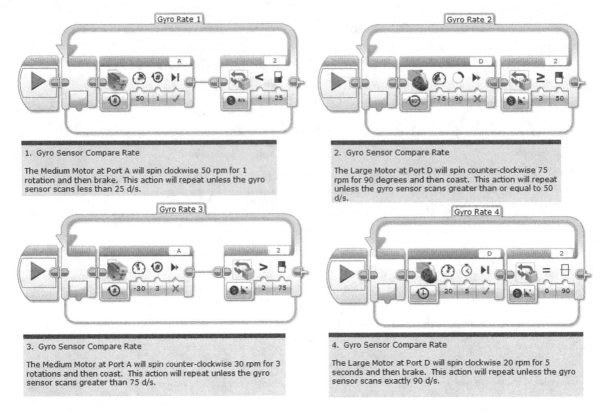

1. Gyro Sensor Compare Rate

The Medium Motor at Port A will spin clockwise 50 rpm for 1 rotation and then brake. This action will repeat unless the gyro sensor scans less than 25 d/s.

2. Gyro Sensor Compare Rate

The Large Motor at Port D will spin counter-clockwise 75 rpm for 90 degrees and then coast. This action will repeat unless the gyro sensor scans greater than or equal to 50 d/s.

3. Gyro Sensor Compare Rate

The Medium Motor at Port A will spin counter-clockwise 30 rpm for 3 rotations and then coast. This action will repeat unless the gyro sensor scans greater than 75 d/s.

4. Gyro Sensor Compare Rate

The Large Motor at Port D will spin clockwise 20 rpm for 5 seconds and then brake. This action will repeat unless the gyro sensor scans exactly 90 d/s.

Figure 2-33. Examples of the Gyro Sensor Rate on the Loop programming block

Infrared Sensor

I've discussed earlier in the chapter what the Infrared Sensor is capable of in Wait Mode. You can use the Modes of Proximity, Beacon Heading, Beacon Proximity, and Remote to end a loop as well. Some examples are provided in Figure 2-34.

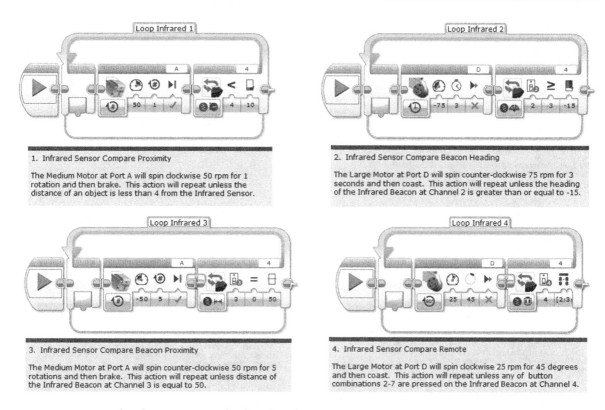

1. Infrared Sensor Compare Proximity

The Medium Motor at Port A will spin clockwise 50 rpm for 1 rotation and then brake. This action will repeat unless the distance of an object is less than 4 from the Infrared Sensor.

2. Infrared Sensor Compare Beacon Heading

The Large Motor at Port D will spin counter-clockwise 75 rpm for 3 seconds and then coast. This action will repeat unless the heading of the Infrared Beacon at Channel 2 is greater than or equal to -15.

3. Infrared Sensor Compare Beacon Proximity

The Medium Motor at Port A will spin counter-clockwise 50 rpm for 5 rotations and then brake. This action will repeat unless distance of the Infrared Beacon at Channel 3 is equal to 50.

4. Infrared Sensor Compare Remote

The Large Motor at Port D will spin clockwise 25 rpm for 45 degrees and then coast. This action will repeat unless any of button combinations 2-7 are pressed on the Infrared Beacon at Channel 4.

Figure 2-34. *Examples of Loop Functions for the Infrared Sensor*

Motor Rotation

Motor Rotation is all about creating an action that will repeat unless a motor turns a certain amount of degrees, rotations, or hits a certain current power. You can see some examples in Figure 2-35, and you will notice that the third one uses two different motors.

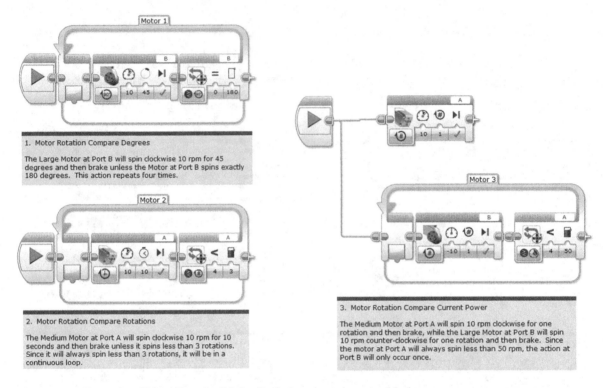

1. Motor Rotation Compare Degrees

The Large Motor at Port B will spin clockwise 10 rpm for 45 degrees and then brake unless the Motor at Port B spins exactly 180 degrees. This action repeats four times.

2. Motor Rotation Compare Rotations

The Medium Motor at Port A will spin clockwise 10 rpm for 10 seconds and then brake unless it spins less than 3 rotations. Since it will always spin less than 3 rotations, it will be in a continuous loop.

3. Motor Rotation Compare Current Power

The Medium Motor at Port A will spin 10 rpm clockwise for one rotation and then brake, while the Large Motor at Port B will spin 10 rpm counter-clockwise for one rotation and then brake. Since the motor at Port A will always spin less than 50 rpm, the action at Port B will only occur once.

Figure 2-35. *Examples of Motor Function Modes for the Loop programming block*

Timer

This allows the program to loop for a certain programmed amount of time, and then the loop closes. See the examples in Figure 2-36.

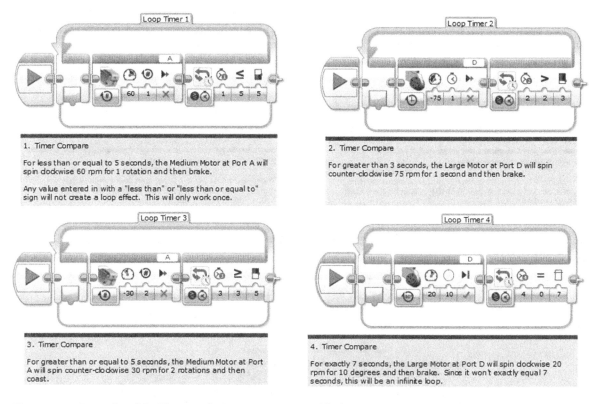

1. Timer Compare

For less than or equal to 5 seconds, the Medium Motor at Port A will spin clockwise 60 rpm for 1 rotation and then brake.

Any value entered in with a "less than" or "less than or equal to" sign will not create a loop effect. This will only work once.

2. Timer Compare

For greater than 3 seconds, the Large Motor at Port D will spin counter-clockwise 75 rpm for 1 second and then brake.

3. Timer Compare

For greater than or equal to 5 seconds, the Medium Motor at Port A will spin counter-clockwise 30 rpm for 2 rotations and then coast.

4. Timer Compare

For exactly 7 seconds, the Large Motor at Port D will spin clockwise 20 rpm for 10 degrees and then brake. Since it won't exactly equal 7 seconds, this will be an infinite loop.

Figure 2-36. *Examples of the Timer on the Loop programming block*

Touch Sensor

This particular mode allows you to stop or start with a release, press, or bump of a button. You can see some examples in Figure 2-37.

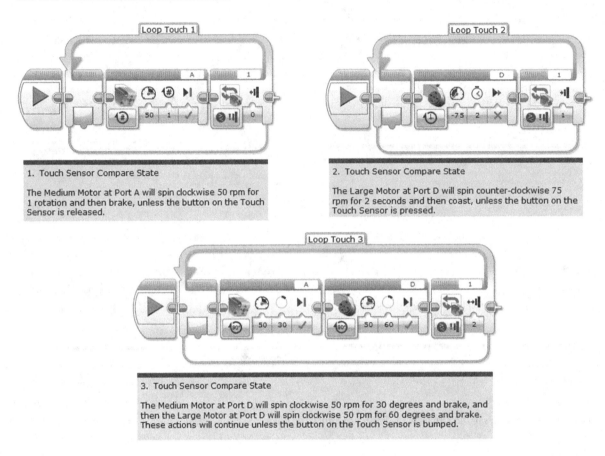

1. Touch Sensor Compare State

The Medium Motor at Port A will spin clockwise 50 rpm for 1 rotation and then brake, unless the button on the Touch Sensor is released.

2. Touch Sensor Compare State

The Large Motor at Port D will spin counter-clockwise 75 rpm for 2 seconds and then coast, unless the button on the Touch Sensor is pressed.

3. Touch Sensor Compare State

The Medium Motor at Port D will spin clockwise 50 rpm for 30 degrees and brake, and then the Large Motor at Port D will spin clockwise 50 rpm for 60 degrees and brake. These actions will continue unless the button on the Touch Sensor is bumped.

Figure 2-37. Examples of the Brick Buttons on the Loop programming block

Ultrasonic Sensor

This is how to program the Loop so it can stop when in scans something within the proper pre-programmed distance. Note the examples in Figure 2-38.

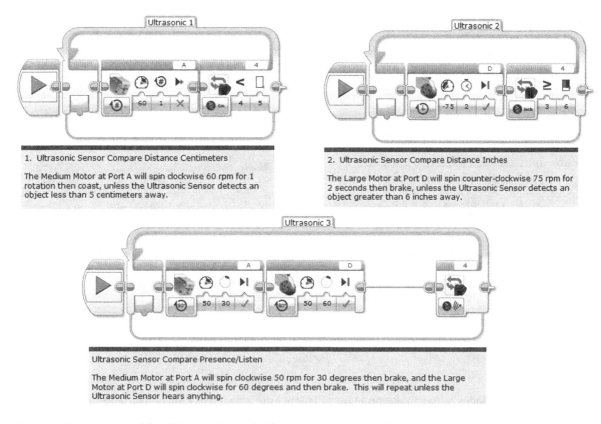

1. Ultrasonic Sensor Compare Distance Centimeters

The Medium Motor at Port A will spin clockwise 60 rpm for 1 rotation then coast, unless the Ultrasonic Sensor detects an object less than 5 centimeters away.

2. Ultrasonic Sensor Compare Distance Inches

The Large Motor at Port D will spin counter-clockwise 75 rpm for 2 seconds then brake, unless the Ultrasonic Sensor detects an object greater than 6 inches away.

Ultrasonic Sensor Compare Presence/Listen

The Medium Motor at Port A will spin clockwise 50 rpm for 30 degrees then brake, and the Large Motor at Port D will spin clockwise for 60 degrees and then brake. This will repeat unless the Ultrasonic Sensor hears anything.

Figure 2-38. *Examples of the Ultrasonic Sensor for the Loop programming block*

Energy Meter

As I mentioned in the Wait programming blocks, this Energy Meter refers to a NXT sensor. With this mode, you can create an action that will repeat unless it detects a certain value in Voltage, Current, Wattage, or Joules. Since this is so similar to other Loop Modes, I did not include any examples.

NXT Sound Sensor

This is another NXT Sensor that has the ability to detect sound in dB or dBa. If you want to create an action that will stop when it senses something in a certain sound range, this is the programming block to use. Like the Energy Meter, I also did not include any examples of this Mode because it is very similar to the Ultrasonic and other Loop Modes.

Messaging

This particular Mode will keep the loop going unless it receives a certain message. The Message will originate from another EV3 Brick, and I will discuss that in Chapter 5.

Unlimited and Count

These particular Loop functions will allow you to specify the amount of time that you want your program to loop. In the case of Unlimited, your Loop will go forever. As for the Count, you specify the amount of times it will run, and it will run that many times. Two examples are provided in Figure 2-39.

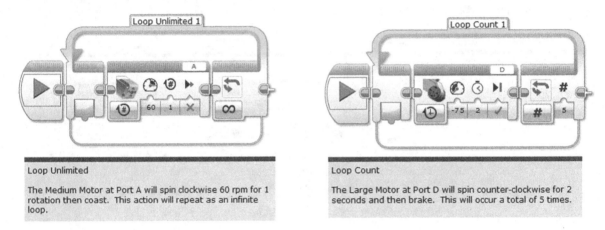

Loop Unlimited

The Medium Motor at Port A will spin clockwise 60 rpm for 1 rotation then coast. This action will repeat as an infinite loop.

Loop Count

The Large Motor at Port D will spin counter-clockwise for 2 seconds and then brake. This will occur a total of 5 times.

***Figure 2-39.** Examples of the Unlimited and Count on the Loop programming block*

Logic and Time

For the last two Loop Modes, setting a value on a logic to True or False is required. I will explain more on that later in the next chapter when I talk about vining and other important details.

As for Time, it is like programming the Timer with the number of seconds that you want it to loop. See the examples in Figure 2-40.

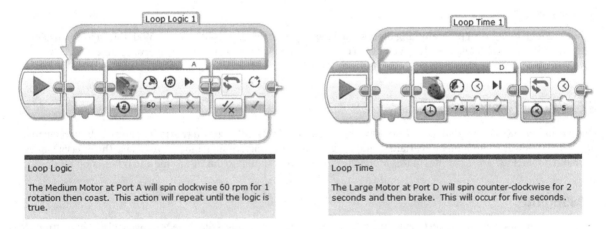

Loop Logic

The Medium Motor at Port A will spin clockwise 60 rpm for 1 rotation then coast. This action will repeat until the logic is true.

Loop Time

The Large Motor at Port D will spin counter-clockwise for 2 seconds and then brake. This will occur for five seconds.

***Figure 2-40.** Examples of the Logic and Time on the Loop programming block*

You can see that these programs will essentially go on forever, but it is possible to end the loop after a certain event occurs, as described in the following section.

Switch

The Switch is essentially a big if/then statement in your program. When you are using a Switch in your program, you are saying: "If this happens, then do this. If this doesn't happen, do that". I'll have more explanations of this below with more examples.

The Switch comes in two forms: Measure and Compare. Measure allows for creating several cases, so it isn't just two options, but several. All you need to do is click on the "+" button. You will also need to click a default setting which is what you tell the program to do when it can't figure out what to do next. As for Compare, this is one measurement or the other.

You might notice that you can view the Switch form in the regular mode or tabbed mode. Tabbed mode allows a smaller view where you can click on the options to see what you can do.

Brick Buttons

As you can see, it is possible to click a button and have something happen, plus a default if nothing is pushed or something other than what is tabbed is pushed. See the example in Figures 2-41 and 2-42.

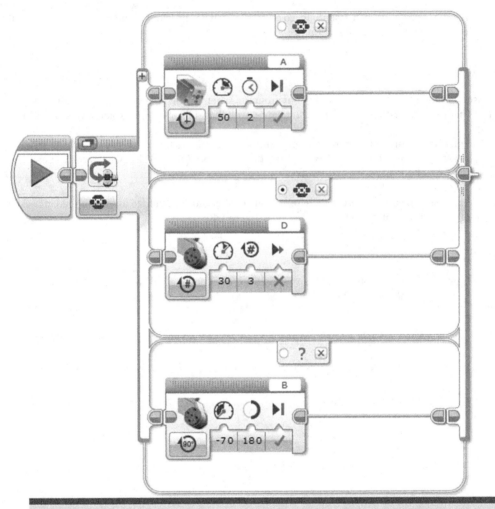

1. Brick Buttons Measure

If no Brick Buttons are pressed, then the Medium Motor at Port A will spin clockwise 50 rpm for 2 seconds and then brake. If Button 1 is pressed, then the Large Motor at Port B will spin counter-clockwise at 70 rpm for 180 degrees and then stop. If Button 4 is pressed, or any other input than listed above, then the Large Motor at Port D will spin clockwise 30 rpm for 3 rotations and then coast.

Figure 2-41. A way of using Brick Buttons to create different Switches for motors on the EV3 Brick

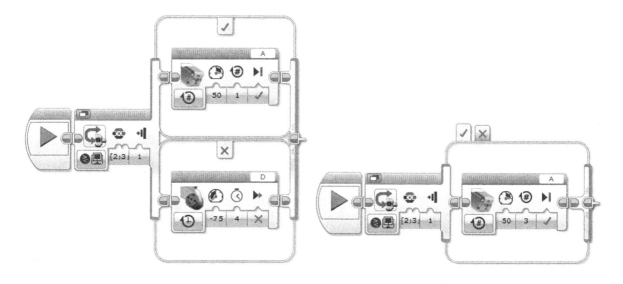

2. Brick Buttons Compare (Regular View and Tabbed View)

If Brick Buttons 2, 3, or 4 are pressed, then the Medium Motor at Port A will spin clockwise 50 rpm for 3 rotations and then brake. Otherwise, the Large Motor at Port D will spin counter-clockwise 75 rpm for 4 seconds and then brake.

Figure 2-42. *Another method of using Brick Buttons on a Switch programming block, with the right being a tabbed view*

Color Sensor

The Color Sensor is set up so you can scan a color and have some different tasks accomplished. You can see how it can be set up for several colors in the Compare section in Figure 2-43.

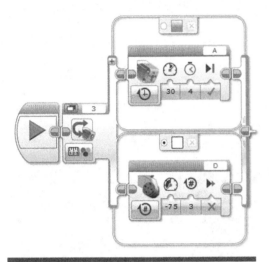

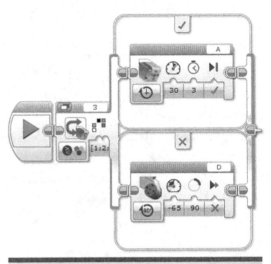

1. Color Sensor Measure Color

If the color scanner scans blue, then the Medium Motor at Port A will spin clockwise 30 rpm for 4 seconds and then brake. If the color scanner scans white, or any other reading, then the Large Motor at Port D will spin counter-clockwise 75 rpm for 3 rotations and then coast.

2. Color Sensor Compare Color

If the color scanner scans black, blue, green, red, or white, then the Medium Motor at Port A will spin clockwise 30 rpm for 3 seconds and then brake. If the color scanner scans anything else, then the Large Motor at Port D will spin counter-clockwise 65 rpm for 90 degrees and then brake.

Figure 2-43. *Examples of the Color Sensor Buttons on the Loop programming block*

Reflected and Ambient Light Intensity

There isn't much difference between the Reflected and Ambient Light Intensity settings, and the examples in Figure 2-44 will show how to set up a Switch for them.

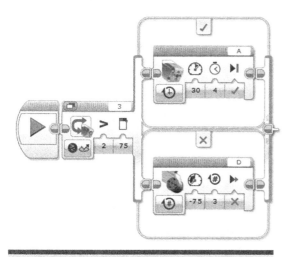

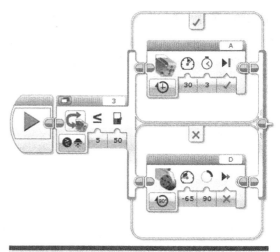

1. Color Sensor Compare Reflected Light Intensity

If the color sensor detects greater than 75 percent reflected light intensity, then the Medium Motor at Port A will spin clockwise 30 rpm for 4 seconds and then brake. If there is any other reading, then the Large Motor at Port D will spin counter-clockwise 75 rpm for 3 rotations and then coast.

2. Color Sensor Compare Ambient Light Intensity

If the color scanner detects less than or equal to 50 percent of ambient light intensity, then the Medium Motor at Port A will spin clockwise 30 rpm for 3 seconds and then brake. If there is any other reading, then the Large Motor at Port D will spin counter-clockwise 65 rpm for 90 degrees and then brake.

Figure 2-44. Examples of the Reflected Light Intensity and Ambient Light Intensity on the Loop programming block

Gyro Sensor

This is a way of doing a switch with the Gyro Sensor, for both Angle and Rate.

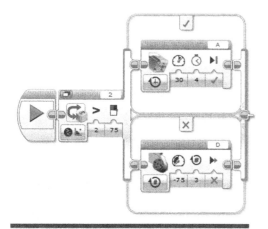

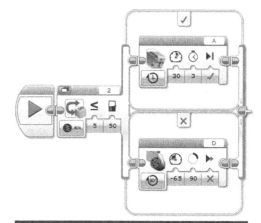

1. Gyro Sensor Compare Angle

If the gyro sensor detects greater than 75 degrees, then the Medium Motor at Port A will spin clockwise 30 rpm for 4 seconds and then brake. If there is any other reading, then the Large Motor at Port D will spin counter-clockwise 75 rpm for 3 rotations and then coast.

2. Gyro Sensor Compare Rate

If the gyro scanner detects less than or equal to 50 d/s, then the Medium Motor at Port A will spin clockwise 30 rpm for 3 seconds and then brake. If there is any other reading, then the Large Motor at Port D will spin counter-clockwise 65 rpm for 90 degrees and then brake.

Figure 2-45. Examples of the Gyro Sensor on the Loop programming block

Infrared Sensor

You will notice that of the four Modes of the Infrared Sensor, Measure only applies to the remote. This is because the Remote requires the input of a specific value or values, and you can see in Figure 2-46 that it is very similar to the Brick Buttons.

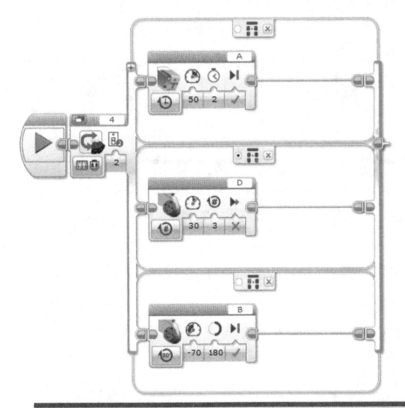

1. Infrared Sensor Measure Remote

If Button Combination 0 is pressed on the Infrared Beacon at Channel 4, then the Medium Motor at Port A will spin clockwise 50 rpm for 2 seconds and then brake. If Button Combination 1 is pressed, then the Large Motor at Port B will spin counter-clockwise at 70 rpm for 180 degrees and then stop. If Button 4 is pressed, or any other input than listed above, then the Large Motor at Port D will spin clockwise 30 rpm for 3 rotations and then coast.

Figure 2-46. A method of using the Switch with the Infrared Remote

When it comes to the other Compare modes, you can see some examples of them in Figures 2-47 and 2-48.

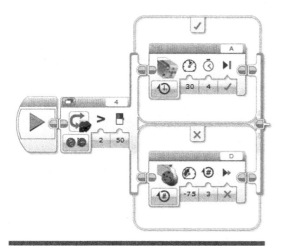

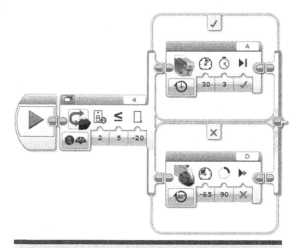

1. Infrared Sensor Compare Proximity

If the Infrared Sensor detects greater than 50, then the Medium Motor at Port A will spin clockwise 30 rpm for 4 seconds and then brake. If there is any other reading, then the Large Motor at Port D will spin counter-clockwise 75 rpm for 3 rotations and then coast.

2. Infrared Sensor Compare Beacon Heading

If the Infrared Sensor detects the Infrared Beacon on Channel 2 at less than or equal to -20, then the Medium Motor at Port A will spin clockwise 30 rpm for 3 seconds and then brake. If there is any other reading, then the Large Motor at Port D will spin counter-clockwise 65 rpm for 90 degrees and then coast.

Figure 2-47. *Examples of the Infrared Sensor Proximity and Beacon Heading for the Switch programming block*

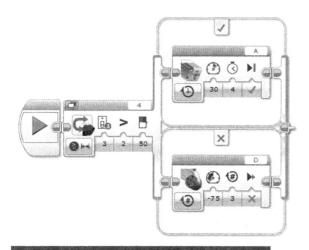

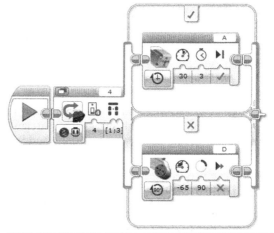

3. Infrared Sensor Compare Beacon Proximity

If the Infrared Sensor detects the Infrared Beacon Proximity at Channel 3 to be greater than 50, then the Medium Motor at Port A will spin clockwise 30 rpm for 4 seconds and then brake. If there is any other reading, then the Large Motor at Port D will spin counter-clockwise 75 rpm for 3 rotations and then coast.

4. Infrared Sensor Compare Remote

If the Infrared Sensor detects a Button Combination the Infrared Beacon at Channel 4, then the Medium Motor at Port A will spin clockwise 30 rpm for 3 seconds and then brake. If there is any other reading, then the Large Motor at Port D will spin counter-clockwise 65 rpm for 90 degrees and then coast.

Figure 2-48. *Examples of the Compare Beacon Proximity and Compare Remote for the Switch programming block*

Motor Rotation

Motor Rotation for the Switch programming block is very similar to the Motor Rotation for the Loop. Both can be programmed with variations of Degrees, Rotations, and Current Power. A program can easily be set up so that output of one motor will affect either occurring or not occurring.

I am only going to give one example of Motor Rotation on the Switch block, and the reason why is because I have currently shown you only certain action blocks that are motors. You can see in Figure 2-49 that the motor in Port A is made to spin one rotation, and that if A spin more than 90 degrees, the first condition (the Large Motor at Port B spinning) will occur.

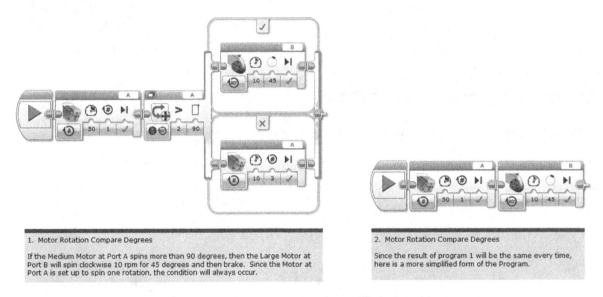

1. Motor Rotation Compare Degrees

If the Medium Motor at Port A spins more than 90 degrees, then the Large Motor at Port B will spin clockwise 10 rpm for 45 degrees and then brake. Since the Motor at Port A is set up to spin one rotation, the condition will always occur.

2. Motor Rotation Compare Degrees

Since the result of program 1 will be the same every time, here is a more simplified form of the Program.

Figure 2-49. *Examples of Motor Rotation for the Switch programming block*

Currently, a Switch would needlessly complicate this program and only two blocks would need to be used, as in the example on the right. I highly suggest that you simplify your programs as much as you can, but once you program your motors to have variable degrees, rotations, and current power, I guarantee this Switch will be more useful.

Temperature Sensor

Of course, you can use the Temperature Sensor to create options for you on the loop, and Figure 2-50 shows how.

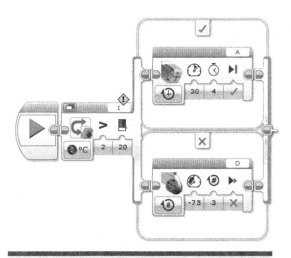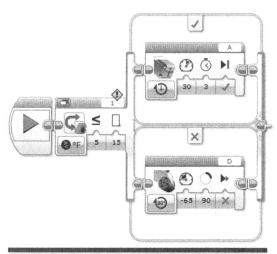

1. Temperature Sensor Compare Celsius

If the temperature sensor detects greater than 20 degrees Celsius, then the Medium Motor at Port A will spin clockwise 30 rpm for 4 seconds and then brake. If there is any other reading, then the Large Motor at Port D will spin counter-clockwise 75 rpm for 3 rotations and then coast.

2. Temperature Sensor Compare Fahrenheit

If the temperature scanner detects less than or equal to 15 degrees Fahrenheit, then the Medium Motor at Port A will spin clockwise 30 rpm for 3 seconds and then brake. If there is any other reading, then the Large Motor at Port D will spin counter-clockwise 65 rpm for 90 degrees and then coast.

Figure 2-50. *Examples of the Temperature Sensor on the Loop programming block*

Timer

This is different from the Time Mode for the Wait and Loop cases. This is for setting time, but you will find that you can set a specific amount. In fact, you can set a clock for eight different amounts, as you can see in the first parameter. Like Motor Rotation, the Timer will be useful when time will be a variable in your program. You can see in Figure 2-51 that it keeps track of the time that your program is running, and since the time in seconds of the first two programming blocks is five, it produces the top output.

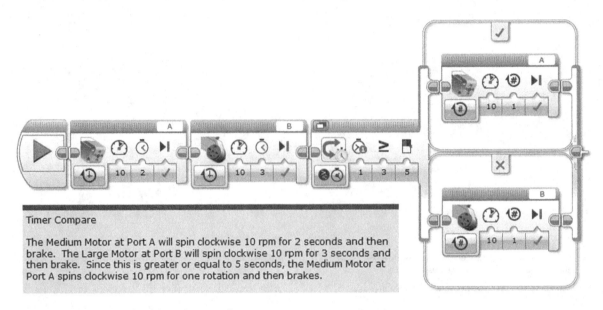

Timer Compare

The Medium Motor at Port A will spin clockwise 10 rpm for 2 seconds and then brake. The Large Motor at Port B will spin clockwise 10 rpm for 3 seconds and then brake. Since this is greater or equal to 5 seconds, the Medium Motor at Port A spins clockwise 10 rpm for one rotation and then brakes.

Figure 2-51. An example of the Timer Switch

Touch Sensor

This is another particular set up for choosing a Touch Sensor button to create a switch in a program. You can see an example in Figure 2-52.

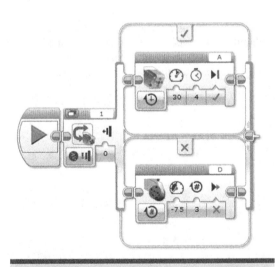

1. Touch Sensor Compare State

If the button on the touch sensor is released, then the Medium Motor at Port A will spin clockwise 30 rpm for 4 seconds and then brake. If the button is pressed, then the Large Motor at Port D will spin counter-clockwise 75 rpm for 3 rotations and then coast.

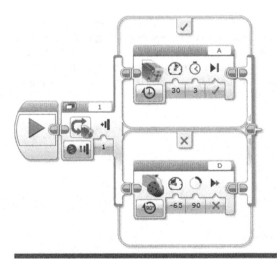

2. Touch Sensor Compare State

If the button on the touch scanner is pressed, then the Medium Motor at Port A will spin clockwise 30 rpm for 3 seconds and then brake. If the button is released, then the Large Motor at Port D will spin counter-clockwise 65 rpm for 90 degrees and then coast.

Figure 2-52. Examples of the Touch Sensor on the Loop programming block

Ultrasonic Sensor

As you can tell, the distance of an object to the Ultrasonic Sensor can determine the next outcome with this Loop Mode. Examples are provided in Figure 2-53.

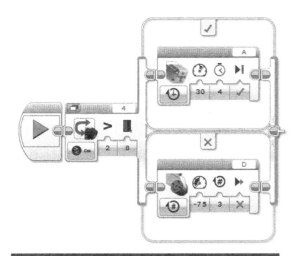
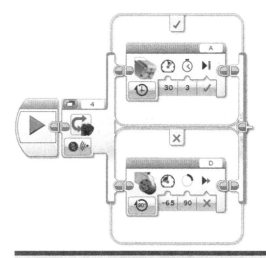

1. Ultrasonic Sensor Compare Distance Centimeters

If the ultrasonic sensor detects and object greater than 8 centimeters away, then the Medium Motor at Port A will spin clockwise 30 rpm for 4 seconds and then brake. If there is any other reading, then the Large Motor at Port D will spin counter-clockwise 75 rpm for 3 rotations and then coast.

2. Ultrasonic Sensor Compare Presence/Listen

If the ultrasonic scanner detects a sound, then the Medium Motor at Port A will spin clockwise 30 rpm for 3 seconds and then brake. If there is any other reading, then the Large Motor at Port D will spin counter-clockwise 65 rpm for 90 degrees and then brake.

Figure 2-53. *Examples of the Ultrasonic Sensor on the Loop programming block*

Energy Meter

As I have previously explained, the Energy Meter is a sensor for the NXT system that I won't be covering in this book, but the Switch program is set up for it, in case you want to create an either/or case with Joules, Watts, Volts, or Amps.

NXT Sound Sensor

Again, I won't be covering the Sound Sensor in this book, but you should try a Switch with dB or dBa if you have this sensor from the last version of LEGO MINDSTORMS.

Messaging

Messaging is a complicated section that I will cover in the section on the Advanced programming blocks in Chapter 5.

Text

I will cover Text in another chapter which deals with the red programming blocks, as well as using wires to import and export information.

Logic and Numeric

The last two topics are applying Logic and Numeric values to the Loop, and I'll explain how to use those to your advantage in Chapter 4. An example of each is provided in Figure 2-54.

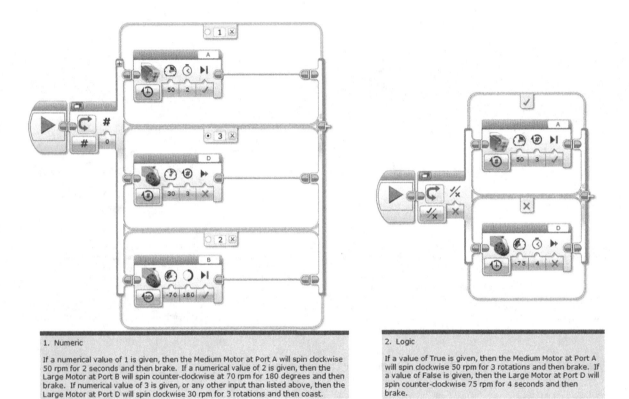

1. Numeric

If a numerical value of 1 is given, then the Medium Motor at Port A will spin clockwise 50 rpm for 2 seconds and then brake. If a numerical value of 2 is given, then the Large Motor at Port B will spin counter-clockwise at 70 rpm for 180 degrees and then brake. If numerical value of 3 is given, or any other input than listed above, then the Large Motor at Port D will spin clockwise 30 rpm for 3 rotations and then coast.

2. Logic

If a value of True is given, then the Medium Motor at Port A will spin clockwise 50 rpm for 3 rotations and then brake. If a value of False is given, then the Large Motor at Port D will spin counter-clockwise 75 rpm for 4 seconds and then brake.

Figure 2-54. *Examples of the Numeric and Logic on the Loop programming block*

Loop Interrupt

The last programming block is the Loop Interrupt, and it is really made for special situations. As you make quite a lot of programs, you might want one where the Loop only needs to work but not completely, as some programmers would call a "break" statement. See Figure 2-55 for an example.

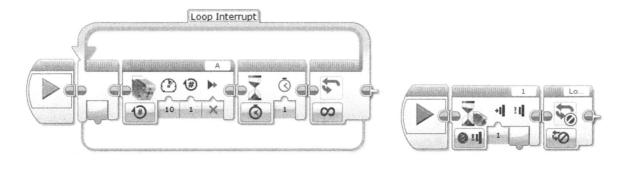

Loop Interrupt

Two Programs run at the same time. The first is an infiite loop where the Medium Motor at Port A spins clockwise for 10 rpm for 1 rotation and then brakes. One second passes and the process repeats on an infiinite loop. A press of the button on the Touch Sensor will trigger a Loop Interrupt during this loop.

Figure 2-55. *An example of Loop Interrupt*

Summary

All LEGO MINDSTORMS projects require a program in order to bring them to life. It is possible to create and alter programs on the EV3 Brick itself, or you can use your computer to download a EV3 Software program to create programs.

Programing with EV3 Software is made simple with the use of programming blocks. All the user needs to do is join them together to get their LEGO MINDSTORMS creation to do what he or she wants.

Part of becoming a successful programmer is understanding the visual EV3 programming block language, and how to use it with commands like Wait, Loop, and Switch. These type of commands can be used with the sensors to really bring a MINDSTORMS creation to life.

CHAPTER 3

Creating a LEGO MINDSTORMS EV3 Vehicle

Now that I have shown some basics of programming on LEGO MINDSTORMS EV3, it is time to talk about a popular project among LEGO MINDSTORMS enthusiasts, building a vehicle. Not only am I going to talk about how to make a decent vehicle, but I am also going to talk about how you can program a vehicle to do all kinds of things such as propulsion, steering, and using the other sensors to work with it.

Instructions for Making a Souped-up Driver's Base Vehicle

The Core Set has instructions for a Driving Base, but it has three wheels. Actually, it has two wheels and one ball bearing wheel in the front. Not only is this Driving Base on the Core Set instruction booklet, but you can find it on the LEGO MINDSTORMS software packet. Just look on the Lobby, under Robot Educator, Building Instructions, Driving Base.

I highly recommend assembling this Driving Base, especially if you are new to LEGO MINDSTORMS or even LEGO in general. The Driving Base has two large motors which power its two back wheels, and it is very simple to program it to move backward or forward using the Move Steering and Move Tank programming blocks that we discussed in the previous chapter. You will discover that its ball bearing wheel makes turning simple, and the instructions show how you can use the other sensors to make this Driving Base do many cool things. Many of the programs that I will list later in this chapter will be compatible with that basic driving unit.

One of the advantages of this Driving Base is that it can literally turn on a dime. Unfortunately, it is not set up to handle all of the sensors, but the vehicle I am about to show you can. Not only that, you are going to set it up with the yellow programming blocks as well. Figures 3-1 to 3-16 describe the steps for building the vehicle.

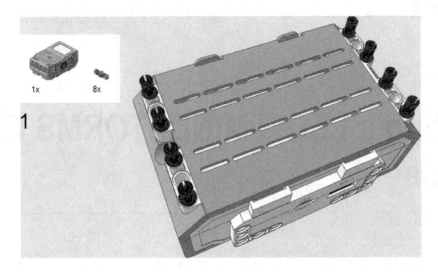

Figure 3-1. *Turn the EV3 Brick over and insert eight connector pegs as shown*

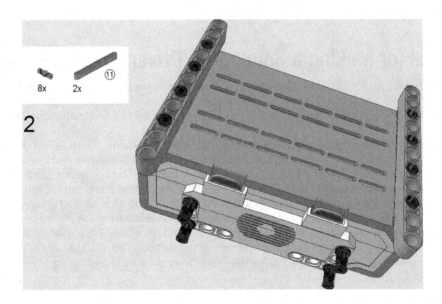

Figure 3-2. *Snap on the two 11M beams as shown. The connector pegs go on each side as shown, with the other side mirroring the same pattern*

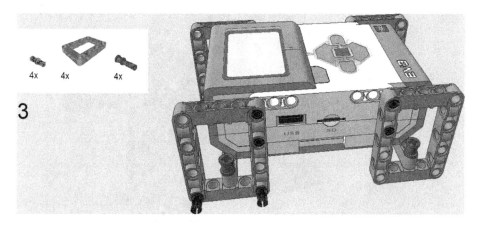

Figure 3-3. *Snap on the four 5 x 7 beam frames on the connector pegs from the last step. Use the four friction snaps to lock the beam frames into place. Insert the four connector pegs as shown*

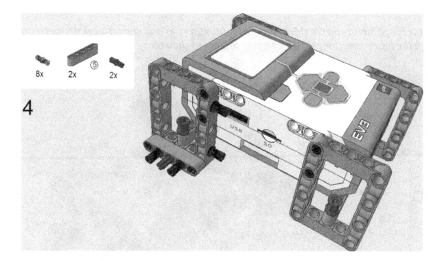

Figure 3-4. *Snap on the 5M beams, and place the connector peg/cross axles in the center through-hole of the 5M beam. Place a connector peg on each side of the connector peg/cross axle*

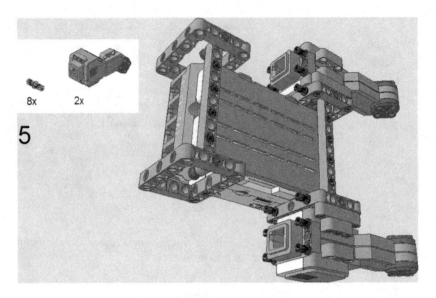

Figure 3-5. *Insert the Large Motors on the sides, atop the connector pegs and connector peg/cross axles from the previous step. Attach the four connector pegs to the Large Motors as shown*

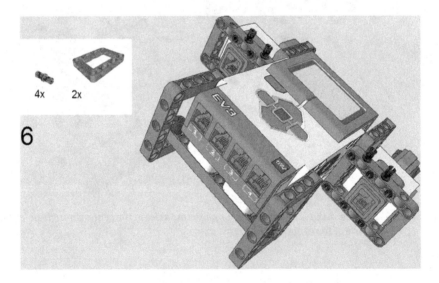

Figure 3-6. *Insert two beam frames on the construction, and insert the connector pegs on as shown*

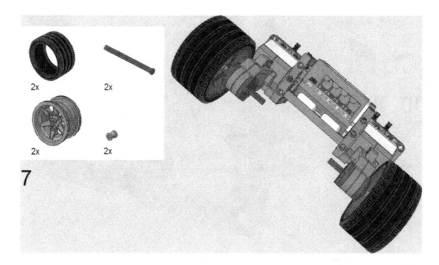

Figure 3-7. *Place the 8 x 36 low wide tires on the 56 x 34 Rims, and slide them on the 8M axles with stop until they hit the stop. Slide on the bushes all the way, and then slide the axles through the Large Motors*

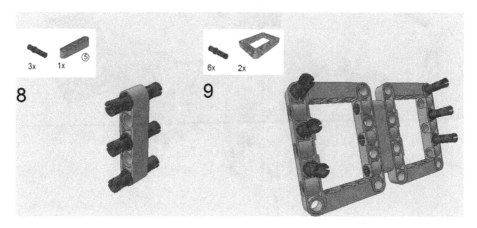

Figure 3-8. *Center three 3M connector pegs on the 5M beam. Attach a 5 x 7 beam frame on each side, and then insert three 3M connector pegs on each side*

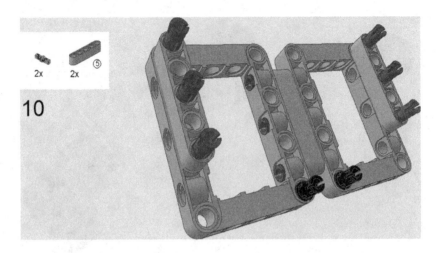

Figure 3-9. *Slide on a 5M beam on each side and add two connector pegs*

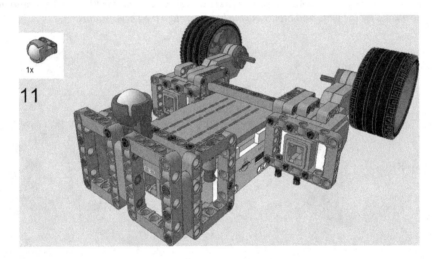

Figure 3-10. *Take the structure from steps 8-10 and snap it into place as shown. Insert the metal ball into the power joint, and snap it into place on the two connector pegs from the last step*

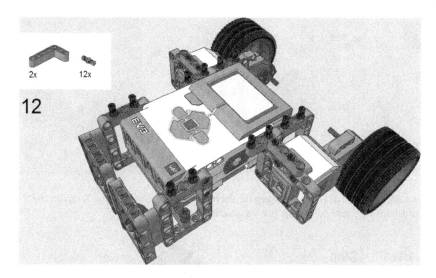

Figure 3-11. *Insert the 5 x 3 beam on the top of the structure as shown, and then the 12 connector pegs as shown*

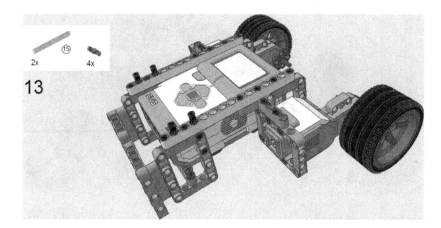

Figure 3-12. *Snap on the 15M beams, which will cap off the structure. Place the four connector pegs as shown*

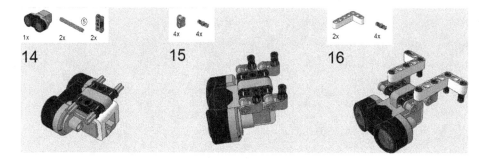

Figure 3-13. *Slide the two 5M axles on the Ultrasonic Sensor, and then cap them off with the double cross blocks. Slide on the 90 degree cross blocks, and insert the connector pegs. Snap on the 5 x 3 beams, and insert the connector pegs underneath*

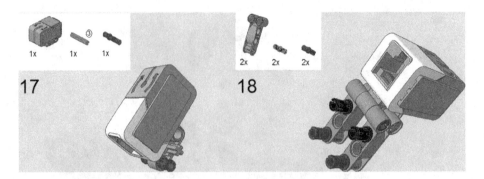

Figure 3-14. *Center a 3M axle and 3M connector peg on the bottom of the Gyro Sensor. Snap on the 2 x 4 cross block on this, as well as the connector pegs and connector peg/cross axles*

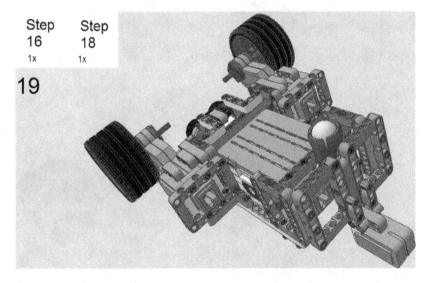

Figure 3-15. *Turn the construction upside down, and you can insert the steps from 14-16 on the bottom as shown. Insert the construction from steps 18-19 on the other side*

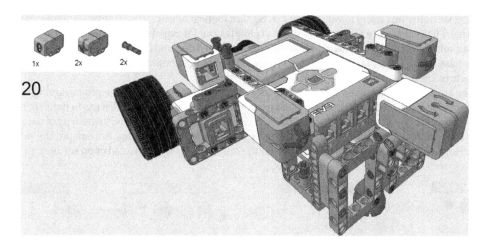

Figure 3-16. *Insert two Touch Sensors on the connector pegs on top. Snap the Color Sensor into place with the friction snaps*

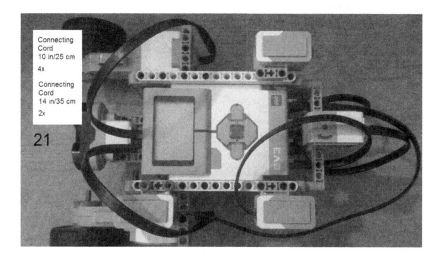

Figure 3-17. *Insert the connecting cords. Connect the Large Motors to Ports B and C. Connect the Touch Sensor to Port 1, the Gyro Sensor to Port 2, the Ultrasonic Sensor to Port 3, and the Color Sensor to Port 4*

Programming the Vehicle with the Yellow Programming Blocks

In the last chapter, I discussed the green and orange programming blocks and how to make them work for you. As I mentioned in that chapter, the orange programming blocks for the Wait or "Wait For" blocks, and they usually waited on a sensor or motor. In the case of the yellow programming blocks, you are informing the program to read a specific Sensor. I thought that I would take the time to discuss how to make the yellow blocks work for the Souped-up driver's base vehicle, with examples. In some of the examples, the yellow blocks do not have much of a role, and there are many ways to use programming blocks that will essentially amount to the same thing.

Before I talk about these particular programming blocks, I must discuss the subject of data wires. Data wires are paths that the user creates in order to take an output value from one programming block and put it in an input value of another programming block. This allows you to take text, numbers, logic, and two different types of arrays to put them in different sections. Text refers to values that can be alphabetical or numeric, just like something you can send on a text message. I'll discuss more about text in the next chapter, but I'll explain numeric. Numeric is simply a value that is a number, and this can be a negative number or number with a decimal in it. Logic refers to whether or not a value is true or false, and I will explain more on Logic later. If you are not familiar with arrays, they are simply groups of either numeric or logic.

You can see examples of data wires in Figure 3-18 (they are the lines underneath the programming blocks that connect the blocks together). Figure 3-18 uses the red programming blocks that I will discuss in detail in the next chapter. These programs don't really do anything, but you will note that you can establish the type of data wire by inspecting the shape on the lower edge of its starting point. By dragging and dropping, you can put the value carried by the wire into an area with a tab of the same shape, but the tab shape is on top instead of on the bottom.

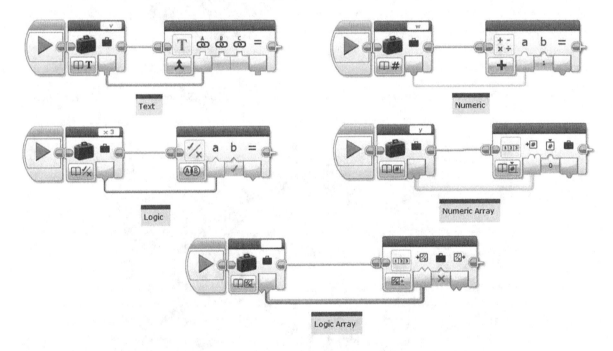

Figure 3-18. *Examples of Wires in EV3 Brick Programming*

Data wires come in five forms:

- Text (square tabs with orange wire)
- Numeric (round tabs with yellow wire)
- Logic (triangle tabs with green wire)
- Numeric Array (double round tabs with thick yellow wires)
- Logic Array (double triangle tabs with green wires)

I'm going to go into greater detail about these wires in the next chapter, but I wanted to point your attention to the numeric and logic wires that will be used in this next section.

Brick Buttons

Figure 3-19 shows the set-up for the Brick Buttons programming block, which allows you to steer the vehicle manually by simply pushing the buttons and holding them down for as long as you wish. The North button is forward and the South is backward. The left and right buttons will steer it left and right.

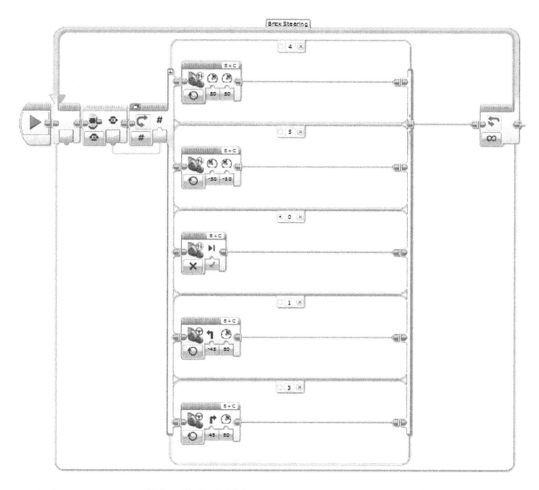

Figure 3-19. *A set up to steer a vehicle with the Brick buttons*

Here's how the program works. You will notice that it is set up with the Numerical Switch, and the value is wired from the yellow block, which is in compare mode. This means the value of the block (equal to the button number) is wired to input with the Switch. Since the entire program is an unlimited loop, the program will accept whatever numerical value is pressed and respond as long as that button is pressed. If you try it out with the Souped-up car, you will see that the vehicle will move forward with 4, backward with 5, left turn with 1, right turn with 3, and the default setting is 0 which will do nothing (0 means no buttons are pushed).

You will note that Brick buttons has two modes: Compare and Measure. Figure 3-20 is an example of Compare, and I want to show you how Measure comes into play. Compare mode will allow you to choose a specific button and state of a button, and will output an action in with Logic and Numeric form.

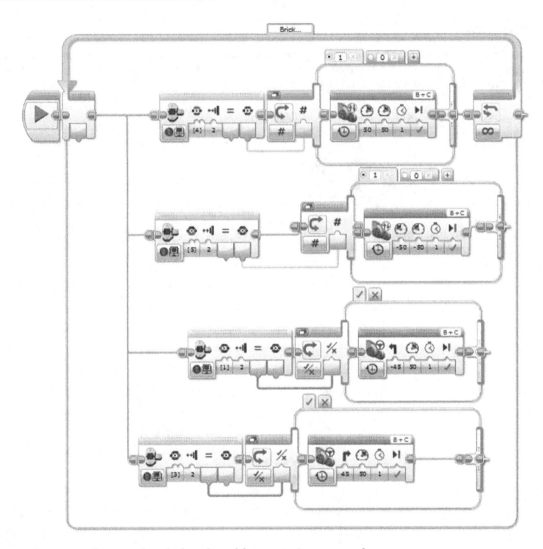

Figure 3-20. *A way of steering the vehicle with Brick buttons in Compare mode*

You can see that Figure 3-20 allows for multitasking, as I have separated the four basic motions (front, back, left, and right) into four different buttons. You can see that each button has to be bumped (quickly pressed and released) to make it go, and this time, I put a time of 1 second to go instead of just being in motion while the button is pushed.

Color Sensor Steering

This particular steering method is similar to the Brick buttons, but this doesn't involve pushing buttons. Instead, it involves scanning a color to produce a certain reaction. This isn't set up to move as a button is pressed or bumped, but two seconds of time after a specific color is scanned. It is set up to go forward with green, go backward with red, go left with yellow, go right with blue, and the default setting is no colors, which means that it does nothing.

I decided to show this with two programs. Figure 3-21 shows the program, and it looks just like the Brick button steering. It is in Color Sensor Compare mode, and it would not be too difficult to convert it into Color Sensor Measure mode by following similar processes in the previous two figures.

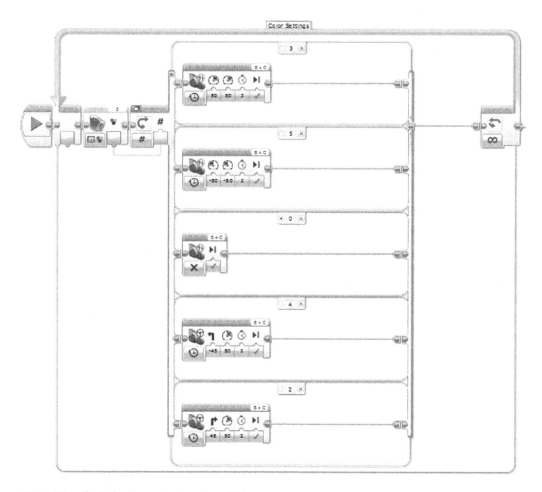

Figure 3-21. *Using the Color Sensor to steer the vehicle*

If you analyze this program, you will find that it can easily be done tabbed view as you can see in Figure 3-22. Look at this Switch again and note that the entire thing is in an infinite loop so this will be in effect as long as the entire program runs.

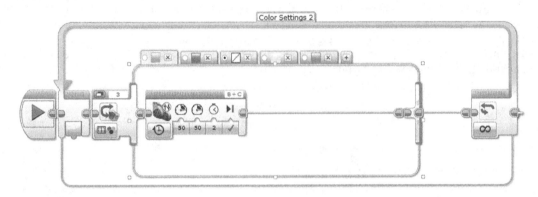

Figure 3-22. *Another way to use the Color Sensor to turn the vehicle*

Again, this is another example of simplicity, and if it is not necessary to use the Color Sensors programming block, then you might want to avoid it.

Reflected Light Intensity

While discussing ways of making the souped-up car go, I thought I should bring up how to use the Reflected Light Intensity for that. Imagine putting a piece of black electrical tape on the floor. Now imagine your car following that path you just made, provided it is a straight line.

If you angle the Color Sensor down, you can program it to follow that line. The formula in Figure 3-23 shows how to do it.

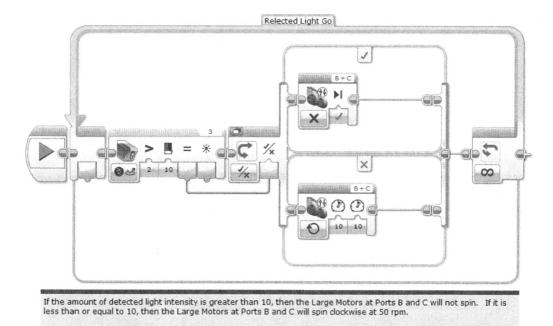

If the amount of detected light intensity is greater than 10, then the Large Motors at Ports B and C will not spin. If it is less than or equal to 10, then the Large Motors at Ports B and C will spin clockwise at 50 rpm.

Figure 3-23. *A way of making your car travel a straight line using the Color Sensor's Reflected Light Intensity ability*

You can set up the program in a similar way with Ambient Light Intensity, programming it to go forward (or backward) depending on the level of lighting in the room. You will notice another mode, which is Calibrate. The Calibrate mode allows you to calibrate the Color Sensor from within the program, and it comes in three forms, as seen in Figure 3-24.

1. Calibrate - Reflected Light Intensity - Minimum

2. Calibrate - Reflected Light Intensity - Maximum

3. Calibrate - Reset

Figure 3-24. *Three versions of Calibrate for Reflected Light Intensity*

For Calibrate Minimum, you can specify the minimum light intensity by manually entering it in on the parameter. Once it is calibrated, the Color Sensor will report this light intensity as 0 or the value specified. The Calibrate Maximum allows you to specify the maximum light intensity, and will report it as 100 or the value specified. Reset mode restores the Color Sensor to its default state.

Gyro Sensor

The Gyro Sensor programming block can be very helpful, as it can measure the rotation angle or rotation rate and get a numeric input. You might discover that you can use the orange programming blocks and achieve the same results.

For example, this particular program uses the Gyro Sensor in order to tell the vehicle when it has made a complete 90-degree left or right turn (see Figure 3-25).

1. Gyro Sensor Angle Turn Right.

Reset the Gyro Sensor. The Large Motor at Port B spins clockwise 20 rpm while the Large Motor at Port C does not spin. The vehicle will turn right until it reaches a 90 degree angle detected by the Gyro Sensor and then brake. The Large Motors at Ports B and C will both spin clockwise 10 rpm for one second and then brake.

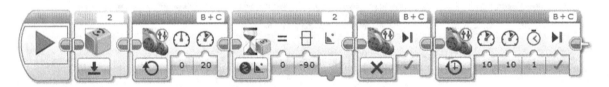

2. Gyro Sensor Angle Turn Left.

Reset the Gyro Sensor. The Large Motor at Port C spins clockwise 20 rpm while the Large Motor at Port B does not spin. The vehicle will turn left until it reaches a -90 degree angle detected by the Gyro Sensor and then brake. The Large Motors at Ports B and C will both spin clockwise 10 rpm for one second and then brake.

Figure 3-25. *A program for turning the vehicle left or right*

You will notice how the Tank Program is being used here. One of the Large Motors will spin, while the other remains stationary. This will turn the vehicle, and the Wait program with the Gyro Sensor tells it exactly when to stop motion of the Large Motors. From there, both Large Motors spin 10 rpm for one second.

You will notice the yellow programming block at the beginning sets the angle to zero. This is Reset mode, and it is similar to the Reset mode on the Color Sensor that I explained earlier in this chapter. The Reset mode rests the rotation angle of the Gyro Sensor to 0, and measurements of the rotation angle measure the motion relative to the last time this sensor was set.

With some modifications, you can program your vehicle to move with these turning programs.

Infrared Sensor

The Infrared Sensor, in Proximity mode, can be very helpful when it comes to detecting a possible obstacle that is in front of the vehicle. If it is mounted the same way that the Ultrasonic sensor is, it can be programed to stop when a certain object is within a certain distance in front of the vehicle, like in Figure 3-26.

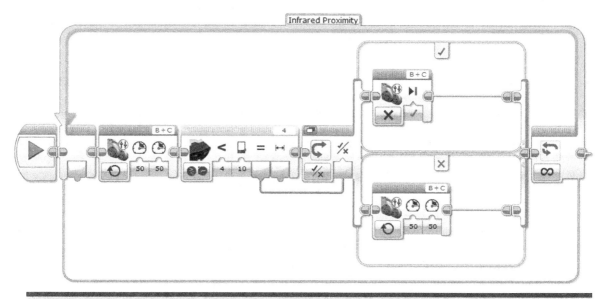

The Large Motors at Ports B and C will spin clockwise at 50 rpm. If the Infrared Beacon detects any object less than a Proximity of 10, then the Large Motors on Ports B and C will brake. If the object is greater than or equal to 10, then the Large Motors will continue to spin clockwise at 50 rpm.

Figure 3-26. *A way of using the Infrared Sensor to stop the car when it gets too close to an object*

Of course, the Infrared can do more than just Proximity. It has a Measure mode for Beacon, which will allow setting the channel to the beacon channel that you want it to detect. There are proximity and heading outputs, and there is a Logic output for True if the beacon is detected, and False if not. In addition to the Measure mode, it also has a Compare mode for the Beacon Heading and Beacon Proximity.

Another Infrared mode is made for the Remote, and you can set it up to control the Souped-up car with a similar set-up as the Brick buttons. In this case, you have a wireless remote that can go forward, backward, and left and right (see Figure 3-27).

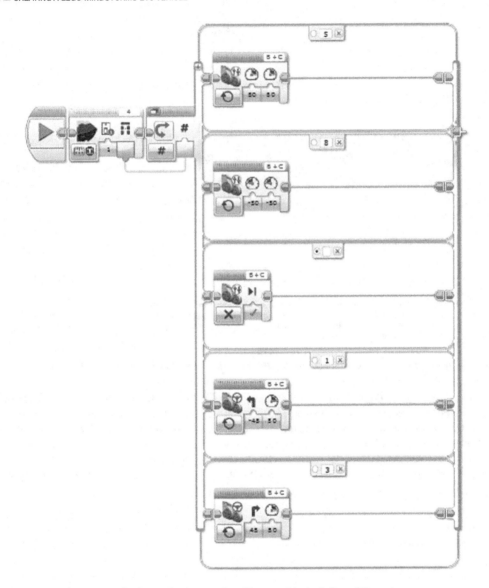

Figure 3-27. *A way of setting up the Souped-up car so it will steer with the Infrared Remote*

Motor Rotation

I've discussed in the previous chapter how Motor Rotation can be used on the Wait, Loop, and Switch programing blocks. The following examples show how it is possible to set parameter values on the Motor Rotation Sensor block. Each of these examples involves you spinning one of the wheels manually to produce a reaction in the other. Before I get to that, I want to quickly discuss the Mode of Reset, which sets the value of the motor to 0 depending on what mode you are running (Degrees, Rotation, or Current Power).

You can see in Figure 3-28 how I have used the Motor Rotation Degrees Compare mode. I started with the Reset block so that the motor at Port B is reset to 0. From here, you can manually turn the wheel on the motor at Port B, and it is set up so that the Large Motor at Port C will turn when the Wheel at Port B turns greater than 90 degrees. This is because this statement has been programmed as "True", and then wired into a Logic Switch. There actually isn't anything in the negative or "X" part of the Switch, so nothing will happen unless the Wheel at Port B is rotated greater than 90 degrees. It should be noted that if the wheel at Port B is rotated back until it is below 90 degrees, the action at Port C will cease. Think of this program as setting up B to be a dial and C to be the action that results from turning the dial.

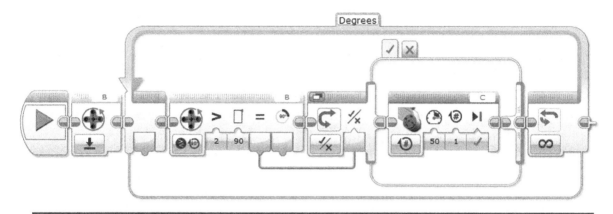

Motor Rotation Degrees

Reset Motor at Port B to 0. If the Motor at Port B spins greater than 90 degrees clockwise, then the Large Motor at Port C will spin clockwise at 50 rpm for one rotation and then stop. The action at Port C will continue unless the Motor at Port B is spun to less than or equal to 90 degrees. If the Motor at Port B spins less than or equal to 90 degrees, then the Large Motor at Port C will not move at all.

Figure 3-28. An example of Motor Rotation Degrees

I used a similar method as an example of Motor Rotation Rotations in Figure 3-29. In this case, I had it set up so the Wheel at Port B will spin one reverse rotation if the Wheel at Port C spins greater than one full forward rotation. Again, if the wheel at Port C is spun backwards for less than or equal to a full rotation, then the action at Port B ceases.

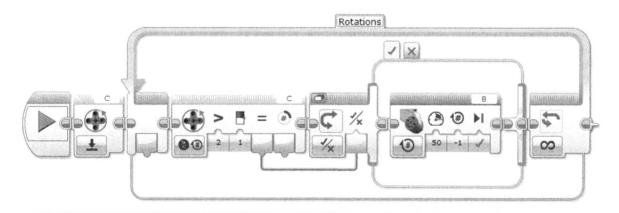

Motor Rotation Rotations

Reset Motor at Port C to 0. If the Motor at Port C spins greater than 1 rotation clockwise, then the Large Motor at Port B will spin counter-clockwise for one rotation and then stop. The action at Port B will continue unless the Motor at Port C is spun to less than or equal to 1 rotation. If the Motor at Port C spins less than or equal to 1 rotation, then the Large Motor at Port B will not move at all.

Figure 3-29. An example of the Motor Rotation Rotations

The last example for motor rotation in Figure 3-30 shows how it is set up for spinning. In this case, it is set up so whatever current power the motor at Port B is spinning causes the motor at Port C to spin at the exact same current power.

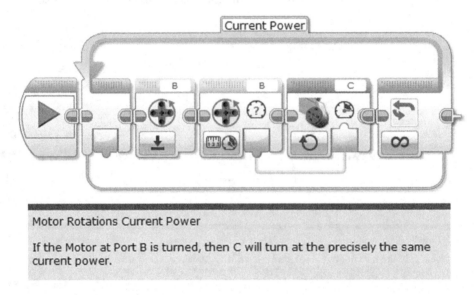

Figure 3-30. *Example of Motor Rotation for current power*

As you can see, the Motor Rotation Sensor block is good for any time you want some action to take place when a motor hits a certain point, such as an angle, rotation, or current power.

Temperature Sensor

The Motor section is about relaying information that happens within the program or the creation, but the Temperature Sensor is all about what happens on the outside. If you want to, you can mount the Temperature Sensor on the front, in place of the Ultrasonic Sensor. Figure 3-31 is an example of that. This will allow you to sense temperature, and allow the vehicle to do some interesting things as it senses cold and hot.

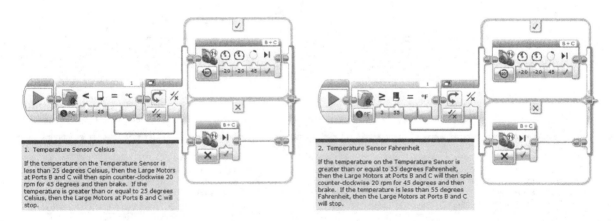

Figure 3-31. *Example of the Temperature Sensor*

Timer

I briefly discussed timers in the last chapter when I discussed the Wait programming block. You will notice that it has the usual Compare and Measure modes, but it also has a Reset. Think of a Reset as like a stopwatch, and you have just set it at zero and started the time. The Timer keeps track of how much time has passed in your program, and you can output that amount as well. Take a look at the example in Figure 3-32.

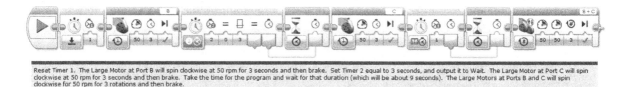

Reset Timer 1. The Large Motor at Port B will spin clockwise at 50 rpm for 3 seconds and then brake. Set Timer 2 equal to 3 seconds, and output it to Wait. The Large Motor at Port C will spin clockwise at 50 rpm for 3 seconds and then brake. Take the time for the program and wait for that duration (which will be about 9 seconds). The Large Motors at Ports B and C will spin clockwise for 50 rpm for 3 rotations and then brake.

Figure 3-32. *An example of using the Timer Sensor*

As you can see from Figure 3-32, Timer 1 has been set to 0 at the very beginning. Then an Action block that takes 3 seconds occurs, followed by Timer 2 set at 3 seconds and waiting just as long. Then another 3 second action block occurs, and Timer 1 is set to wait again. By this time, Timer 1 is now at about 9 seconds, and waits that long before the final Action block at Ports B and C commences.

Touch Sensor

Setting up for the Touch Sensor means that you are programing something to happen at the touch of a button. You can see in Figure 3-33 that I have programmed the vehicle to start at the touch of a button, and it will stop if the button is not pressed.

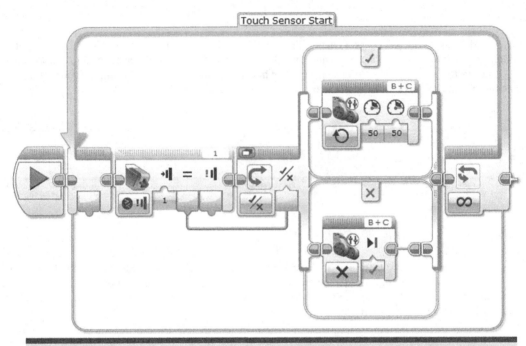

1. Touch Sensor

If the button on the Touch Sensor is pressed, then the Large Motors at Ports B and C will spin clockwise 50 rpm. If the button is not pressed, then the Large Motors will be still, unless the button is pressed again.

Figure 3-33. *A set-up to start the vehicle with the Touch Sensor*

Ultrasonic Sensor

I mentioned earlier how the Infrared Sensor can be used to stop a vehicle if it is in Proximity mode. I highly recommend that this manner of setup be used for the Ultrasonic Sensor, as it can detect an object in front of it within inches. I have laid out an example in Figure 3-34.

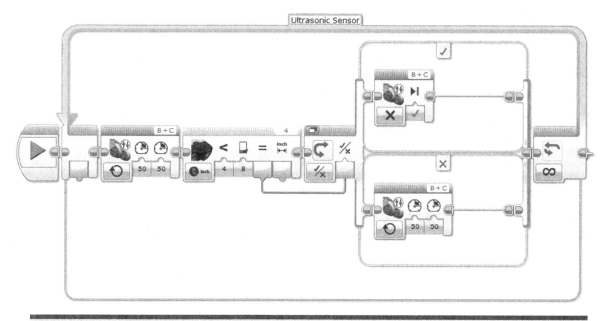

The Large Motors at Ports B and C will spin clockwise at 50 rpm. This will continue until the Ultrasonic senses an object that is less than 8 inches away. If the object is greater than or equal to 8 inches, then the Large Motors at Ports B and C will spin clockwise at 50 rpm.

Figure 3-34. *A way of making the souped-up car stop by connecting it to the Ultrasonic Sensor*

Energy Meter and NXT Sound Meter

Since I am bringing up every one of the EV3 sensors and motors, I felt it necessary to bring up the NXT Energy Meter and the Sound Meter; the set-ups are the same as the other sensors with Compare and Measure modes.

Other Methods for Building Vehicles

I recommended a Driver's Base type of vehicle because it is easy to program and assemble. However, if you want a challenge of another type of vehicle, I highly recommend the following options.

Rack-and-Pinion Steering

In my first book about Lego, *Practical Lego Technics*, I showed how to assemble a vehicle with rack-and-pinion steering in Chapter 3. This is a method that uses a rack with a gear in order to move the front wheels. I will recommend consulting that book and using variations of the model with the Medium Motor to steer it. You can download the illustrations at http://www.apress.com/9781430246114.

Four-Wheel Steering with Four-Wheel Drive

One of the first vehicles in my other Lego Technic book, *Lego Technic Robotics*, focused on creating a wheeled base for a robot that is capable of four-wheeled steering with four-wheel drive. This model appeared in Chapter 3 and it could be adapted, but you would probably need three Medium Motors to do so.

Tank Tread Model

As I mentioned in Chapter 1, the Core and Expansion Kits contain Tank Treads. With the use of the sprockets and rubber attachments, you can have tank-like treads for your wheels if you like. If you are looking for a model to emulate, I would recommend the Tank Bot on the Expansion set.

Summary

There are many ways to make a LEGO MINDSTORMS vehicle. I suggest the Driving Base in the Core set of instructions to help you get started. I have provided instructions for another Driving Base that can fit all the sensors.

Just as important as building a driving vehicle is knowing how to program it so it can move like you want it to. The Brick buttons and Color Sensor can allow you to both propel and steer the vehicle, and I have included other programs for the sensors as well.

The beauty of EV3 MINDSTORMS vehicles is there are many ways to build them, such as a rack-and-pinion model, one with four-wheeled drive (and four-wheel steering), as well as one with tank treads.

CHAPTER 4

Creating Visuals, Making Sounds, and Using Data on the EV3 Brick

Since I already discussed how to connect the motors to the EV3 Brick to make things happen in the last chapter, I think it is time that I discuss the particulars about sight, sound, and lights on the EV3 brick. This is somewhat complex, and I wanted to devote an entire chapter to this.

While discussing the display, sound, and Brick Status Light, I thought I would spend part of this chapter discussing the importance of the data operations, or red programming blocks. Data operation blocks can do a lot of things, but sometimes the results will not be as visible as the programs for the model in Chapter 3. As their name implies, the data operations blocks will be performing highly complex data processing and mathematics, and the results may not be seen unless the program asks. This is the reason I chose to discuss the data blocks in the same chapter as the display, because you can program the display to show you what the data operation blocks have achieved.

Display Programming Block

The Display programming block is capable of creating a graphic to be shown on the screen, and even though the screen is not in color, it does have good resolution. You will see that the Display block has four modes: Text, Shapes, Image, and Reset Screen that you can see in Figure 4-1.

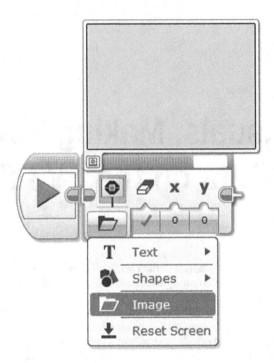

Figure 4-1. *The four modes of the Display programming block, along with the Preview*

You will notice that when you switch modes, this will change the parameters for each, but the one constant is the preview that you can access by clicking on the left-hand corner. You will see it underneath the big blank section in Figure 4-2.

Text

Text allows you to create words, and the bar on the right-hand corner allows you to type in whatever text that you want to put on the EV3 Brick display, provided it fills only one line on the display preview. This is a maximum of 21 characters with the smallest font provided, and 11 characters with the largest. Unfortunately, the program does not allow you to do more than one line per Display programming block. If you want to have more than one line on the screen, see Figure 4-3.

You will also notice that an option that says "Wired", and this is when you want to wire your text in from another programming block, which I explained in Chapter 3. I will have a demonstration of that later in this chapter when I discuss the variable data operation block.

Some of your options include Pixels and Grid, and you can see examples of both of those sub modes and parameters of Text in Figure 4-2.

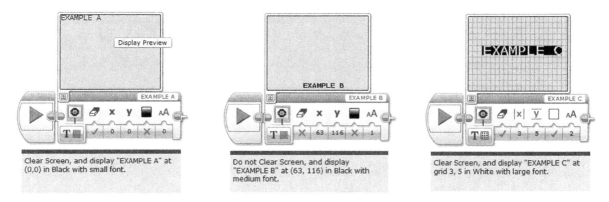

Figure 4-2. *Three examples of Text on a Display*

Examples A and B in Figure 4-2 are in Pixel mode, which means that it will essentially give a blank background in the example as opposed to the Grid mode. You can see in Example C that the text is on a grid, which is very helpful in spacing words on the display screen. Please note that when you run the program on the EV3 Brick, the grid will not be seen.

Now I will talk about the other parameters.

- The first is the True and False option under the clear screen, which does exactly as it says. You may notice that it says "MINDSTORMS" and "Program" every time you run any program on the LEGO EV3 Brick. By setting the value to "Clear Screen True" you ensure that you don't see the "MINDSTORMS Program" when you run your program. You can see this demonstrated in Examples A and C, which means that you will see exactly what is on the previews when you run the program. Example B will print the words on whatever is on the screen. The Clear Screen is also useful for when you want to have multiple lines on one display screen, as the example shows in Figure 4-3.

- The X and Y parameters control the horizontal (x) and the vertical (y). You will notice that there are bar controls to adjust the length and width of the placement of the words. In the Pixel mode, the text moves pixels and has a large range (–177 to 177 for x and –127 to 127 for y). In the grid mode, you can adjust from 0 to 21 on X and 0 to 12 on y. Example A has coordinates at 0, 0, which insures the words are up and to the left. Example B puts the words on the bottom with (63,116). Example C uses the grid to place it at 3, 5, and the parameter values center the text. You will note that negative numbers can be used, as well as decimals. The problem is you might even put the words so far off the screen that they won't be seen.

- As for the Color, it is possible to make it be white on black or black on white. Examples A and B are in black, while Example C has the white on black look. All that is required is to set the color to White or False.

- There are only three options for the Font Size: 0, 1, and 2. I call them Small, Medium, and Large, and examples of them are respectively in Examples A, B, and C.

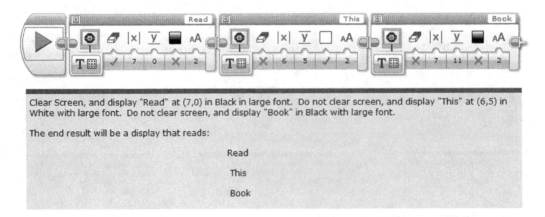

Clear Screen, and display "Read" at (7,0) in Black in large font. Do not clear screen, and display "This" at (6,5) in White with large font. Do not clear screen, and display "Book" in Black with large font.

The end result will be a display that reads:

Read

This

Book

Figure 4-3. A way of displaying multiple lines using the Display programming blocks

Shapes

This mode allows you to make shapes on the screen; the ones that you can make are geometric such as the line, circle, rectangle, and point. Like the text program, it is possible to make more than one shape on the screen at once, with the proper use of "Clear Screen". I will demonstrate how to do that later, but for now, I want to explain the parameters of each shape individually.

Line

This is for creating your basic straight line segment that will appear on the screen. You will notice that, like the text option, there are options for x and y that show where the line begins and ends. You can also see that you can change the color of the line as well, but I have discovered that changing it to white makes the line difficult to see on the display. You can see that it requires setting parameters and you can see some examples in Figure 4-4.

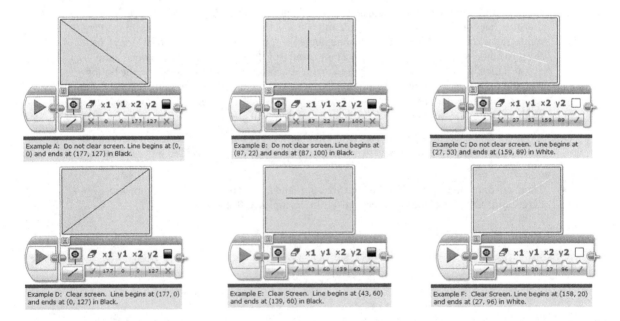

Example A: Do not clear screen. Line begins at (0, 0) and ends at (177, 127) in Black.

Example B: Do not clear screen. Line begins at (87, 22) and ends at (87, 100) in Black.

Example C: Do not clear screen. Line begins at (27, 53) and ends at (159, 89) in White.

Example D: Clear screen. Line begins at (177, 0) and ends at (0, 127) in Black.

Example E: Clear Screen. Line begins at (43, 60) and ends at (139, 60) in Black.

Example F: Clear Screen. Line begins at (158, 20) and ends at (27, 96) in White.

Figure 4-4. Examples of making lines on the display

Making a line segment is about setting one point for the beginning (x1, y1) and another point for the ending (x2, y2). You can see that by altering the coordinates how it changes the slope of the line as well as the length.

Circle

With the text making a circle, you first establish where the center is, and then establish a radius. You then have to choose if you want the circle filled and the color. You can see examples of this in Figure 4-5.

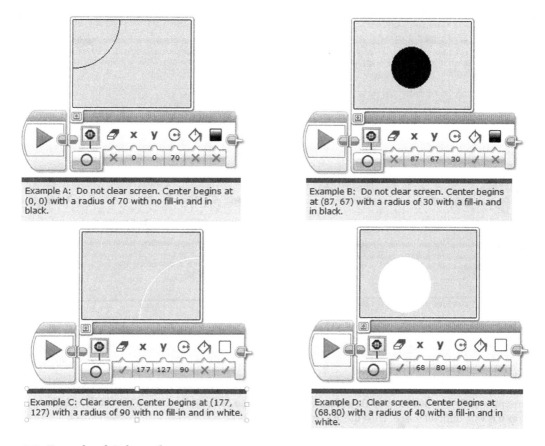

Figure 4-5. *Examples of circles on the program*

You will note that in some of the examples, the center is off the screen. In some cases, the entire circle is visible.

Rectangle

This allows you to make rectangles by beginning with the X and Y point of origin. You can adjust the length and width of these rectangles by increasing or decreasing its size as well as filling it in. You can see some examples in Figure 4-6.

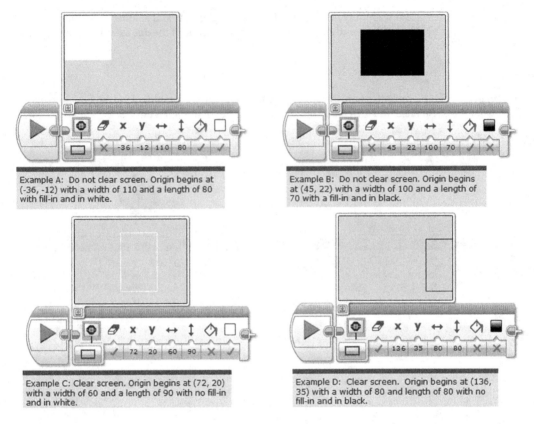

Example A: Do not clear screen. Origin begins at (-36, -12) with a width of 110 and a length of 80 with fill-in and in white.

Example B: Do not clear screen. Origin begins at (45, 22) with a width of 100 and a length of 70 with a fill-in and in black.

Example C: Clear screen. Origin begins at (72, 20) with a width of 60 and a length of 90 with no fill-in and in white.

Example D: Clear screen. Origin begins at (136, 35) with a width of 80 and length of 80 with no fill-in and in black.

Figure 4-6. *Some examples of rectangles on the display*

Like the samples with the circles, you can have the rectangles or squares off the edge, and they will show.

Point

In this particular mode, it only puts a single point on the screen. You can adjust its X and Y. I didn't include any examples as it is very difficult to see. Trust me, it works.

As I promised earlier, I wanted to give a demonstration of how to place multiple shapes on the display, so here is an example in Figure 4-7.

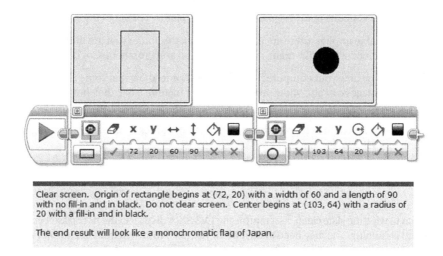

Clear screen. Origin of rectangle begins at (72, 20) with a width of 60 and a length of 90 with no fill-in and in black. Do not clear screen. Center begins at (103, 64) with a radius of 20 with a fill-in and in black.

The end result will look like a monochromatic flag of Japan.

Figure 4-7. *How to do multiple shapes on the EV3 display*

Image

This allows for any kind of image, and the EV3 brick comes with several built in. All that is required is to click on the upper-right corner and click on the file folder marked LEGO Image Files. Any time you use any image for the LEGO Image Files, it will automatically show up in the Project Images file. See the examples in Figure 4-8.

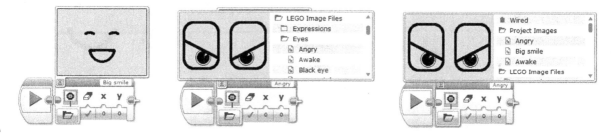

Figure 4-8. *Examples of Images available on the Display programming block, and their files. Images are the creation of the LEGO Group*

The following are the types of images that the EV3 Brick has:

- Expressions. These are essentially the emoticons of the EV3 Brick display, and they range from facial expressions to various hearts or other graphics that convey a feeling.

- Eyes. All of the eyes in this particular category are two rectangles with curved edges. Each of them can convey a different feeling, and sometimes the pupils can turn into interesting shapes. It is good for situations where the EV3 Brick becomes like a head.

- Information. I highly recommend using these symbols to display any kind of instruction to the user. For example, there is a stop display graphic that looks like a stop sign, as well as a question mark, thumbs up/thumbs down, etc.

- LEGO. This folder contains many Lego logos, as well as pictures of the EV3 sensors, and so on.

- Objects. As the name implies, there are a lot of objects in this folder that are difficult to classify, but they convey associations like night, snow, pirate skull and crossbones, or other objects.

- Progress. You know how your computer has a progress bar to show that some new program is loading? These images can also show progress and they include a bar, dial, hourglass, timer, and water level.

- System. This is similar to the Progress category, as it has graphics of indicators showing the status on the EV3 Brick.

Reset Screen

This is a simple function to wipe the slate clean, as it returns the EV3 Brick display to the normal screen of information on display when a program is running. You may need to do it when you need to switch from one display graphic to another.

The Image Editor

You have the option for creating your own image. All you need to do is go to the Tools on the Main menu and click on "Image Editor". There you will see a program similar to a paint or graphics program, as in Figure 4-9.

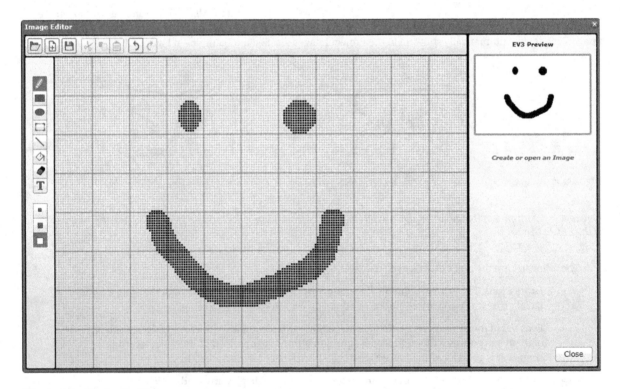

Figure 4-9. *The Image Editor*

You can see the horizontal menu bar on the top, and it gives you a lot of options, including:

- Open: It is possible to go into an image file and open it in this particular format. I will explain how to upload a photo onto the display later in this chapter.

- New: Clears the screen so a new image can be made. Whatever you have been drawing on the Image Editor there is not automatically saved.

- Save: You will find that this will open up a window that says "Name for Image in project". This allows you to type in a name for your program, which you can open on the Project Images file folder on the Display programming block in Image mode.

- Cut: An option for the Select tool which I will explain when I get to the vertical menu bar. This removes a selected area so it can be pasted elsewhere.

- Copy: Another option for the Select tool, but this one does not remove the area selected. It does give you the option of pasting it.

- Paste: What you can do with a selected area after it is cut or copied.

- Undo: A way to remove an action that was just complete. I have no idea how many levels of undo there are, but I used it with 16 examples before I realized that was all that I needed.

- Redo: A way to cancel your undo.

As for the vertical bar, this is where you can select drawing tools, such as:

- Pencil: This allows you to draw whatever line or shape that you wish using your mouse or other tracking controller.

- Rectangle: Allows you to make rectangles or squares.

- Ellipse: Allows you to make ellipses or circles.

- Select: Allows you to select a rectangle or square-shaped area that you can move as well as Cut, Copy, or Paste.

- Line: Allows for making line segments.

- Fill: Allows you to fill in any shape that you have, provided it is a closed off area.

- Erase: Allows you to remove any graphics with the same type of controls as the Pencil.

- Text: Allows you to type out text in two different text styles.

- Small, Medium, and Large Pencil: This is a separate menu bar below the drawing tools bar, and it will control the size of the pencil. In addition to the Pencil, it works on the Circle, Rectangle, Line, and Eraser functions as well.

As I have stated before, the Image Editor looks like any particular paint program. I have also stated that it is possible for you to upload an image file and make it so it can be put on the EV3 Brick display. For example, I was able to load a picture of my son that I took at Arches State Park that you can see in Figure 4-10.

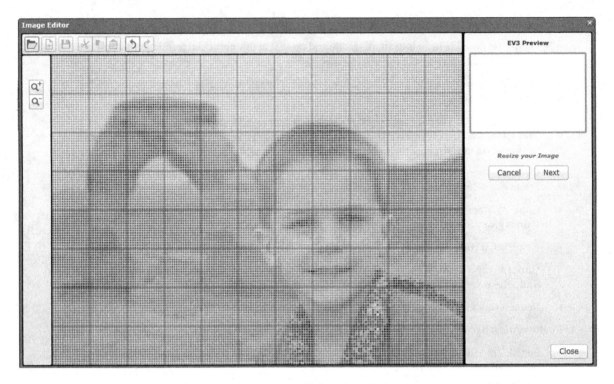

Figure 4-10. *The Image Editor allows you to load pictures that you have on your computer or mobile device*

You can see the magnifying buttons on the left side, which allow you to focus on the area that you want to focus on. The picture that you see here was originally taken in portrait mode, but I focused on the area that I thought was most interesting. I then hit the "Next" button on the right, and I got what you see in Figure 4-11.

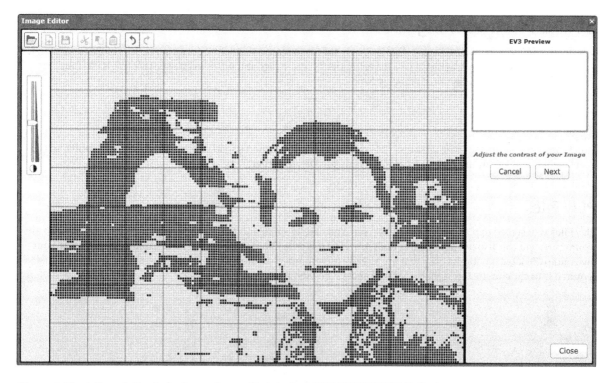

Figure 4-11. A "translation" of a former image file into the LEGO MINDSTORMS display

Once I hit the "Save" button, I have a permanent image, which I titled "Arch and Son". As you can see in Figure 4-12, the project is saved in the Project Images folder, and easily accessible.

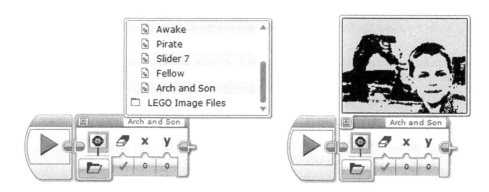

Figure 4-12. Accessing a file from the Image Editor program

As you can see, the Display programming block is a very versatile tool. Before I go any further, I want to explain that the programs above will require more if you want the images to stay on screen. For example, you can use the Wait programming block in Time mode if you want the image to stay on screen for a few seconds, and an Infinite Loop can keep it on indefinitely. I have some examples on the programs below with the data operations programming blocks.

Sound Programming Block

Now that I showed you how to display visuals, it only stands to reason that I introduce sound. This block is designed solely to make some noise, whether it be a note, frequency, pre-programmed, or even user-created. It has four functions: Stop, Play File, Play Tone, and Play Note.

Stop

Stop is designed to simply cease all sound. It is good for situations when sound needs to stop; it is very similar to the Reset Screen that I mentioned when I was discussing the Display programming block.

Play Files

Play Files is designed to play a particular audio file. You can select an audio file from many categories. In case you are wondering, you can also use your own sound, provided it is only about ten seconds. I will explain how to make your own audio file later, but for the ones that are already programmed on the EV3 Brick, they are easy to access. All that is required is to click on the top-right corner and access the files, as seen in Figure 4-13.

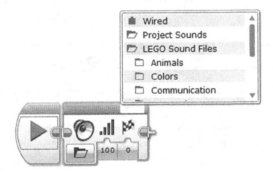

Figure 4-13. *Accessing the audio files for the Sound programming block*

I highly recommend playing with all the sound files, as they might add some interesting audio treats to your program. The Sound files are in several categories, including:

- Animals: The sound that a particular animal makes.

- Colors: A voice that states the color.

- Communication: Another voice that states some expression, saying things like "Fantastic" and "Good Job" in a very text-to-speech sounding robot voice.

- Expressions: Cute sounds that might be heard as filler for a radio morning show.

- Information: Any sound that communicates direction or action.

- Mechanical: Sounds that indicates that technological things are happening.

- Movements: More indicators of actions, specifically robot or motor oriented.

- Numbers: An audio recording speaking a number from zero to nine.

- System: An audio sound to confirm that some mechanical system is operational.

You will notice that one of the parameter controls are for the volume, which can range from 0 to 100. There are also three methods of Play Type to program here in the parameters.

- Play to Completion plays the sound effect once, and then the program waits for the specific sound to finish before continuing.

- Play Once plays the sound effect once, and then the program immediately continues.

- Repeat plays the sound effect multiple times, looping ad infinitum.

Play Tone

The Play Tone measures a note by Hertz or its note value. You can see a good example of it working in Figure 4-14.

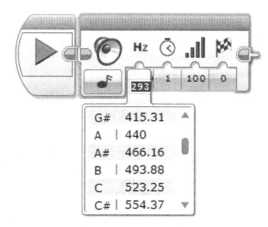

Figure 4-14. *An example of the Play Tones*

You will notice that you can enter the frequency manually by simply typing it in. You can also enter the amount of seconds that you want the tone to play. The Volume and Play Type is also here for you to control as well.

Play Note

As for the Play Note, this will set up a note to play, like a piano keyboard. You can see an example of it in Figure 4-15.

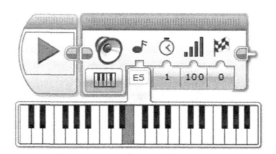

Figure 4-15. *An example of the Play Note function, with a keyboard to select a note*

121

Make your own Sound

It is possible to use the LEGO MINDSTORMS programming software to create your own kind of sound. All that is required is to go to the top of the menu bar and select Tools and Sound Editor. You will then see a small window that looks like Figure 4-16.

Figure 4-16. *The Sound Editor on the MINDSTORMS Software on the left, and the Project Sounds programming blocks on the right*

The Sound Editor works a lot like a standard voice recording software program. You essentially hit the big red button to record your voice or anything else, and then you can save it after you are done (see Figure 4-16, left). Keep in mind that the maximum length of a sound is about 10 seconds, so nothing too long can be saved. Accessing the Sound files is as easy as clicking in the upper-right corner and selecting the one in the Project Sounds folder.

In case you wanted to know whether or not you can put your favorite MP3s on your EV3 brick, I will have to say that the answer is a sad no. As I have stated before, the maximum length of a recorded sound is about 10 seconds, which is not the length of a song. You can upload an audio file, like a song, and you can select a section of a song, and then save it. These files can be saved, and they can be retrieved on the Project Sounds on the upper-right corner. It is possible to save your entire song in 10-second sections, then string them together on different recording blocks (see Figure 4-16, right).

Brick Status Light Programming Block

It is also possible to change the color of the status light on the EV3 Brick. It is pretty simple to set up, as you can see in the following examples in Figure 4-17.

Figure 4-17. *Three examples of changing the brick status light (note the change in number as well as color)*

I highly recommend using the Brick Status as an indicator. For example, you might want to create a program where the light is green when something is a normal condition, but red when it is not.

The Brick Status Light is the last of the green programming blocks, and now I want to spend some time talking about the red programming blocks, which are for data operations. As I stated in the introduction, the data operations blocks are used to calculate internal operations within the EV3 Brick. Oftentimes, you won't be able to see what is going on, any more than you can read someone's thoughts. However, you can connect the outputs of the data operation blocks to the motors as well as the display, sound, and Brick Status Lights. I have several examples below of how these can be used.

The Data Operations Programming Blocks

You are going to find the data operations programming blocks to be very helpful, as numerical values will be used in your programs a lot. Much of what you will read in this section might remind you of middle school or high school level mathematics class, and you will find that the EV3 is set up to do very high math.

Variable

If you know anything about algebra, then you know you are usually solving for x (and sometimes y). In an algebraic textbook, the variable is a container that contains an unknown quantity which you try to determine; in the case of the Variable programming block you can create your own value for your variable, and even change the value later in the program.

You will see that the Variable is a briefcase, which implies that it is a value that is closed up, until you open it. You will note its two main modes of Read and Write, with Read symbolized by a book and Write being a pencil. The Write mode is where you establish the variable name and value like writing something in a book, while Read mode is where you use that value, like reading some piece of information from a book.

The name of the variable is established by simply clicking on the upper-right corner and entering in a name, which can be pretty much anything depending on the values you are working with. You will note that Read and Write come in the form of values like Text, Numeric, Logic, Numeric Array, and Logic Array.

You can then go to the lower-right corner of the Variable block in Write mode and enter the value. After you have created a Variable, it will be saved for easy access later. So the next time you put a Variable programming block in your program, you can click on it and access the Variable by name.

Text

As we discussed earlier with the Display programming block, a text program uses words that you enter in. You can see in Figure 4-18 that this new variable is named "Test Text", and the value is a very simple abc. You can see by the single LEGO brick on the Display Programming Block that it is in Micro mode, which means it will accept input that is wired to it.

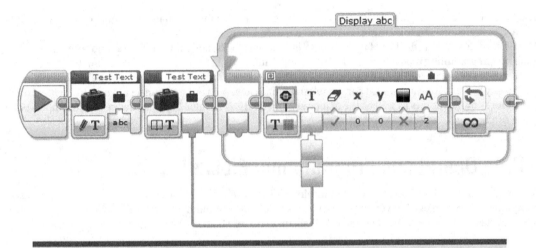

1. Variable Text

The Test Text variable is set to "abc". The variable is then read by the Display, and posted at (0,0) in black in Large Font (the upper left of the screen). Since the Display Brick is in Unlimited Loop Mode, the "abc" text will remain on screen indefinitely.

Figure 4-18. *An Example of using Variable for the Text*

It's pretty simple to wire the value of Test Text into the Display programming block. You will notice that the Display block is in a loop, so the value of Test Text will display indefinitely. I recommend running this program yourself, and even changing the value of the Test Text to something else. I am not certain how many characters you can have in your text, but the display size is limited if you want to try to display entire paragraphs without using multiple Display programming blocks.

Numeric

Numeric is for reading and writing variables that are numbers. You can see the example of its writing and reading in Figure 4-19.

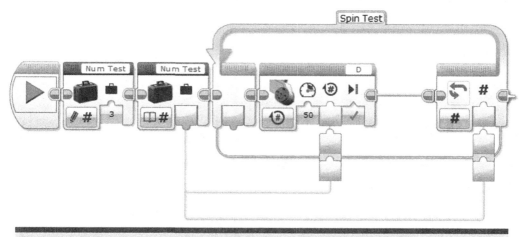

2. Variable Numeric

The Numeric Variable has been set to "3". The Red Programming brick reads the set value and plugs it into the Loop Equation for Count. This causes the Large Motor at Port D to spin clockwise 50 rpm for 3 rotation, three times. This is a total of 9 rotations.

Figure 4-19. *An example of the Variable Numeric*

You will notice that the number is plugged into the amount of rotations for the Large Motor's On For Rotations parameter. It is also plugged into the Loop programming block, and it is on the Count Setting's number of time. This means that the action on Port D will play three times for a total of nine rotations.

Logic

You may recall lessons in your mathematics class that dealt with logic, and much of it consisted of establishing values as "true" or "false" and working within those conditions. In the case of the logic Variable, you are essentially establishing a case of True or False, and then using it, like in Figure 4-20.

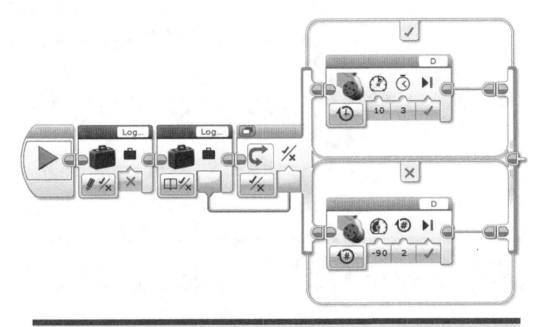

3. Variable Logic

The Variable known as Logic Test has been set to "False". This value has been read in a Switch Programming Brick, which means it will follow the "False" preset. The Large Motor at Port D will spin counter-clockwise 90 rpm for 2 rotations and then brake.

Figure 4-20. *An example of Variable Logic*

You will notice that the name of the Variable is "Log…". It is actually "Logic Test", but the space in the upper-right corner abbreviates it to make it fit. You can see that Logic Test has been set to a value of "False", and this value is plugged into a Logic Loop. The Logic Loop was something that I only touched upon in the last chapter, but it is essentially a way of telling the program: "If the value is true, then do this. But if the value is false, then do that." In the case of Figure 4-20, the value is set to false (the cross in the variable block), so it will spin a faster –90 rpm for 2 rotations instead of the slower 10 rpm for 3 seconds (i.e., it uses the block in the cross section, rather than the block in the tick section).

Numeric Array and Logic Array

You have probably noticed that Array has its own category on the data operations programming blocks. If you aren't familiar with an array, think of it as a group of something. In the case of Variable, it comes in two forms, Numeric and Logic. The Numeric Array is essentially a group of numbers, while the Logic Array is a group of True/False statements.

To write an array, all you have to do is click on the lower-right corner of the block and then enter in your values. You can see the Numeric example in Figure 4-21 has three values of 1, 4, and 5. Individual values can be deleted by clicking on the "X" beside the individual value, while more values can be added by clicking on the "+" button.

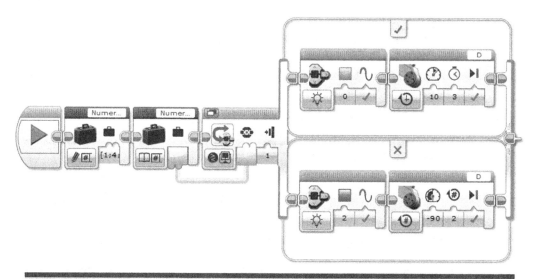

4. Variable Numeric Array

The Variable known as Numeric Array Test has been set to "1,4,5". This value has been read in a Brick Buttons Switch Programming Brick, which means it will read 1, 4, or 5. If buttons 1, 4, or 5 are pressed, then the Status Light will change to green, and the Large Motor at Port D will spin clockwise 10 rpm for 3 seconds and then brake. If buttons 1, 4, or 5 are not pressed, then the Brick Status light will change to red, and the Large motor at port D will spin counter-clockwise 90 rpm for 2 rotations and then stop.

Figure 4-21. *An Example of a Variable Numeric Array*

In Figure 4-21, the values of 1, 4, and 5 are wired into a Brick Button's Switch programming block, and correspond to the numeric values of the Brick Buttons. This means if the left button, top button, or bottom button are pressed, then the Large Motor at Port D will spin clockwise 10 rpm for 3 seconds. If these buttons are not pressed, it will go into a default setting, spinning counter-clockwise at 90 rpm for 2 rotations. Note that the program is configured so the Brick Status Light will glow green with the proper button is pressed and red when it is not.

I will explain more about Logic Arrays when we get to the Arrays section, but right now, I want to focus on the Constant.

Constant

If you can remember using variables in your mathematics class, then you probably remember constants. Unlike Variables, Constants are values that are known and never change. You will notice that the icon of the Constant is a locked briefcase, which symbolizes how unchanging it is. Once you have typed the value of the Constant in the upper-right corner, it is established. You will notice that the value can only be Read, and it is in the same forms as the Variable with Text, Numeric, Logic, Numeric Array, and Logic Array.

Constants are helpful when you have a program where the same number is used over and over again, such as the rpm. It is easy to simply establish this constant at the beginning, and then wire it in all the places where it will be used. If you want to change this constant, it is simple and will affect all the blocks that it is wired to. There are several examples in Figure 4-22.

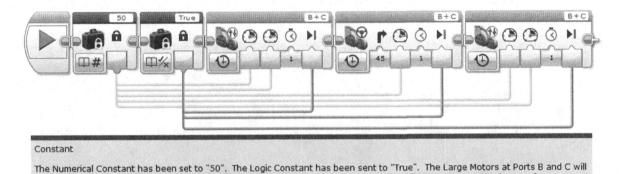

Constant

The Numerical Constant has been set to "50". The Logic Constant has been sent to "True". The Large Motors at Ports B and C will spin clockwise 50 rpm for 1 second and then brake. The Large Motors at Ports B and C will turn 50 rpm at 45 degrees for one second and then brake. The Large Motors at Ports B and C will spin clockwise 50 rpm for 1 second and then brake.

Figure 4-22. *Example of a Constant in a Program*

In Figure 4-22, you will note that a Constant Numeric value of 50 is plugged into the rpm of the three green programming blocks. The value of True is a Constant, and plugged into the blocks as well. If you wanted to change the rpm, all you would need to do is change the value of the constant in one spot instead of many. The same goes for the braking constants. Keep in mind it is not possible to change some of the three cases, unless you add more constants or enter in the parameters manually.

Arrays

As I explained in the Variables section, it is helpful to create an Array if you want to use multiple numeric values, or multiple true/false values. The Array is very helpful, and it comes in four modes: Array Append, Read at Index, Write at Index, and Length.

Array Append

This first Append mode will add a value onto your established array. So if you have a group of four values in your array, you will have five after you run it through this programming block. The value is established as a parameter, as seen in Figure 4-23.

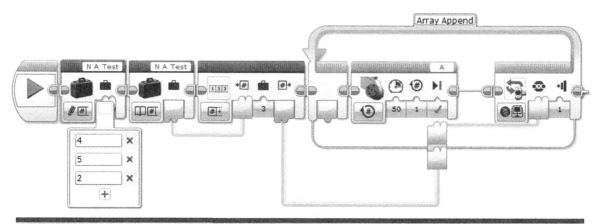

1. Array Append

Numeric Array known by variable "N A Test" is written with 4, 5, and 2. N A Test is ran through Array Append, and the new value of 3 is added to the array. These values are plugged into a Brick Buttons Loop. As a result, the Large Motor at Port A will spin clockwise 50 rpm for 1 rotation and then brake. This action will continue unless buttons 4, 5, 2, or 3 are pressed.

Figure 4-23. *An example of Array Append*

You can see that the Variable of "N A Test" is initialized as a Numeric Array of 4, 5, and 2. Once I put it through the Array Append, a new value of 3 is now a part of this array, making it 4, 5, 2, and 3. Since the Brick Buttons Loop is set to spin a Motor for one rotation, it will only stop if the numeric value of certain brick buttons (4, 5, 2, and 3) are pressed.

Read at Index

With Read at Index, it is possible to create an array, and then access one of the values at a specific point in the array. You can see an example of it in Figure 4-24 with a newly created Logic Array.

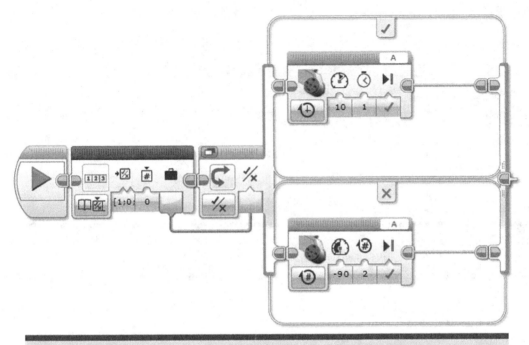

2. Array Read at Index

Logic Array written with values of 0: True, 1: False, 2: True, and 3: False. The value of 0 is plugged into the Switch Logic Loop. Since value 0: False, then the Large Motor at Port A will spin counter-clockwise 90 rpm for 2 rotations and then brake.

Figure 4-24. An example of an Array Read at Index

You will notice the Logic Array values start at 0 and end at 3. That is slightly confusing, but this is how the Array programming block organizes your information. You can see that the parameter is set to "0", so it takes the first input of the array, which is "true" and plugs it directly into the Switch Logic. Note this always causes the same action, but switching it to a parameter of "False" will cause something different.

Write at Index

Write at Index also allows you to create arrays, but you can also alter one of the values at the address or index. You can see in the example of Figure 4-25 how the number for parameter 3 was changed from 4 to 5.

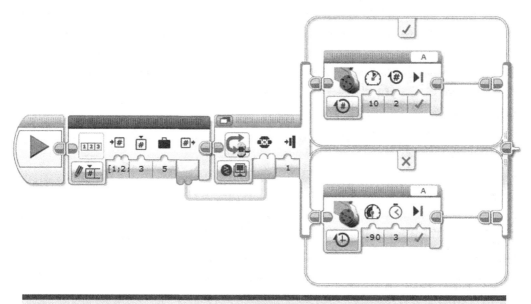

3. Array Write at Index

Numeric Array written with values of 0:1, 1:2, 2:3, and 3:4. The Write at Index changes the value of 3 so now 3:5. As a result, if the Brick Buttons 1, 2, 3, or 5 are pressed, then the Large Motor at Port A will spin clockwise 10rpm for 2 rotations and then brake. Otherwise, it will spin counter-clockwise 90 rpm for 3 seconds and then brake.

Figure 4-25. *An example of Array Write at Index*

You can see that the numerical values for the Brick Buttons have now been changed from 1, 2, 3, and 4 to 1, 2, 3 and 5. The Write at Index is perfect for situations in which you only want one value to change and not the entire array.

Array Length

The purpose of Array Length is to take the number of cases in an array and export the number. There is an example in Figure 4-26.

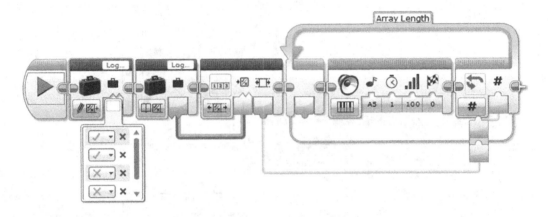

4. Array Length

Variable of Logic Array Test set to 0=True, 1=True, 2=False, and 3=False. Logic Array Test is read and plugged into Array Length, which exports the numeric value of Length into the Count Loop. Since the Length Number is equal to 4, the A5 Note will play for 1 second at 100 volume for four times.

Figure 4-26. *An example of Array Length*

As you can see, the Logic Array Test has four distinct cases, and therefore exporting the number of them via wire into a Count Loop allows the A5 note to play four distinct times.

Logic

Logic is all about establishing if a first value is true or false, a second value is true or false, and what the result will be when you apply a logic operator to the values. You have four choices of logic operator, and this includes the "Not" which will reverse the value from true to false, or vice versa:

- a AND b
- a OR b
- a XOR b
- Not a

You can then select true or false values for a and b, and then use the result of the logic operation to determine if an event happens or doesn't happen. I have examples of each, starting with a simple example of AND.

Logic AND

For AND, it is about two conditions that must be true in order to make the AND statement true. The easiest way to describe this is using the Touch Sensors, which can either be True (pressed) or False (unpressed). Figure 4-27 is an example of an AND statement where both must be pressed to create the "True" condition.

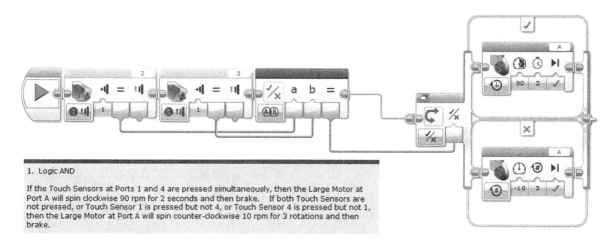

1. Logic AND

If the Touch Sensors at Ports 1 and 4 are pressed simultaneously, then the Large Motor at Port A will spin clockwise 90 rpm for 2 seconds and then brake. If both Touch Sensors are not pressed, or Touch Sensor 1 is pressed but not 4, or Touch Sensor 4 is pressed but not 1, then the Large Motor at Port A will spin counter-clockwise 10 rpm for 3 rotations and then brake.

Figure 4-27. *The use of Logic AND in an EV3 Program*

Figure 4-27 has two Touch Sensors rigged at Ports 1 and 4, and both of them must be pressed to pass the Logic Switch. You can rig up this program pretty easily, and note what happens when one Touch Sensor is pressed but not the other, or no Touch Sensors are pressed. Keep in mind that the timing is important for this, as the programming will dictate going from one block to the other. In other words, it is important to press both Touch Sensors at the very beginning to produce the positive result. Timing is also important for the OR, XOR, and Not functions.

Logic OR

If we were to change the program in Figure 4-27 to an OR statement, then it would only require one of the switches to be pressed to create a True statement. In short, we are creating a condition where only one element has to be true to make the entire situation true. Here is another example in Figure 4-28.

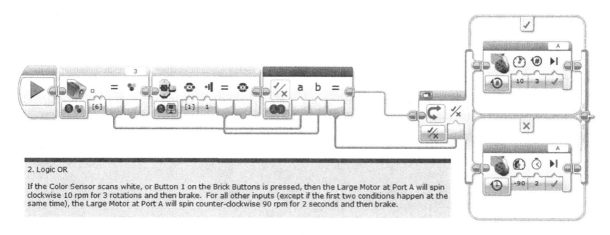

2. Logic OR

If the Color Sensor scans white, or Button 1 on the Brick Buttons is pressed, then the Large Motor at Port A will spin clockwise 10 rpm for 3 rotations and then brake. For all other inputs (except if the first two conditions happen at the same time), the Large Motor at Port A will spin counter-clockwise 90 rpm for 2 seconds and then brake.

Figure 4-28. *An example of Logic OR*

You can see that the first condition is the Color Scanner must scan White, also known by its numeric value of 6. The second condition is that button 2 must be pressed. If you tried this program yourself, then you will find it only takes one of these conditions to get the Large Motor at Port A to spin slowly. The value of True will also occur if both of these conditions are present.

Logic XOR

The XOR stands for Exclusive Or, which will only read True provided both conditions are the opposite of each other. I used the Brick Buttons in Figure 4-29 to illustrate this.

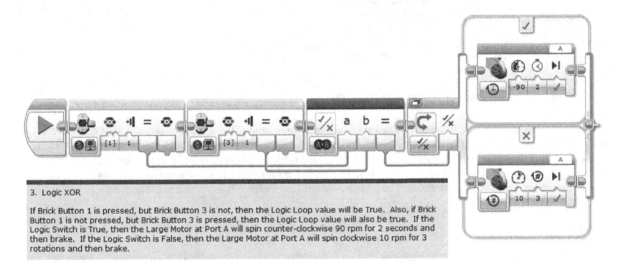

3. Logic XOR

If Brick Button 1 is pressed, but Brick Button 3 is not, then the Logic Loop value will be True. Also, if Brick Button 1 is not pressed, but Brick Button 3 is pressed, then the Logic Loop value will also be true. If the Logic Switch is True, then the Large Motor at Port A will spin counter-clockwise 90 rpm for 2 seconds and then brake. If the Logic Switch is False, then the Large Motor at Port A will spin clockwise 10 rpm for 3 rotations and then brake.

Figure 4-29. *An example of Logic XOR*

For these two conditions, all it takes is for just one to be pressed to be True while the other is not pressed. In other words, the inputs have to be the opposite of each other. Try this out for yourself.

Not A

The condition of Not A simply takes what would have been a True output and shifts it immediately to a False one, and shifts a False output to a True one. I went ahead and added a Not A to Figure 4-30, and put it in the program below.

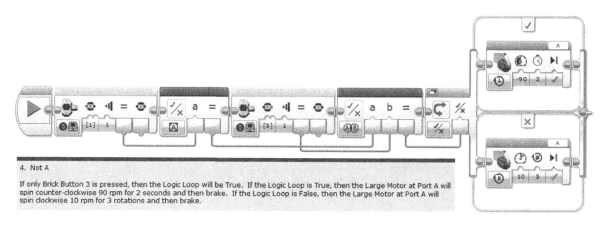

4. Not A

If only Brick Button 3 is pressed, then the Logic Loop will be True. If the Logic Loop is True, then the Large Motor at Port A will spin counter-clockwise 90 rpm for 2 seconds and then brake. If the Logic Loop is False, then the Large Motor at Port A will spin clockwise 10 rpm for 3 rotations and then brake.

Figure 4-30. *An example of Not A*

If you run the program, you will find that it only reads True if Brick Button 3 and only this button is pressed. This is because this represents a positive input, while not pressing 1 produces the True result.

Math

In addition to the logic operations you might want to do some math problems while you program. You may need to use mathematics in your programs, and this will help you for when you want to use addition, subtraction, multiplication, or division of two numeric values. You can see a complex example in Figure 4-31, and I used a Count Loop to create a problem that will display the answer in text form.

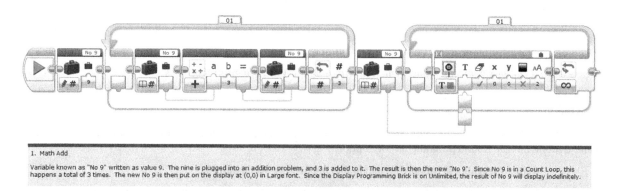

1. Math Add

Variable known as "No 9" written as value 9. The nine is plugged into an addition problem, and 3 is added to it. The result is then the new "No 9". Since No 9 is in a Count Loop, this happens a total of 3 times. The new No 9 is then put on the display at (0,0) in Large font. Since the Display Programming Brick is on Unlimited, the result of No 9 will display indefinitely.

Figure 4-31. *An example of the Math programming block, with an emphasis on Addition*

If you tried this program, then you should see "18" on the display, because 3 was added to the original 9 three times, so 9+3=12, 12+3=15, and 15+3=18. If you didn't, check your program or your arithmetic. You might want to tinker around with the formula and see what results you can get. The EV3 Brick is as good as a calculator.

The Math programming block is also good for when you want to find the absolute value or square root of one numeric value. You can also find an exponent if you have a number and the exponent. You can see this example in Figure 4-32 which demonstrates the application of the Pythagorean Theorem on a triangle whose opposite and adjacent sides are 6 and 8.

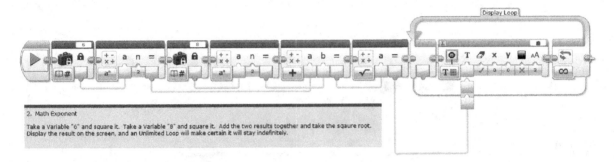

2. Math Exponent

Take a Variable "6" and square it. Take a Variable "8" and square it. Add the two results together and take the sqaure root.
Display the result on the screen, and an Unlimited Loop will make certain it will stay indefinitely.

Figure 4-32. An example of the Math programming block with exponents and square roots

This time, I won't bother spoiling the answer for you with this one. You probably already know it if you took trigonometry and studied basic Pythagorean triplicates.

You can even do real complex math with four numeric units, with a, b, c, and d. With the Advanced function, you can do a lot of other complex equations like sine, cosine, and tangent, and a lot more. You can see some examples in Figure 4-33.

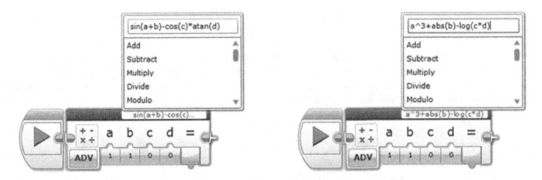

Figure 4-33. Examples of more advanced math functions on the Math programming block

Round

Occasionally, while you are doing math, you might end up with a repeating decimal or irrational number that you want to round off. The Round program has four options:

- To Nearest. This will round your decimal to the nearest whole number.

- Round Up. This will round up to your decimal to the nearest whole number, whatever it may be.

- Round Down. This will round down your decimal to the nearest whole number, whatever it may be.

- Truncate: Here is where you can set the parameters for your number in decimal places.

I have included examples in Figure 4-34 so you can see the varied results, and you will see different outputs on the display all with the same Constant of 43.5687.

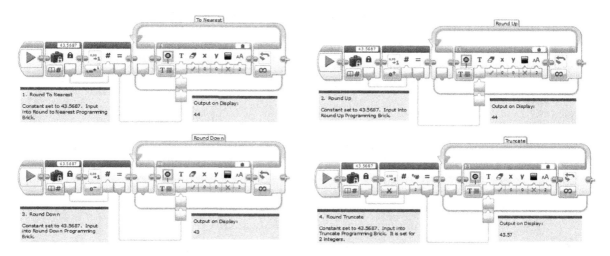

Figure 4-34. *Some examples of how to use the Round programming block*

Compare

Compare allows you to compare two numeric values with Equal To, Not Equal To, Greater Than, Greater Than or Equal To, Less Than, or Less Than or Equal To. Using the Math programming block and a Switch, you can set it up to have different reactions depending on the result. There is an example in Figure 4-35.

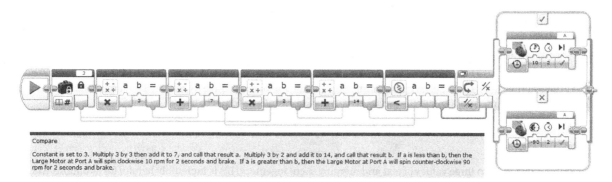

Figure 4-35. *An example of the Compare programming block*

You can see that the set-up is for a certain equation, and whatever is the lesser amount will trigger the positive action. You can easily change the constant to something else if you want to see a different result, and change the inequality sign as well.

Range

Range is helpful for situations where you want to establish a lowest and highest value for something. For example, you can call a vehicle to come only within a certain range of something and then stop. You can command it to stay inside or outside of its range which can be established between any two numeric values. There is an example in Figure 4-36 of a program designed to do just that.

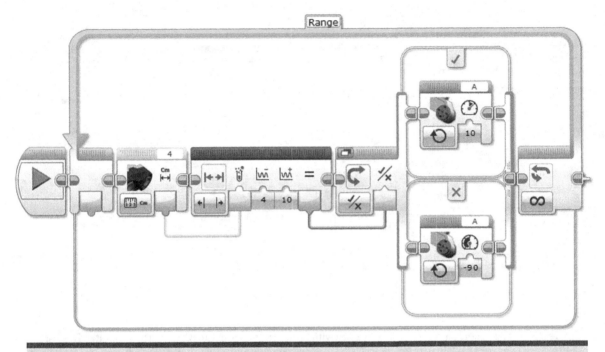

Range

The Ultrasonic Sensor scans, and any item that comes less than 4 cm or greater than 10 cm will cause the Large Motor at Port A to spin clockwise at 10 rpm. If it gets within the range of 4-10, then the Large Motor at Port A to spin counter-clockwise at 90 rpm.

Figure 4-36. *An example of using the Range programming block*

In the example in Figure 4-35, it is programmed in Outside mode to produce its results. The same results can be done with the Inside mode, although the parameters and cases would need to change.

Text

Text is about taking up to three values of text and merging them together. This is incredibly helpful for situations when you want the display to show you values of something. For example, if you want to hook up the Ultrasonic Sensor so it can measure things a distance away, this is what you use in Figure 4-37.

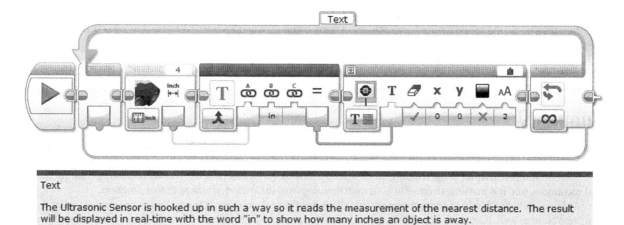

Text

The Ultrasonic Sensor is hooked up in such a way so it reads the measurement of the nearest distance. The result will be displayed in real-time with the word "in" to show how many inches an object is away.

Figure 4-37. *An example using Text*

If you run the program, you can put your hand right in front of the Ultrasonic Sensor and watch as the display shows the distance between your hand and the sensor in real time.

Random

Recall how you set up values with the Range: Random is all about letting the EV3 Brick come up with a value that it selects on a whim, with no bias. It can be used for Logic, such as a yes or no percentage from 0 to 100. For instance, an input of 20 would create a situation that has an output of 20% True and an 80% False output. It can also be used as a random number generator as seen in Figure 4-38.

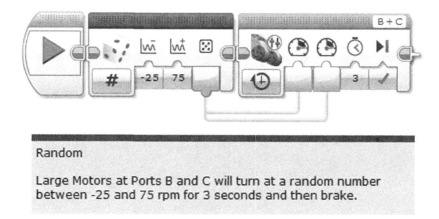

Random

Large Motors at Ports B and C will turn at a random number between -25 and 75 rpm for 3 seconds and then brake.

Figure 4-38. *A demonstration of the Random programming block*

As you can see from Figure 4-38, the Random Number Generator will discover a number in between –25 and 75, and then plug it into the speed for the Large Motors at Ports B and C. Will it be fast? Will it be slow? It is truly a roll of the dice.

With the right application of Random, you can create a vehicle that will go all over the floor in completely random directions and speeds.

Summary

In creating programs for the LEGO MINDSTORMS EV3, it is helpful to know how to insert a graphic for the display, a sound, or even change the Brick Status light. Fortunately, it comes with programming blocks that will help with that.

For example, the Display programming block is set up for text, lines, and point. It can also do shapes like circles and rectangles, and it is possible to enter in your own drawing with the included Image Editor program.

As for sound, the Play File program comes with all kinds of sounds to enter. It is possible to program it to play a Tone or a Note as well. Like the Image Editor, it is possible to record one's own sound with the Sound Editor program, included on the EV3 Software program.

The Brick Display Light can also be constructed to turn whatever color that you wish as well with its personal programming block.

In addition to the sight and sound, LEGO MINDSTORMS equips the user to manipulate data with the data programming blocks. These red blocks are very handy for setting values, not to mention all kinds of arithmetical operations.

I highly recommend playing with all of these functions. Not only will you become more adept at placing them in your programs, but it is really a lot of fun.

■ ■ ■

CHAPTER 5

Data Logging and Advanced Programming Blocks

As discussed in the introduction, one of the reasons that LEGO MINDSTORMS was originally conceived was for scientific data logging. If you are familiar with any of the sciences, it is all about collecting information or data and using it to prove (or disprove) some sort of hypothesis. That is the scientific method in a nutshell, and EV3 has software built into the EV3 Brick and Software to help you collect whatever data you need to prove or disprove your theories.

The interesting thing about the Data Logging feature of LEGO MINDSTORMS EV3 is that it can help you analyze and organize your data as well as collect it. It is possible to read data while a program is running, and it is possible to use the EV3 Brick screen to obtain this information as well. You will use the Brick Datalog on the Apps tab, as discussed in Chapter 2.

Open a New Experiment

To create an experiment, you open up a page of data the same way you opened up a New Program, as shown in Chapter 2. Go to "File", and "New Project". Instead of selecting "New Program", select "New Experiment" (see Figure 5-1).

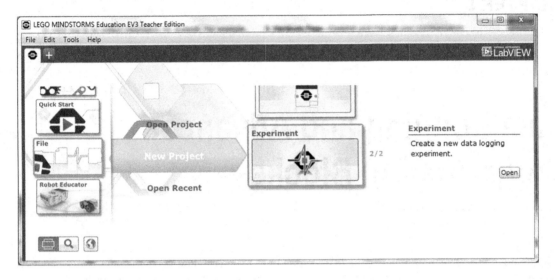

Figure 5-1. *The section of the Lobby where you can open an experiment*

When you click on "Open", you will see some charts and other information that might seem confusing at first (see Figure 5-2). I highly recommend plugging the EV3 Brick into your computer's USB port, and then plugging all the motors and sensors into the EV3 Brick with the Connecting cables. You will then see that some information is already collecting.

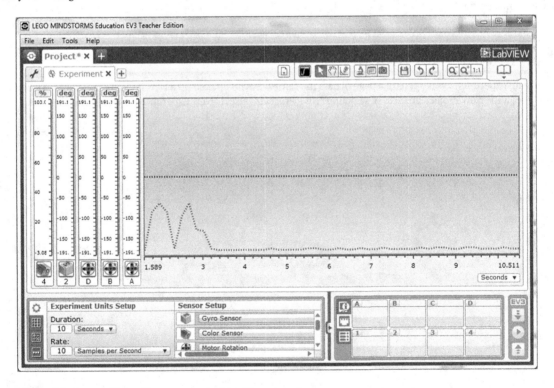

Figure 5-2. *What you will see when you open a New Experiment*

Graph Area

On the left is the Graph Area, which will allow you to see what is being plotted as far as what is connected to the EV3 Brick. You will notice that the X-axis or horizontal axis represents a unit of time, and it defaults to seconds. It can be changed to minutes by clicking on the tab that says "Seconds" in the lower-right corner of Figure 5-2.

As for the vertical or y-axis, you will see that it is different for every sensor that is plugged into it. Note that any of the sensors that are connected to the EV3 Brick show up here, provided the EV3 Brick is connected to your computer via the USB cable. You will also notice that what the y-axis represents is different for every sensor, and I will explain that after the following example.

If you are familiar with graphing, then you know how you can use this data. For example, I connected the Color Sensor, Gyro Sensor, and Ultrasonic Sensor and let the computer grab the data.

You can see that there are three lines on the graph in Figure 5-3. The bright line on the bottom of the graph represents the data from the Ultrasonic Sensor, and you can see that it is constant (straight) on the graph at first, and then slowly tapers off by the 7th second. This is because I began the experiment with my hand at a distance from the Ultrasonic Sensor, and then slowly brought it closer. As my hand came closer to the Ultrasonic Sensor, it was reflected in the data.

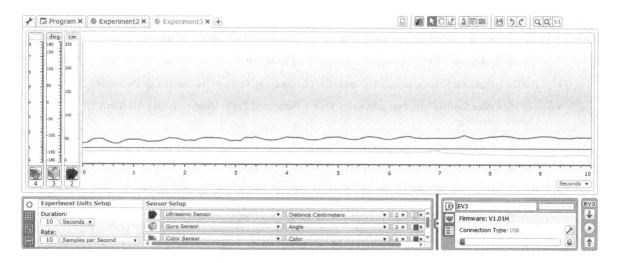

Figure 5-3. *The results of an experiment using the Color, Gyro, and Ultrasonic Sensors*

The line at the top of the graph in Figure 5-3 represents the data from the Gryo Sensor. This sensor is designed to measure the angle, and you will notice that the line has peaks and valleys like a mountain range. See if you can guess what was happening to the Gyro Sensor during this time. If you guessed that I was shaking it up and down, you are right. Again, the data reflects this.

As for the line in the middle, that line represents the Color Sensor. As you might have guessed on the flat line that represents constant value, I did absolutely nothing to it.

I highly recommend playing with the sensors on the graph until you become comfortable reading the information on it. You can then analyze the information with the window below the Graph Area and to the left, otherwise known as the Configuration Panel. ˙

Configuration Panel

The Configuration Panel allows for setting up an experiment and managing a dataset. It has four tabs that you can select here, which are very useful in obtaining data.

Experiment Configuration

Under the Experiment Configuration tab, you can see many tabs that you can alter which will change the values obtained that are in your experiment. For example, under the column labeled "Experiment Units Setup", you can choose to change the Duration and Rate.

The Duration defaults to 10 seconds. You can input how long you want the experiment to be, and this will change the x-axis accordingly. Note that it can be set to seconds or minutes. See Figure 5-4 for a better example.

Figure 5-4. *Experiment Configuration allows you to set up the values for Duration and Rate, as well as the settings for all sensors*

You can see all the sensors that are attached to the EV3 Brick. If there are more than three, you can scroll down to see more. You can manually add more sensors and motors, and you can also adjust the mode.

- For the Touch Sensor, you cannot change anything, as it only detects the State.

- For the Ultrasonic Sensor, you can change the distance in Centimeters, Inches, or Presence.

- For the Color Sensor, you can adjust for Color, Reflected Light Intensity, and Ambient Light Intensity.

- For the Gyro Sensor, you can adjust the Angle or the Rate.

- For the Temperature Sensor, you can set for Celsius or Fahrenheit.

- For the Energy Meter, you can set it to measure Voltage, Current, Wattage, or Joules.

- For the NXT Sound Sensor, you can set it to measure dB (unadjusted measurement of sound pressure above or below human range of hearing) and dBa (adjusted measurement of sound pressure taking into account the human range of hearing).

- For the Medium and Large Motors, you can plot for Degrees, Rotations, or Current Power.

In addition to adjusting the modes, you can also adjust the Ports. For example, if you want to switch the Gyro Sensor to Port 3, you can, provided you physically do this on the EV3 Brick as well.

You can also adjust the color of the line on the graph, but if you want to change the color after the information is entered, you'll have to use the DataSet Table.

If you hit the red X, it will eliminate the sensor from the setup.

DataSet Table

The next tab down is the DataSet Table, and this will show your data in certain increments. You can rename the data set, change the color of its representation on the graph, and even the type of data. See Figure 5-5 for an example.

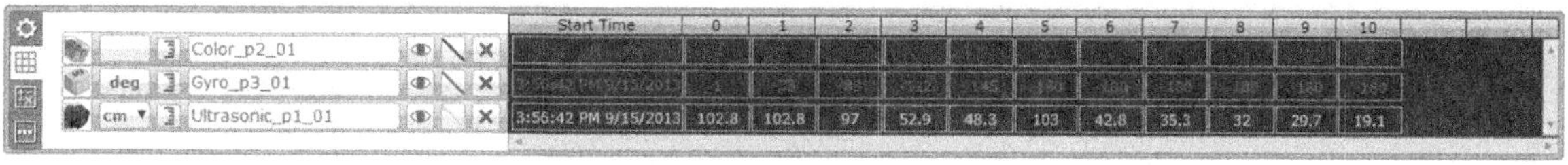

Figure 5-5. *The DataSet Table Tab allows you to look at the data obtained in your experiment*

In Figure 5-5, you can look at data obtained from an experiment similar to the one in Figure 5-3, and I set it at one reading per second. You can set it at more readings per second, and you will get a much wider graph.

You can see that the program has formed the datasets and named them. The one for the Color Sensor is Color_p2_01, and since the sensor was not tampered with, it registers a zero for every reading. As for the Gyro one (Gyro_p3_01), it registers with negative angles, as it was shaken up. The really interesting reading comes with the dataset for the Ultrasonic Sensor, Ultrasonic_p1_01. You can see that it steadily decreases from seconds 0–4, but then suddenly jumps up to 103 cm at point 5 before steadily declining from 6–10. I believe that this result was from my hand moving out of the way of the Ultrasonic Sensor, and then it locking on to the nearest thing in sight. As with all scientific experimentation, you have to account for very odd readings.

Anyway, you will notice that you have a lot of options here. If it permits, you can change the mode. For example, I can change the Ultrasonic Sensor values from centimeters to inches. I can't change the Gyro Sensor from Degrees to Rate.

There is also a button that looks like a ruler, complete with markings for smaller units. Clicking on that allows the dataset to be moved to the axis. By the way, if you want to change the dataset names, that is possible.

You can also hide the dataset by hitting the eyeball button, and make it return by hitting the same button. You can also change the color of the dataset, and highlight the sample times with certain shapes like squares, plus signs, circles, or X's. You can also eliminate the dataset entirely by hitting the red X.

DataSet Calculation

As for the DataSet Table, this is what you can do with your dataset after you have the data. You can run it through a lot of arithmetical calculation and even graph the result.

As an example, I did an experiment using two results with the Ultrasonic Sensor.

- The first reading revealed dataset Ultrasonic_p1_01, which resulted in a semi-constant rate that led to a gradual decline starting at the 3rd second until it almost hit 0 cm at the tenth second. This was because I was moving my hand toward the Ultrasonic Sensor, slowly.

- The second reading (Ultrasonic_p1_02) was more erratic because my hand was very quickly moving toward the Ultrasonic Sensor. You can see the peaks and valleys are very frequent in between the 3rd and 5th second.

You can see the results in Figure 5-6.

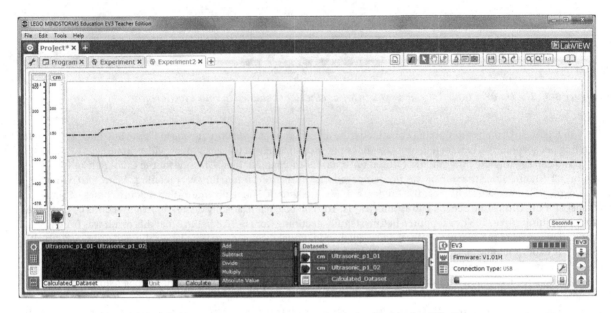

Figure 5-6. *Using the DataSet Calculation on two readings, with the third being the difference*

Using the DataSet Calculator, I was able to take both the datasets and find the difference. All I need to do is click on the first dataset, click "Subtract", and then hit the other database near it. By hitting "Calculate", I could put that Difference on the graph, which is the third line graphed on Figure 5-6.

Just to let you know, you can go back to the DataSet Table and find your Calculated DataSet there. You can rename it if you like.

You should also take note of the other mathematical functions that you are able to derive with this. In addition to subtract, you can add, divide, multiply, and do a whole lot more.

Graph Programming

As for Graph Programming, this is about dividing an experiment into different sections, and having something happen when a result is reached. In graph programming, you can program something to happen to the EV3 Brick when a certain threshold is reached, provided you use the green programming blocks.

Here is an example in Figure 5-7, again using the Ultrasonic Sensor. What happened is that I programmed the light on the EV3 Brick to glow a certain color when my hand was less than 84.15 cm from the Ultrasonic Sensor. This is the circle zone, as you can see on the tab in Figure 5-7.

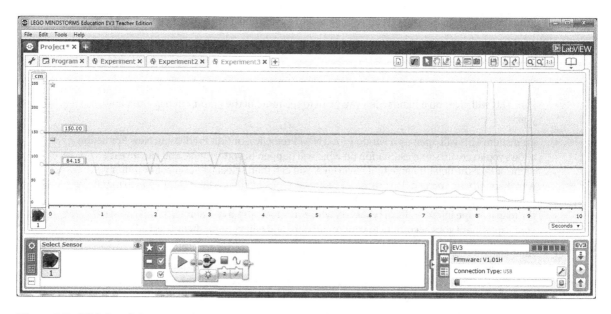

Figure 5-7. *With Graph Programming, you are able to program something happening at a certain threshold*

You will notice that there are three thresholds here: one with a star, one with a rectangle, and one with a circle. Clicking on one of these will automatically put the threshold on top. Clicking on two will split the y-axis in half, but you can set the value for that threshold. Clicking on all three will split the screen into three sections, with you being able to set the value of two thresholds.

You can program the EV3 Brick to do anything when it hits a threshold, provided it is one of the Action programming blocks. You can program it to run a motor like we demonstrated in Chapter 2, or do sight and sound like I demonstrated in Chapter 4.

Hardware Page

To the right and on the bottom of Figure 5-7 is the Hardware Page, which is what it was while setting up a program, a place to see what is attached to the EV3 Brick. It will only work if the EV3 Brick is attached to the computer.

It has the Brick Information, which displays the Firmware type as well as the Connection type. Then there is the Port View, allowing you to see what sensors are connected to the ports. The next tab down is available blocks, allowing you to see what other EV3 Bricks you are connected to via USB, Bluetooth, or Wi-Fi.

Content Editor

All the way to the right is the Content Editor, which works the same as the one on the Program screen. You can minimize it with the button on the end, and since it works pretty much the same as the one on the Program, I won't bother going into detail about it.

Data Logging Toolbar

Above the Content Editor is the Data Logging Toolbar, and it has a series of buttons that I will describe from left to right.

- Program/Experiment List: You can select a recent experiment in this pull-down menu.

- Stop Oscilloscope mode: You will note the Oscilloscope mode when you log in, and here is a button for clicking it on or off.

- Select: Like in Program mode, this is what you use for selecting pretty much anything.

- Pan: This will give you a hand when you want to see more of the graph, such as the x and y-axis.

- Prediction: This will open up a window for a New Prediction or Edit Prediction. New Prediction allows you to create some estimation on what will happen to your results. You can give it a name or take the default name that it will give. You can then select what sensor or motor you want to put there. You can then chose a Prediction type of Pencil, which allows you to manually draw on the graph with your mouse. Then there is Linear, which allows you to create a line on the map in slope intercept form (y=mx+b, where m=slope and b=y-intercept). You can see if your experiment goes according to your prediction, and edit your prediction as well.

- Analysis: This comes in two forms, Point Analysis and Section Analysis. Point Analysis allows you to click on a single value on the x-axis, and you can see the values of the y-axis at that point. Section Analysis allows you to select an entire section of the x-axis and obtain information like the minimum, maximum, mean, median, standard deviation, integral, and curve fit.

- Comment: Like in Programming, this is where you can put whatever text that you want to see in the graph.

- Screenshot: If you want to particular still shot of your experiment, click on this and you can save it to wherever you want on your computer.

- Save: Saves whatever experiment you are working on, along with every secondary tab underneath.

- Undo: In case you do something on your program that you regret, feel free to hit this to remove a move. I am not certain how many levels of Undo are allowed, but I did it over ten times.

- Redo: If you hit Undo and decide that what you undid you really wanted, hit this.

- Zoom Out: You will want to hit this if you want to increase the range on your graph.

- Zoom In: This allows you to really narrow your focus on your graph, and you might be surprised what you can see.

- Reset Zoom: This gives you a 1:1 view.

Now that you have been acquainted with the Data Logging feature of LEGO MINDSTORMS EV3, I want to take some time to talk about the Advanced programming blocks and how they can help you with Data Logging, as well as other functions that are somewhat related.

You will note that I include fewer examples in this particular section, as many of these Advanced programming blocks are similar to those that I have previously introduced.

Advanced Programming Blocks

Since I have covered all types of programming blocks in Chapters 2, 3, and 4, it only seems appropriate to cover the dark blue or Advanced programming blocks in this section. As for the light blue area, these are the macros or "My Blocks", and you'll have to wait until Chapter 6 before I cover them.

File Access

File Access is very similar to the Variable Programming block that I discussed in the last chapter, but it can do a lot more. If you recall, the Variable allows you to plug in a numeric, logic, text, or array value, but File Access allows you to enter in values that it converts into Rich Text Format (rtf). The Files Access block comes in four modes which are ordered Read, Write, Delete, and Close. Using the File Access block involves using these modes in a different order, though.

Write

Like the Variable block, you can name your File on the upper-right corner. You can then manually type a text or numeric value in the parameter section.

Close

Since the Numeric or Text value is in rich text format (RTF), this means that you can actually fit quite a few lines of code within the file that you just wrote. Before a file is to be read, you must use this command, which will make it possible so the first line of the files can be read.

Read

Like the Variable Program, the Read function is represented by a book, which means that whatever is on the file will be read, like it was in a book. Be sure that it was closed first, using the Close command. Also, you will have to output the value in the form of Text or Numeric, so be certain you have the right setting.

Here is an example of how the File Access modes work together in Figure 5-8.

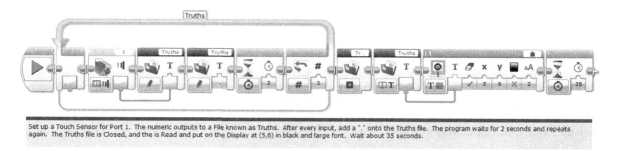

Set up a Touch Sensor for Port 1. The numeric outputs to a File known as Truths. After every input, add a "." onto the Truths file. The program waits for 2 seconds and repeats again. The Truths file is Closed, and the is Read and put on the Display at (5,6) in black and large font. Wait about 35 seconds.

Figure 5-8. *A way to use the File Access Programming Brick*

As you can see, the File has to be written, then Closed, and then it can be Read. If you want to see the value on this file, you can access this on the Memory Browser, which is located on the "Tools" section of the memory bar (see Figure 5-9).

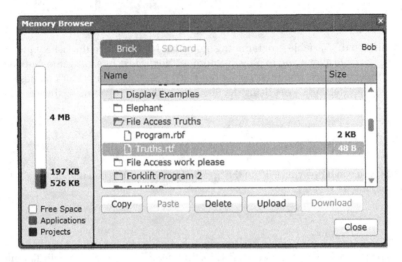

Figure 5-9. *The Memory Browser Tool for accessing the File Access values*

You can find your File here, and the rtf file can be uploaded by selecting it and hitting "Upload". You can then open it on programs like Notepad and see the file for yourself.

Delete

When you are finished with the file, go ahead and just delete it. It is as simple as entering in the file name and making the program execute this block.

Data Logging

If you want to log data, but do not want to have the USB cable connected to the computer, you can program the Data Logging block to gather the data for you, and then upload it in Experiment.

It comes in four modes that include On For Time, On, Single Measurement, and Stop. In the first mode, you select the length of time in which you are interested, in seconds or minutes. From there, you can select the rate and the rate unit with 0 meaning samples per second and 1 meaning seconds between samples.

You can see in Figure 5-8 that I can set up data to be read at several ports. All that is needed is to select a port, and then the mode, which include the following:

- Color Sensor (including Color, Reflected Light, and Ambient Light)

- Gryo Sensor (including Angle and Rate)

- Infrared Sensor (including Proximity, Beacon Heading, Beacon Proximity, and Remote)

- Motor Rotation (Degrees, Rotations, and Current Power)

- Temperature Sensor (Celsius and Fahrenheit)

- Touch Sensor (Off and On readings only)

- Ultrasonic Sensor (Advanced, Distance Centimeters, Distance Inches, and Presence)

- Energy Meter

- NXT Sound Sensor (dB and dBa)

You can click on the "+" button to add on more sensors, and the red "X" button to get rid of them.

On For Time

This particular mode comes in two forms, seconds or minutes. I set up a program that you can see in Figure 5-10, and the first parameter is at 10 seconds.

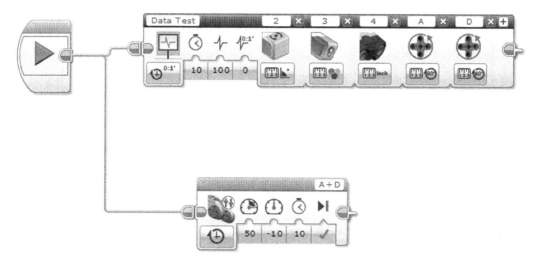

Figure 5-10. *An example of the "On For Time" section of the Data Logging programming block*

You can see that I set up the Data Test to read the Gyro Sensor at Port 2, the Color Sensor at Port 3, the Ultrasonic Sensor at Port 4, plus two Large Motors at Ports A and D. I then set the motors moving and just shook up the other sensors.

I made certain that the EV3 Brick was unhooked from my computer, and then ran the program from the Brick on the menu screen. The program ran, and I shook the other sensors while the motors ran.

Once the program was timed out and finished, I plugged the USB cord and opened an experiment tab. I then went to the Hardware page on the bottom right and hit the upload button.

You can see in Figure 5-11 that my data was saved in the Data Logging block file, as this was the saved file for the project. By opening this file folder, I can see that my data was saved under Data Test_2.rdf, as this was my most recent reading. By selecting this file and hitting "Import", my data appears on a graph of its own, which you can see in Figure 5-12.

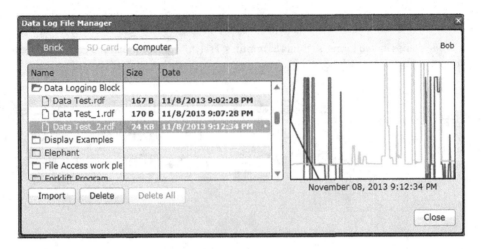

Figure 5-11. *Uploading data from the Data Logging programming block*

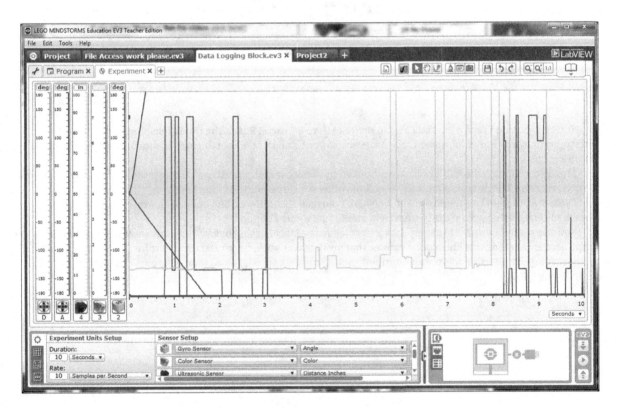

Figure 5-12. *An example of data uploaded to my computer after using the Data Logging programming block*

On

The second mode for Data Logging, simply called On, just turns it on. There is no time parameter set, and it records until the Program has ended or if you use the command of Stop, which you can read about later in this section.

Single Measurement

This mode is exactly what it sounds like, as it allows measurements to be taken only at one point.

Stop

You will notice that there are no parameters that have to be set here, as all it does is issue a command to stop datalogging.

Messaging

If you have more than one EV3 Brick, then you can actually send messages from one to the other via wireless Bluetooth connection. In order to do this, the EV3 BRICKs have to be synced with each other using Bluetooth. Pairing with an EV3 Brick or even a smartphone is possible with the Settings menu on the EV3 Brick itself, as discussed in Chapter 2. It is also possible to turn on and off the Bluetooth Connection with the appropriately named Bluetooth Connection programming block, which I will discuss in the next section. It comes in three communication modes: Send, Receive, and Compare.

Send

In order to send a message from one EV3 Brick to the other, you need to have three things.

1. Message Title, which is typed in the upper-right corner.

2. The name of the EV3 Brick that will receive the message, typed in the first parameter.

3. EV3 the message itself, which can be typed in or wired from another source. Note that you want to specify the type of values that you are sending, in the form of Text, Numeric, or Logic. Think of this Send mode as a "Write".

Receive

If the Send mode is the "Write" block, then the Receive mode is the "Read". The Receive block needs to have the message title of Send block typed in the upper-right corner, and the Receive file has to be set up to receive the proper value (Text, Numeric, or Logic) of the Send file. You can see an example in Figure 5-13.

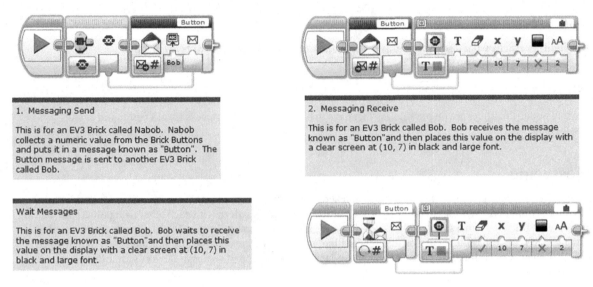

1. Messaging Send

This is for an EV3 Brick called Nabob. Nabob collects a numeric value from the Brick Buttons and puts it in a message known as "Button". The Button message is sent to another EV3 Brick called Bob.

2. Messaging Receive

This is for an EV3 Brick called Bob. Bob receives the message known as "Button" and then places this value on the display with a clear screen at (10, 7) in black and large font.

Wait Messages

This is for an EV3 Brick called Bob. Bob waits to receive the message known as "Button" and then places this value on the display with a clear screen at (10, 7) in black and large font.

Figure 5-13. *Ways of doing the Send and Receive Messaging Block*

The programs on the top left and right are highlighted, so that they will run at the same time. It actually uses two EV3 Bricks, one named Nabob and the other Bob. Nabob sends a message known as "Button" which is the input of a Brick Button pressed. Bob then receives this message and outputs it to the display. You will notice another program on the bottom of Figure 5-13 which is essentially the same, but with a Wait or Wait For Programming Brick in Messaging Update mode.

Compare

This mode takes the Receive one step further, as it takes a received message and then compares it to another value. This is set up in the form of an equation with the usual equality and inequality symbols, with outputs of True or False. Compare is especially good if you want to create a Switch case for the next block.

Bluetooth Connection

This block is one that you may or not have to use in your program, depending on whether or not you established a Bluetooth connection with the EV3 display screen. As I mentioned in the Messaging section, the EV3 Brick can be paired with other EV3 Brick, but they can also be paired with a smartphone, tablet, or a computer.

Bluetooth Connection has four modes. The first is On, which allows you to switch on the Bluetooth mode on the EV3 Brick. The second is Off, which switches the Bluetooth off. For Initiate, this is for establishing a connection with a very specific Bluetooth device which you can name in the first parameter. The opposite of Initiate would be Close, which will close the connection. See Figure 5-14 for examples.

1. Bluetooth On

Turns Bluetooth on the EV3 Brick running this program.

2. Bluetooth Off

Turns off the Bluetooth on the EV3 Brick running this program.

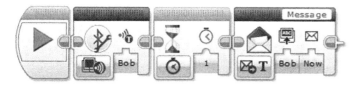

3. Bluetooth Initiate

This EV3 Brick named Nabob wants to Initiate a Bluetooth connection to another EV3 Brick named Bob. After one second, Nabob will send a message entitled "Message" to Bob with the text of "Now".

4. Bluetooth Close

The EV3 Brick named Nabob ends its Bluetooth connection to Bob.

Figure 5-14. *Examples of Bluetooth Connection*

Keep Awake

You may have noticed on the EV3 menu how you can program the EV3 Brick to sleep, or automatically shut off if no command is received after a certain amount of time. You can program it from about 2 minutes to 60 minutes, and it will shut off even if the EV3 Brick is plugged into the computer.

Keep Awake allows the EV3 Brick to keep on going, even though your program is nowhere finished running. If you like, you can output the Keep Awake to the display, and the number will be whatever you set it up with in the Brick's Main Menu. You can see an example of this in Figure 5-15.

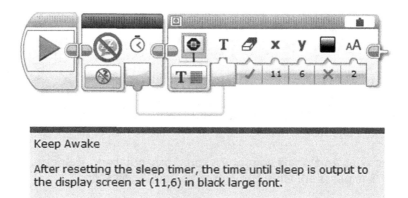

Keep Awake

After resetting the sleep timer, the time until sleep is output to the display screen at (11,6) in black large font.

Figure 5-15. *How to use the Keep Awake to display the time before the EV3 Brick goes to sleep*

Raw Sensor Value

This particular Programming block is set up for an unprocessed sensor reading, and it can read a range of 0 to 0123. This is good for third-party sensors, which I have not worked with yet (you use ports 1–4 to set this up).

You can see an example in Figure 5-16. All you need to do is connect the Color Sensor to port 3 and you will see all kinds of readings when you scan things with the Color Sensor. I wasn't able to make sense of it, but I am guessing that future EV3 kits might have more of a use for this particular programming block.

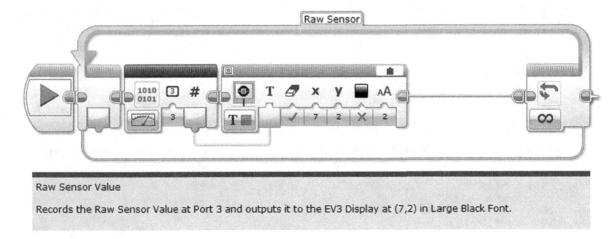

Figure 5-16. *An example of how to use the Raw Sensor Value with Port 3*

Unregulated Motor

This allows you to have absolute power over a motor. You may have noticed how they will automatically stop if put in a bad situation, but not in this case. Use with discretion on this one, as the Special Construction Projects in the next chapter need to be pretty precise.

You can see an example in Figure 5-17 of a motor that spins at 75 rpm, which means that it will spin continuously even if you try to physically stop it, like with your hand. Doing this could damage the motor, which is why I don't recommend it. Instead, use the Wait or Wait for Programming Brick and just push Brick Button 3.

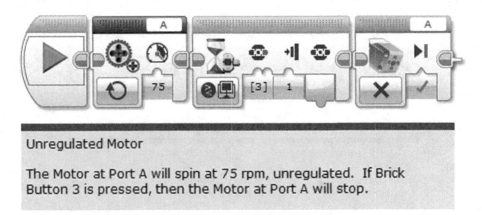

Figure 5-17. *An example of an Unregulated Motor programming block*

Invert Motor

This is a tool that you want to use in case you don't want to use negative values to make the motor spin in the other direction. You might remember that I had to use negative numbers to represent the power level in Chapter 3. If I wanted to keep my values positive to represent forward motion, I would just put the Invert motor in front of it like in Figure 5-18.

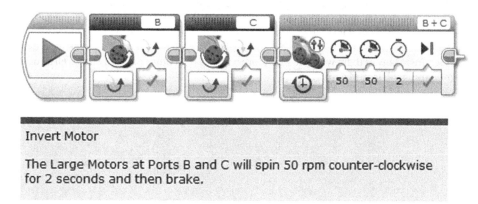

Figure 5-18. *This formula will spin the motors in a negative direction, without the negative values*

Keep in mind that two Invert Motor programming blocks do not cancel each other out. They simply take the motor and invert the rpm from positive to negative, or vice versa.

Stop Program

If you do enough programs, you will discover that sometimes they will not quit. If that should happen to your program, you might want to put this End Program block in to instantly cease activity on your program, leaving you the ability to start another program. An example is provided in Figure 5-19.

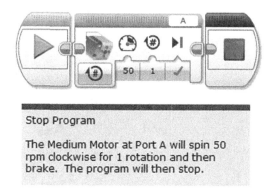

Figure 5-19. *An example of Stop Program programming block*

Summary

LEGO MINDSTORMS is very scientific in nature, and both the software and the EV3 Brick contain many ways of gathering data. It is very simple for the user to open a new experiment, and get all the data they will need (and more) from it.

In addition to graphing the data, a LEGO MINDSTORMS user can organize it easily. The Configuration Panel allows for the user to play with the Experiment Configuration, as well as making DataSets. The user can even run their DataSets through mathematical formulae and graph the results with the DataSet Calculator. It is also possible for the EV3 Brick to give warnings when the data reaches certain thresholds, thanks to Graph Programming.

Data Logging is also assisted by the Advanced programming blocks, which allow data to be used within LEGO MINDSTORMS programs. Many of them work via Bluetooth wireless with other EV3 Bricks as well as other Bluetooth devices like smartphones, tablets, and computers.

CHAPTER 6

Special Construction Projects and Macros

Now that I covered creating a vehicle in Chapter 3 as well as advanced programming steps in Chapter 5, I imagine you want to make that vehicle do all kinds of things. This chapter discusses how to create a lot of specialized vehicles like forklifts, cranes, scissorlifts, and other types of construction equipment.

Before I begin, I want to explain that even though I will be explaining how to program these specialized features, I am not going to really explain how to build vehicles that will house these constructions. It would take me too long and too many pages of instructions to do that, so you will see things like the lifting part of a forklift, but not the wheels. As I have stated in the introductory part of my book, the purpose of this book is that you create cool LEGO MINDSTORMS creations, not imitate the models here.

Swivel

I will start with one of the easiest and most necessary projects for the swivel. I use the term swivel to describe any time you want some apparatus to turn, and this can spin at 360 degrees. If you follow the instructions below, you can easily create a decent swivel. You will need the turntable piece, which is shown in the following instructions. It is possible to use a bigger turntable piece if you wish.

Project 6-1: The Swivel

I highly suggest using the Gyro Sensor to make certain it will work correctly. Please keep in mind that since you will need to connect them with connector cables, the ability to spin freely could be limited. The instructions are shown in Figures 6-1 to 6-17.

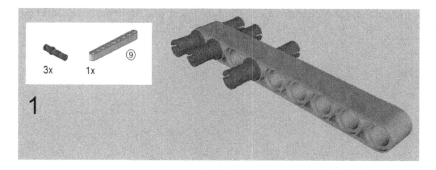

Figure 6-1. *Take a 9M beam and center three 3M connector pegs in the following through-holes as shown*

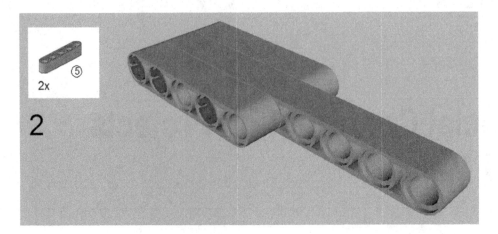

Figure 6-2. Snap on a 5M beam on each side of the creation

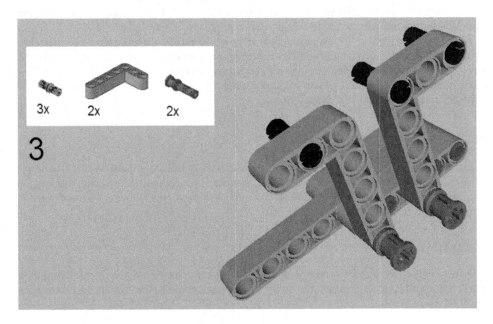

Figure 6-3. Use the friction snaps to click in two 5 × 3 beams as shown, and insert the three connector pegs

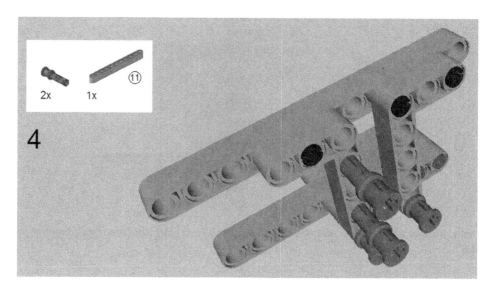

Figure 6-4. *Install the 11M beam on top. Snap on two friction snaps, but only halfway on*

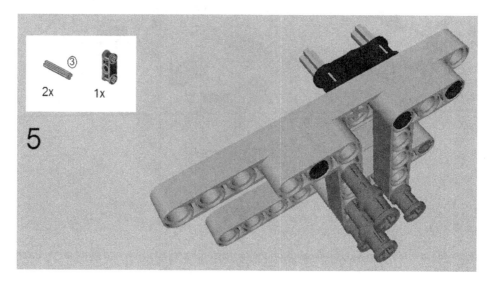

Figure 6-5. *Center two 3M axles on the double cross block, and insert it on the 9M beam*

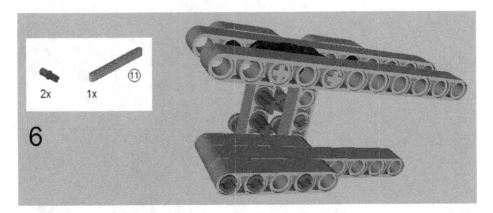

Figure 6-6. *Insert another 11M beam on the other side of the double cross block, and insert the connector peg/cross axles as shown*

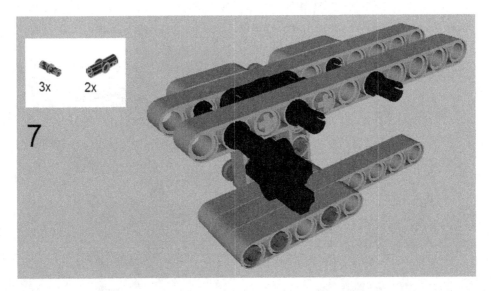

Figure 6-7. *Place the two 180 degree angle elements on the connector peg/cross axles, and place the connector pegs on the 11M beam on top*

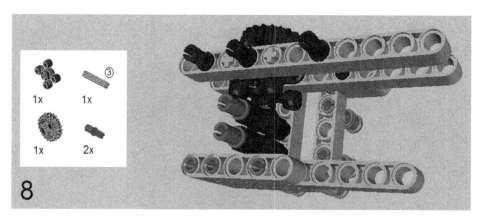

Figure 6-8. *Stick a 3M axle through the angular wheel just above the 180 angle elements, then place the Z20 bevel gear on top of that. Stick on the connector peg/cross axles on the 180 degree angle elements*

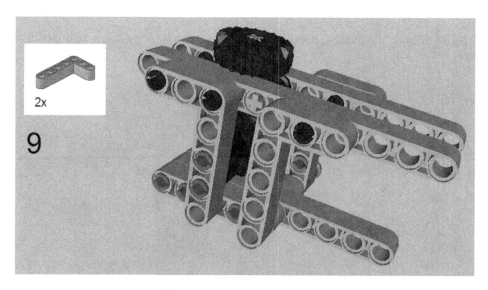

Figure 6-9. *Snap on the two 5 × 3 beams on the side to hold the structure together*

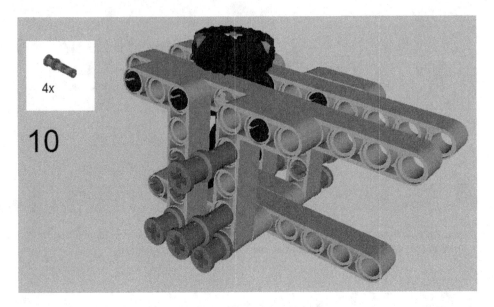

Figure 6-10. *On the bottom of the structure, push in two Friction Snaps all the way through. Push the other two friction snaps halfway in*

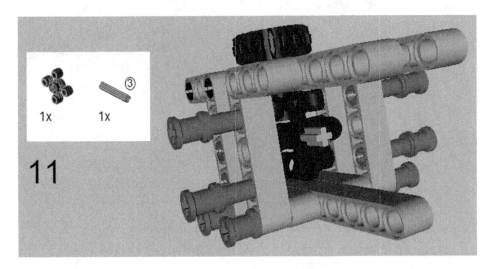

Figure 6-11. *Center an angular wheel on the 3M axle, and place it in the center of the 180 degree angle element*

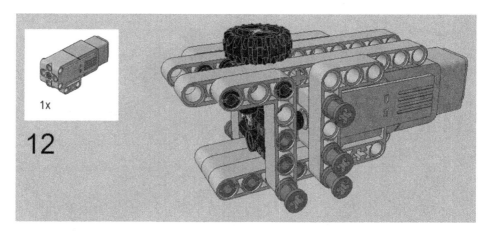

Figure 6-12. *Slide the Medium Motor on the 3M axle from the last step, and secure it by pressing in the friction snaps that were halfway in steps 4 and 10*

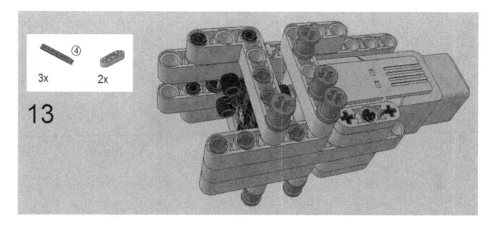

Figure 6-13. *Secure the Medium Motor on the bottom with the two 3M levers and three 4M axles*

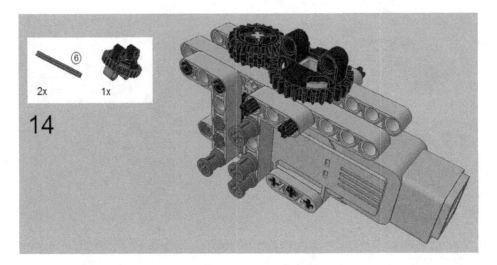

Figure 6-14. *Insert the small turntable on top so it meshes with the Z20 bevel gear. Secure the turntable on the sides with two 6M axles and it will be secured in the next step*

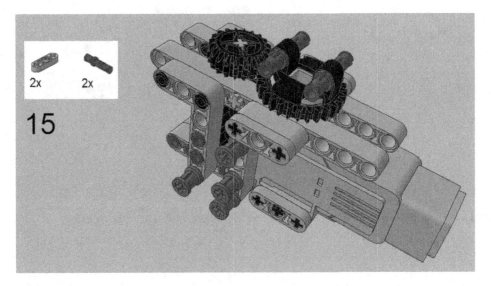

Figure 6-15. *Use the two 3M levers to secure the two 6M axles from the previous step. Center the two 3M Connector Pegs on top of the small turntable*

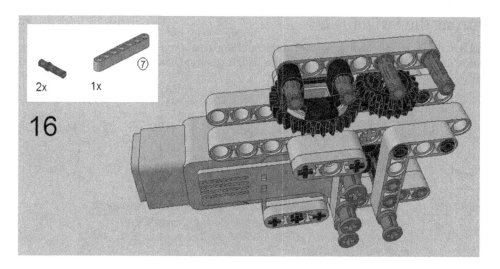

Figure 6-16. *Insert the 7M beam along the 3M connectors, and snap on two 3M Connector Pegs*

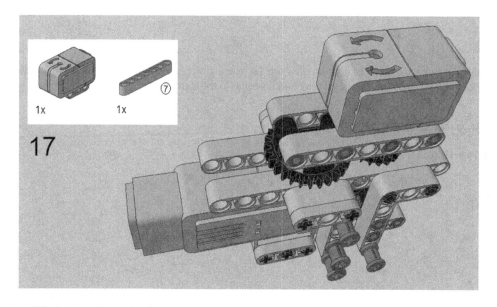

Figure 6-17. *Slide the Gyro Sensor in the center of the 3M Connector Pegs, and snap on another 7M Beam on top*

Programming the Swivel

LEGO MINDSTORMS has an easy to program tool to spin and stop where you want it. Using the Wait Program block with the mode of the Gyro Sensor, you can input whatever angle you want it to stop at, as seen in Figure 6-18.

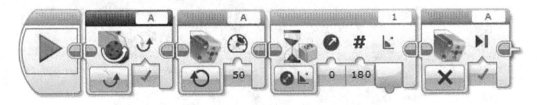

The Medium Motor at Port A will turn until the Gyro Sensor sees that it is at 180 degrees, at which point it will stop.

Figure 6-18. *A program for spinning the Swivel program in Project 6-1 at 180 degrees, but it can be easily reprogrammed for any angle*

Forklift

There are instructions for some sort of lifter on the Core Set instruction booklet, but the following instructions will allow it to work like a traditional forklift. You may find it similar to the stair climber in the Expansion Set.

Project 6-2: The Forklift

Follow Figures 6-19 to 6-38 to build the forklift.

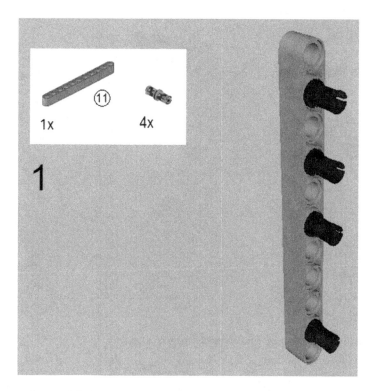

Figure 6-19. *Take an 11M beam and place the four connector pegs on it as shown*

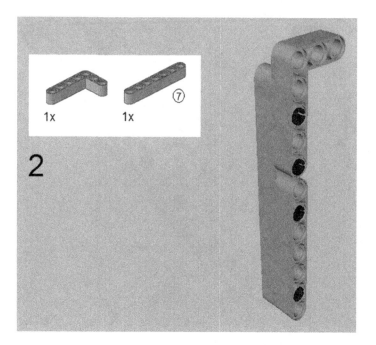

Figure 6-20. *Snap on the 5 × 3 beam and 7M beam on the 11M beam*

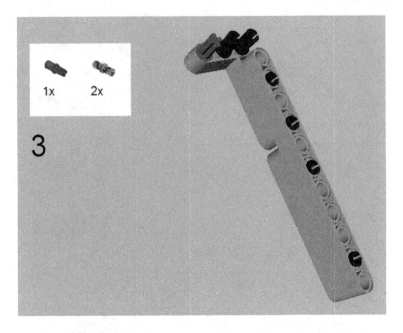

Figure 6-21. *Click in the two connector pegs and connector peg/cross axle*

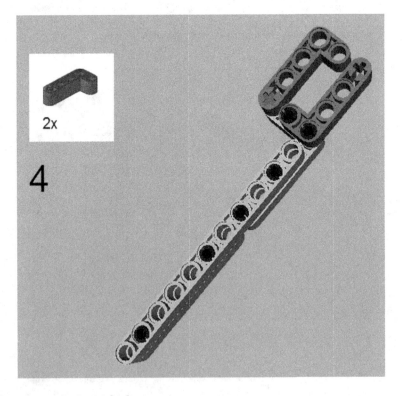

Figure 6-22. *Click on the two 4 × 2 angular beams*

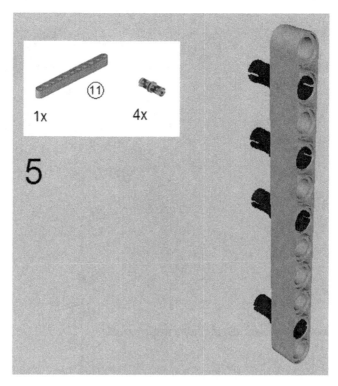

Figure 6-23. *Steps 5-8 are a separate section that mirrors steps 1-4. Take an 11M beam and place the four connector pegs on it as shown*

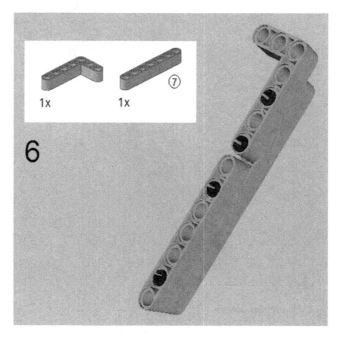

Figure 6-24. *Snap on the 5 × 3 beam and 7M beam on the 11M beam*

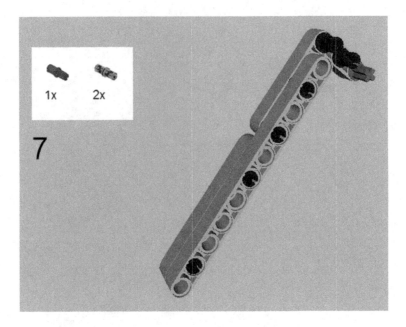

Figure 6-25. *Click in the two connector pegs and connector peg/cross axle*

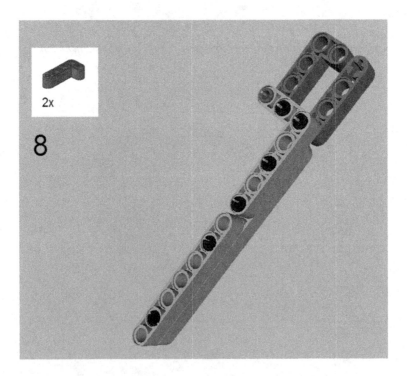

Figure 6-26. *Click on the two 4 × 2 angular beams*

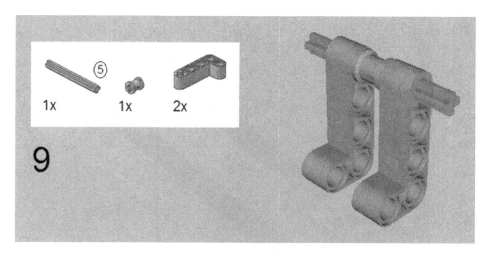

Figure 6-27. *Center a bush on a 5M axle, and then place a 4 × 2 beam on each side*

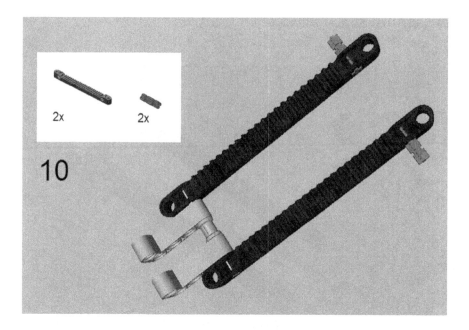

Figure 6-28. *Slide on a 13M rack on each side, and slide on a 2M axle on each of those racks*

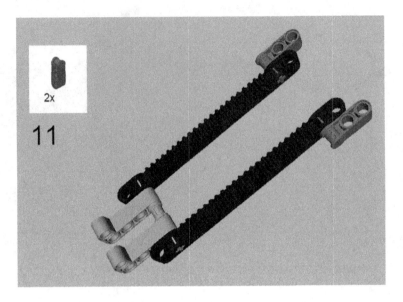

Figure 6-29. Slide on a 3M cross block on the 2M axles

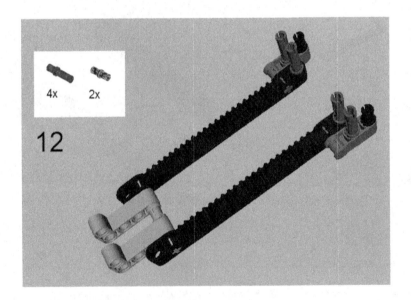

Figure 6-30. Insert the 3M connector pegs and regular-sized connector pegs as shown

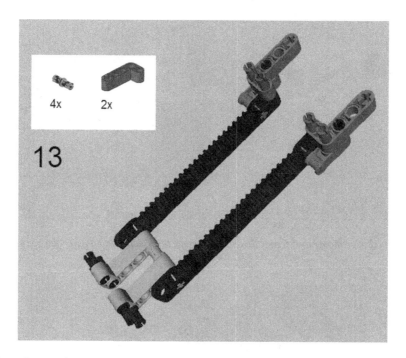

Figure 6-31. *Slide on the 4 × 2 beams on top. Insert the four connector pegs on the 4 × 2 beams on the bottom*

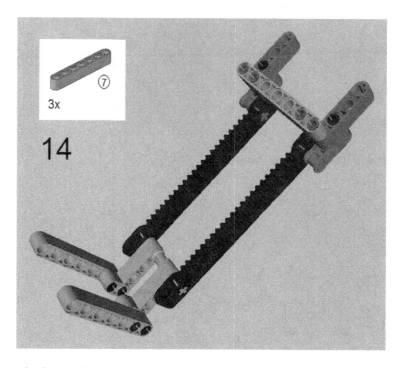

Figure 6-32. *Snap on the three 7M beams. Two are on the bottom, one is on top*

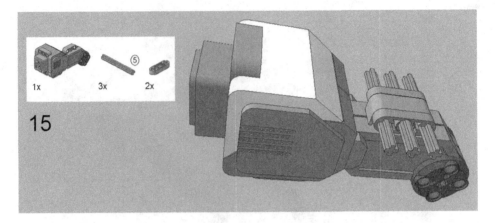

Figure 6-33. *Take out a Large Motor and center three 5M axles on top. Secure them with two 3M levers*

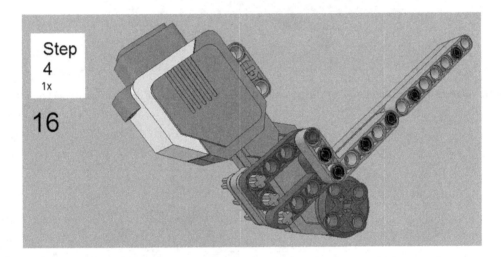

Figure 6-34. *Insert the right-side section done in steps 1-4*

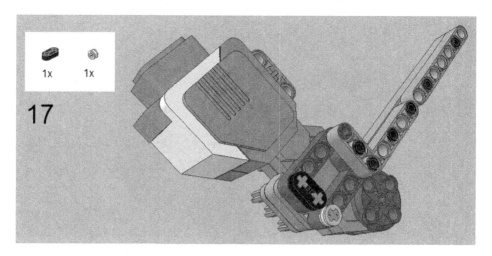

Figure 6-35. *Slide on the half-bush and 2M lever to secure the right-side section*

Figure 6-36. *Insert the left-side section done in steps 5-8*

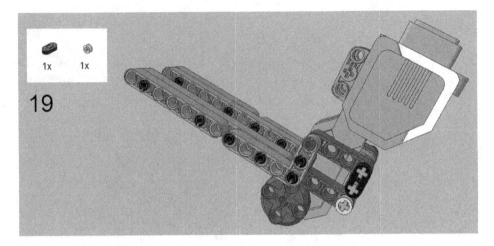

Figure 6-37. *Slide on the half-bush and 2M lever to secure the left-side section*

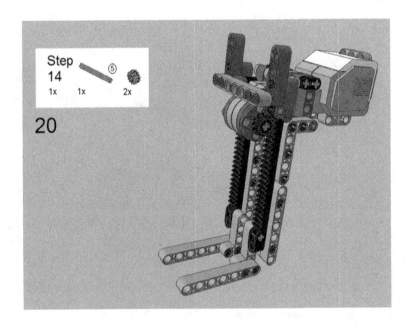

Figure 6-38. *Slide in the 5M axle with the two bevel gears, and secure the center section at the top*

Programming the Forklift

Since the Large Motor is attached directly to the two bevel gears, all you need to do is tell them how long to spin, and they will raise or lower the central section. I discovered that asking the EV3 Brick to spin the gears at 540 degrees or 1.5 rotations allowed the prongs to go from top to bottom, as seen in Figure 6-39. Be careful with any tampering with this formula, as you don't want the gears to jam on the racks. This is why I recommend using the formula in Figure 6-39 with the forklift prongs all the way at the bottom, but if you want to make the forklift go halfway up, you can just program it to spin 270 degrees.

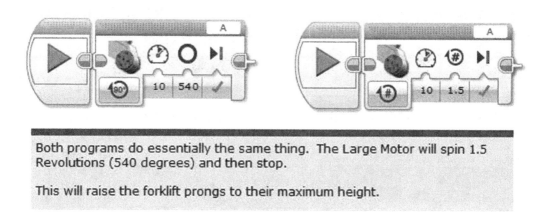

Both programs do essentially the same thing. The Large Motor will spin 1.5 Revolutions (540 degrees) and then stop.

This will raise the forklift prongs to their maximum height.

Figure 6-39. A program for operating the forklift of Project 6-2

Scissorlift

This is a variation of a project I made in the LEGO Technic Robotics book, but it is greatly simplified with the addition of a Large Motor. If you aren't familiar with a scissorlift, it uses a pantagraph method of taking someone or something higher up. If you are not familiar with a pantagraph, look to Figure 6-71. You might see something like it at construction sites or other places where higher levels must be reached.

Project 6-3: The Scissorlift

To build the scissorlift, follow the instructions in Figures 6-40 to 6-70.

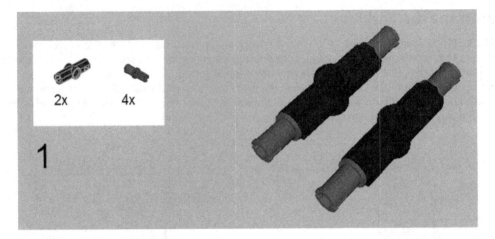

Figure 6-40. *Place connector peg/cross axles on each end of the two 180-degree angle elements*

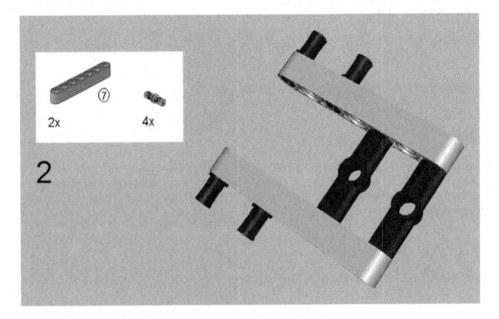

Figure 6-41. *Snap on the 7M beams and the four connector pegs*

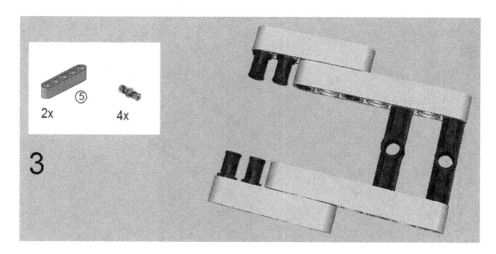

Figure 6-42. *Snap on the 5M beams and four connector pegs*

Figure 6-43. *Snap on the 5 × 3 beams along with the connector pegs*

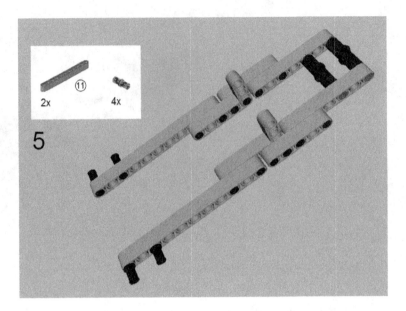

Figure 6-44. *Click on the 11M beams and the connector pegs*

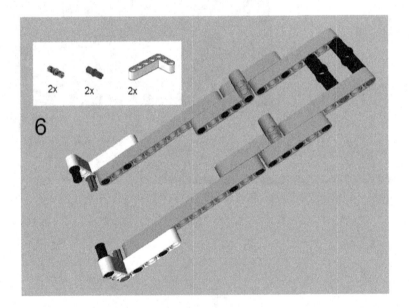

Figure 6-45. *Snap on the 5 × 3 beams and connector pegs as well as the connector peg/cross axles*

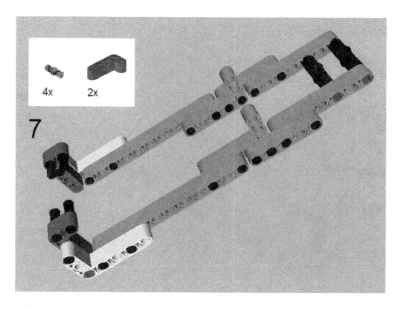

Figure 6-46. *Snap on the 4 × 2 beams and the connector pegs on that*

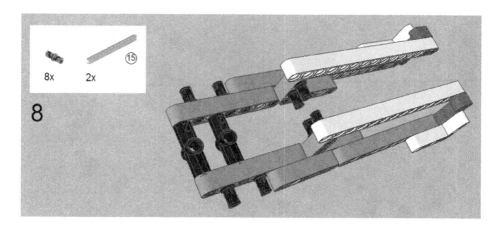

Figure 6-47. *Snap on the 15M beams and the eight connector pegs as shown, with four connector pegs on the front and four in the middle*

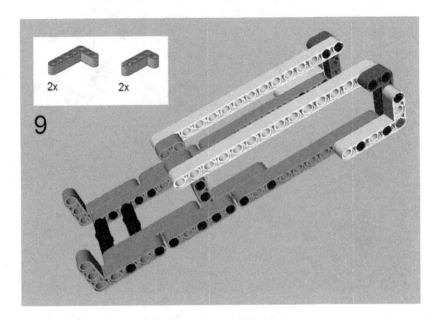

Figure 6-48. *Snap on the 5 × 3 beams as well as 4 × 2 beams*

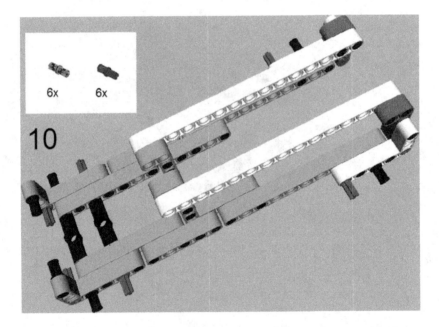

Figure 6-49. *Click on the six connector pegs and connector peg/cross axles*

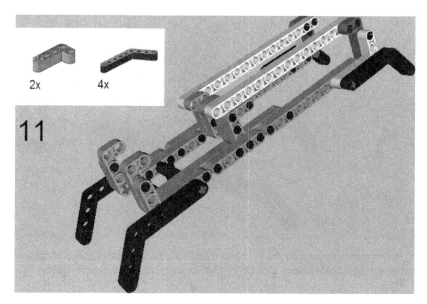

Figure 6-50. *Click on the two 4 × 2 beams and the four 6 × 4 beams below*

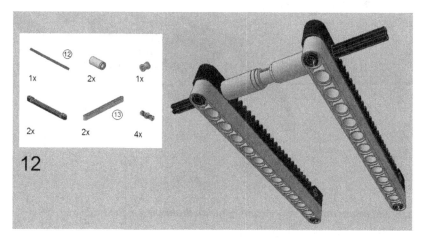

Figure 6-51. *This step is separate from the rest of the construction. Attach the 13M beams on the 13M racks with the four connector pegs. Connect them together with the 12M axle with the two tubes and bush in the middle*

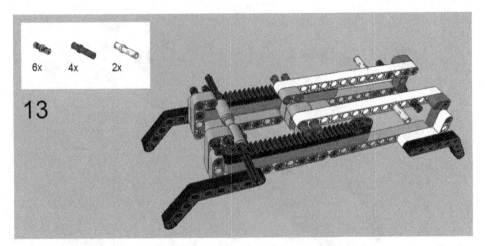

Figure 6-52. *Attach the six connector pegs on the 4 × 2 beam and 15M beams. Slide in the 3M connector pegs all the way, through the middle 4 × 2 and 15M beams. The 3M connector pegs without friction as shown*

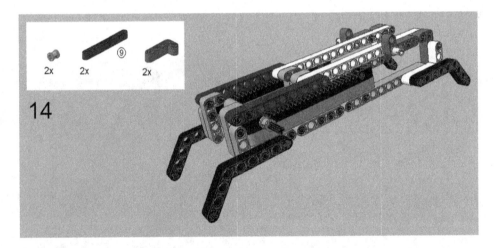

Figure 6-53. *Insert the 9M beams and the 4 × 2 beams. Slide on the bushes on the 12M axle*

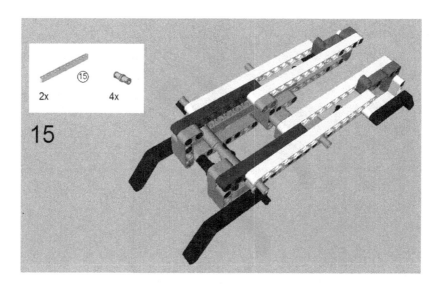

Figure 6-54. *Slide on the 15M beams with the connector pegs with without friction*

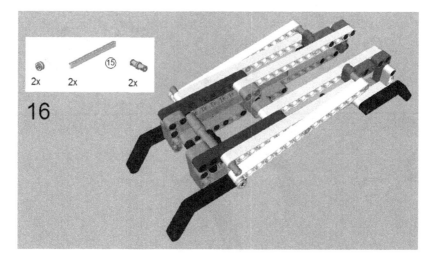

Figure 6-55. *Slide on end of the 15M beam on the 12M axle, and cap it off with the half bushes. The center of the 15M beam snaps onto the connector pegs (without friction) and another connector peg (without friction) on the other end of the 15M beams*

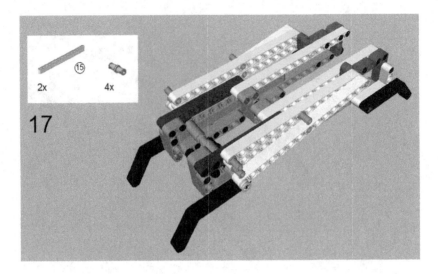

Figure 6-56. *Snap on the 15M beams and connector pegs*

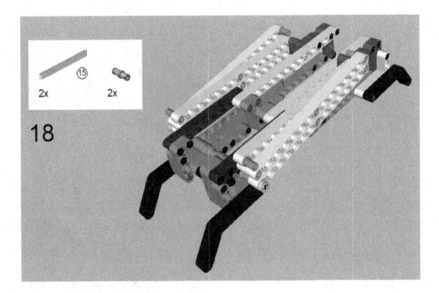

Figure 6-57. *Snap on the 15M beams and connector pegs*

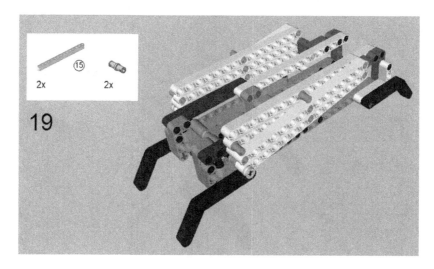

Figure 6-58. *Snap on the 15M beams and connector pegs*

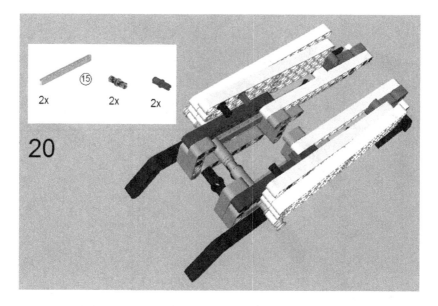

Figure 6-59. *Snap on the 15M beams, connector pegs, and connector peg/cross axles*

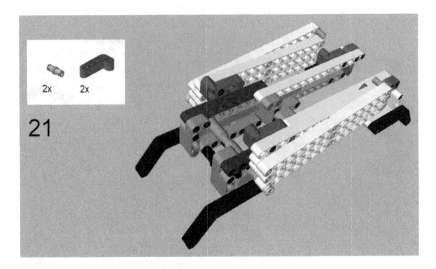

Figure 6-60. *Snap on the 4 × 2 beams and connector pegs*

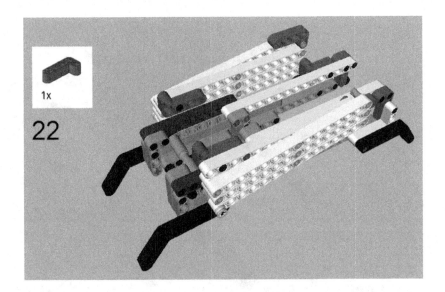

Figure 6-61. *Snap on the 4 × 2 beam*

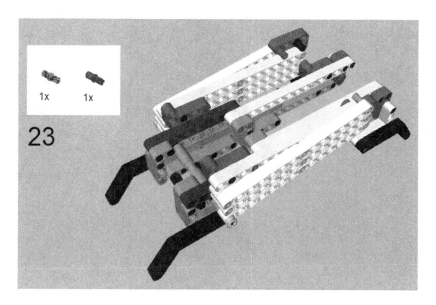

Figure 6-62. *Snap on the connector peg and connector peg/cross axle*

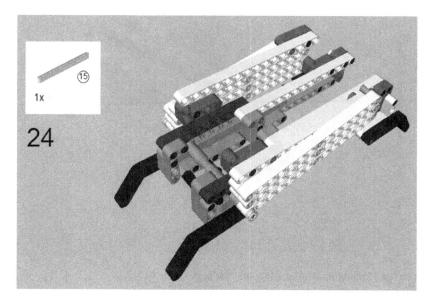

Figure 6-63. *Snap on the 15M beam*

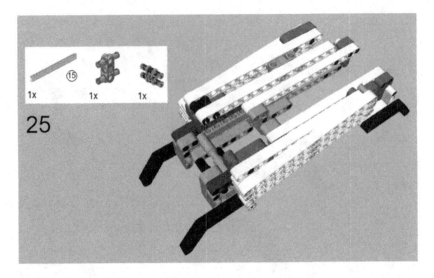

Figure 6-64. *Snap on the 15M beam, modular connector peg, and 1 × 3 peg*

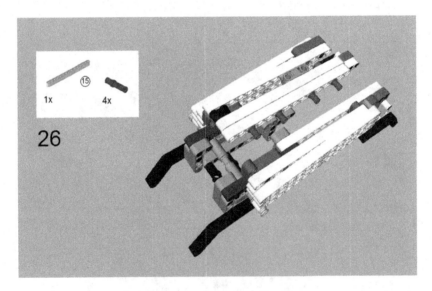

Figure 6-65. *Snap on the 15M beam and four 3M connector pegs*

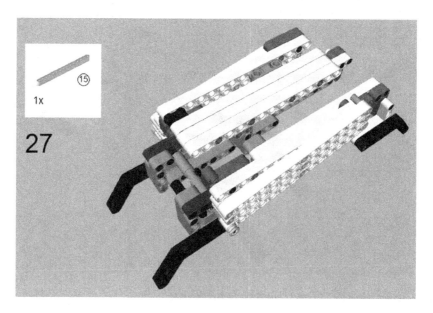

Figure 6-66. *Snap on the 15M beam*

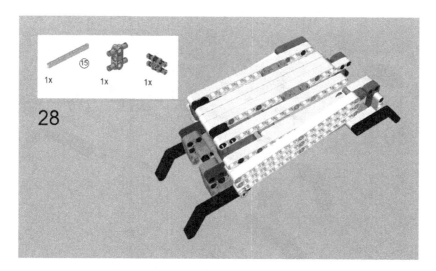

Figure 6-67. *Snap on the 15M beam, modular connector peg, and 1 × 3 peg*

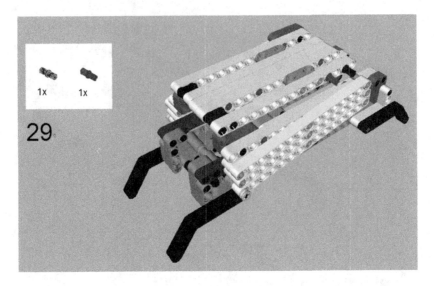

Figure 6-68. *Snap on the connector peg and connector peg/cross axle*

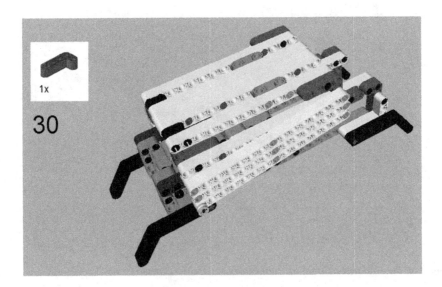

Figure 6-69. *Snap on the 4 × 2 Beam to complete the top of the scissorlfit*

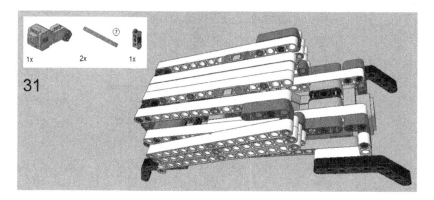

Figure 6-70. *Place the Large Motor on the construction, and put the double cross block in the middle. Slide the two 7M axles in to lock it in place*

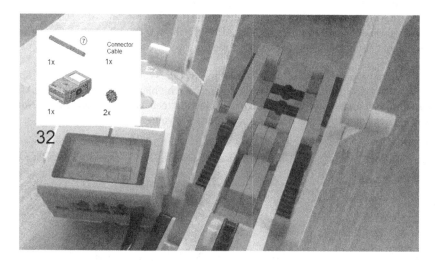

Figure 6-71. *I raised up the pantagraph and took a photo so you can see the step here more clearly. You need to slide the 7M axle through the Large Motor and then add the gears at each end, making certain that they mesh with the racks. Attach the connector cable and EV3 Brick, and it is ready to lift*

Programming the Scissorlift

Like the forklift, the twin bevel gears are set to spin when the Large Motor turns. This causes the racks to move, and I discovered that one full rotations is all that is needed to get the scissorlift platform to rise to its highest point. Again, I warn you on your own programming endeavors, as you can jam the gears.

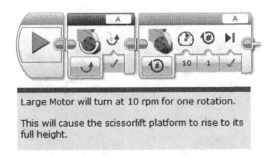

Large Motor will turn at 10 rpm for one rotation.

This will cause the scissorlift platform to rise to its full height.

Figure 6-72. *A program for the scissorlift*

Make Me a Macro

If you know anything about programming, then you know the importance of macros. If you are not familiar with them, then it is simply a way that you can do several things with just the push of a button.

You will discover as you are programming on LEGO MINDSTORMS that you are often doing the same things over and over again. Instead of cutting and pasting the same code from one location to the next, I highly recommend using macros.

Macros are the last type of programming block that I want to address. All that is required is to simply create a bunch of programming blocks that you want to be a macro and then highlight all of it. Go into the Menu bar and select Tools and "My Block Builder". Input your information in the Macro screen as seen in Figure 6-73. Note that you can add your parameter and its icons, so all you need to do is enter a few values.

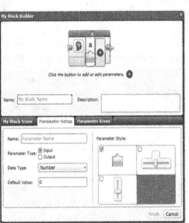

Figure 6-73. *The steps required to create your own individual programming block*

Once you have created your macro block, it will be in the Indigo section on the programming blocks, ready to be used. For example, let's say you built Project 6-2, the forklift, and you just want to simplify the lifting of the prongs. Figure 6-74 shows a way.

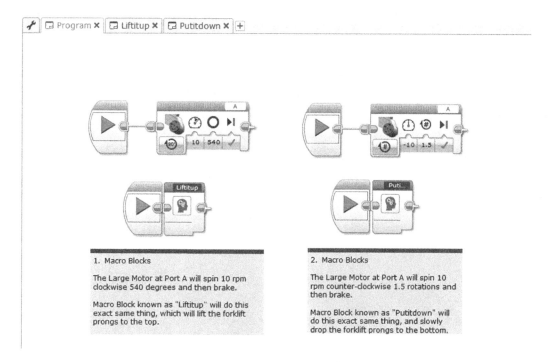

Figure 6-74. *A way to use the forklift using the Macro blocks*

Note that the programs of lifting the forks up and putting them down have been reduced to a single block. So if they ever need to be used again, they can be accessed down below without ever needed parameters entered in. You will notice that if you click on a Macro block, it will open up a tab that will show all the blocks within.

Now that you have created a macro, you will discover that it can be a major shortcut in your program. In fact, you can even create macros that have macros.

Summary

In addition to programming simple vehicles that can travel across flat areas, you will want to create LEGO MINDSTORMS vehicles that can do special features, like construction equipment.

This chapter details how to use the Medium and Large Motors to create such real-life examples of a swivel that can turn it 360 degrees and more, a forklift with prongs that can lift items, and a scissorlift which can rise quite high.

Programming these types of vehicles is also simple, but be careful when manipulating them as they could cause gears and motors to jam. Therefore, I recommend that you start the swivel, forklift, and scissorlift in the same place and end them in the same place each time they are used.

Once you have your construction into what you want it to be, you can start with the programming. You may discover that you will often be repeating certain actions, so it might be simpler to make a macro. Macros allow you to put a lot of code onto one block, and these macros can even contain macros themselves.

■ ■ ■

CHAPTER 7

The LEGO MINDSTORMS EV3 Robot Arm

In the last chapter, we covered how to make some interesting EV3 creations that are similar to those found on a construction site. In this chapter, I'm going to discuss how to create some fascinating robot parts for some unique combinations, starting with the Robot Arm.

Just to let you know, the Core Set already has instructions for a Robot Arm. Just like all the instructions, I recommend building them at least once. You will discover how to be a better builder through repetition of creating models by LEGO professionals. As you build more models, you will discover different processes and will be able to improve upon your designs with each new version that you make. This is why I am devoting this book to not just a series of instructions for you to imitate, but basic models that you can imitate and improve upon.

I am going to show you how to create an arm that can bend at a joint, just like a real elbow. I will also show how to create a wrist that can work as a swivel, like your wrist does. As for the hand, it will close like a real hand. Like the models of last chapter, I will only show you the basic and somewhat crude construction of what is required. How you want to use this is entirely up to you.

The Core Instructions have a Robot Arm with a claw that closes over its intended targets, but the one that I have created instructions for in this chapter allows the wrist and hand to be used together, more like a real hand. This is not to say that the version of a Robot Arm is "better" than the one in the Core Instruction kit, it is saying that I have put my own spin upon the instruction and come up with a design that feels a bit more like a human arm. It is not without limitations, but perhaps you can improve upon that.

In addition to showing how to create a robotic arm, I will also give some programs that show how to control these particular constructions. I have split this project up into two separate projects: Project 7-1 is the hand and wrist portion, while Project 7-2 is the base to hold it together.

Just to let you know, these models use a slightly different technique from the ones created in the rest of the book. Earlier models could be built if you had the Core and Expansion set. That is, you could take the pieces from these sets and not run out. If you build both Projects 7-1 and 7-2, you will discover that you will have to borrow from other sets to get this working. I highly recommend ordering more pieces or just getting other sets.

Project 7-1: The Robot Claw

The purpose of the next set of instructions (Figures 7-1 to 7-14) is to show how to make a hand like the one on a normal human arm, with an ability to flex and pivot. This is accomplished with a Large Motor giving the "fingers" the ability to grip, and a Medium Motor providing the ability to swivel like a wrist. It should be noted that this particular wrist could swivel 180 degrees, unlike a human wrist.

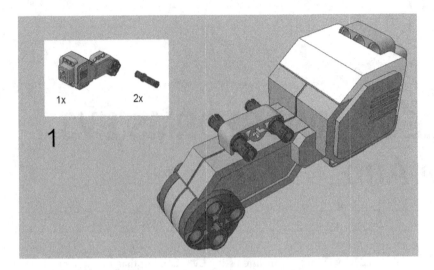

***Figure 7-1.** Take the two 3M connector pegs and center them on the Large Motor as shown*

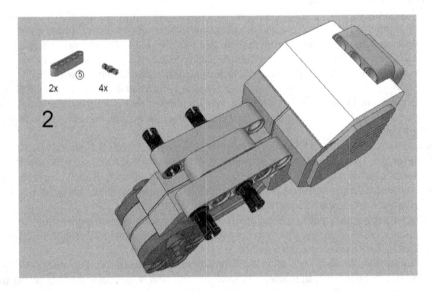

***Figure 7-2.** Snap the four 5M beams into place as shown, and then snap in the two connector pegs on each side*

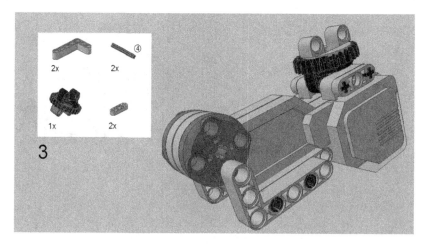

Figure 7-3. *Snap on two 5 x 3 beams on the connector pegs from last step. Take the small turntable and use the two 6M axles to hold it on place on the Large Motor. Cap off the 6M axles with the two 3M levers*

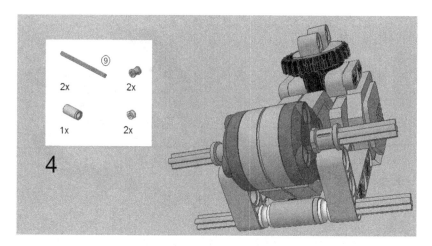

Figure 7-4. *Center the 9M axle on the corner of the 5 x 3 beams, making certain that the tube and two half bushes are as shown. Center the other 9M axle on the Large Motor itself and put on the bushes on the edges*

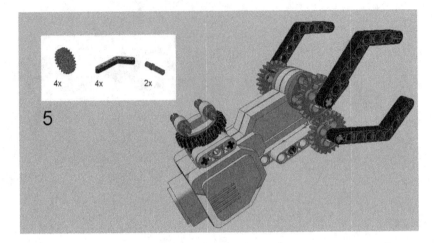

Figure 7-5. *Center the 3M connector pegs on the small turntable. Slide on the 24 tooth gears and make certain that they mesh. Slide on the 6 x 4 beams as shown*

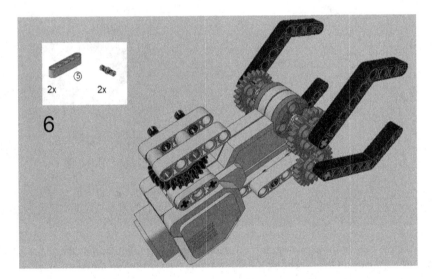

Figure 7-6. *Snap on the 5M beams on the 3M connector pegs. Then snap on two connector pegs on one side*

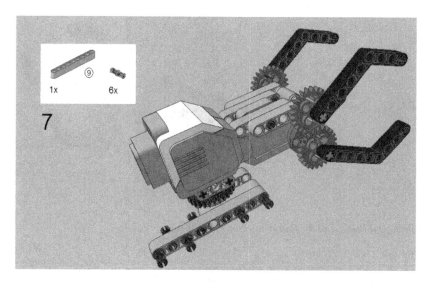

Figure 7-7. *Snap on the 9M beam on the bottom, and then add the connector pegs*

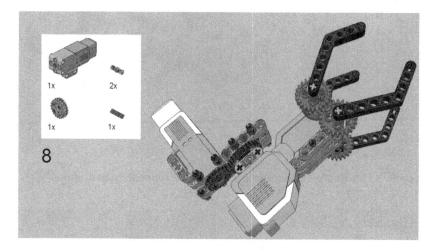

Figure 7-8. *Snap on the Medium Motor, and snap on two connector pegs on that. Slide on the 2M axle on the front of the Medium Motor, and slide on the 20Z bevel gear to mesh with the small turntable*

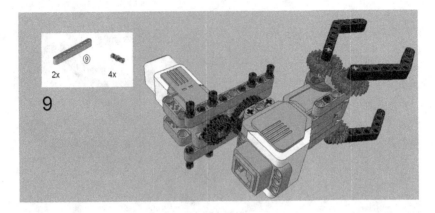

Figure 7-9. *Snap on the 9M beam and the four connector pegs*

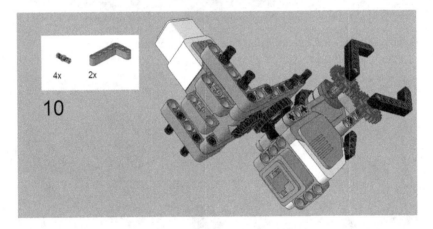

Figure 7-10. *Snap on the 5 x 3 beams as shown, and then snap on the connector pegs as shown*

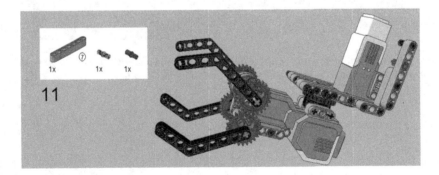

Figure 7-11. *Snap on a 7M beam, along with the connector peg and connector peg/cross axles*

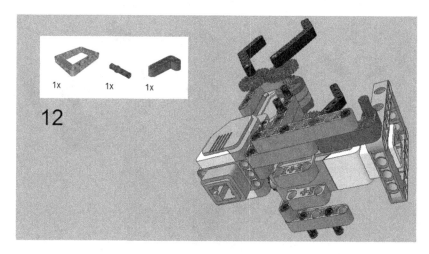

Figure 7-12. *Following the example below, insert a 4 x 2 beam on one side. Center a 3M connector peg on the 4 x 2 beam, and snap on a 5 x 7 beam frame*

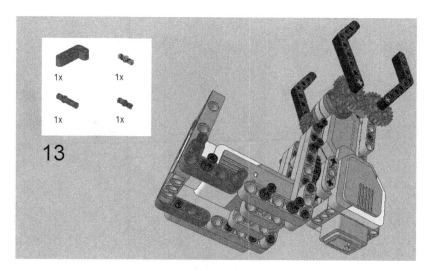

Figure 7-13. *Snap on another 3M connector peg on the beam frame, and then slide on a 4 x 2 beam on that. Insert the connector peg and connector peg/cross axle on the 4 x 2 beam*

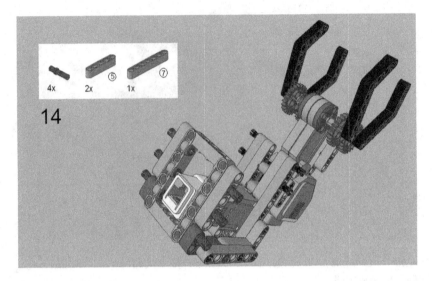

Figure 7-14. *Insert four 3M connector pegs on the beam frame, and then slide on two 5M beams on that. Snap on a 7M beam on the bottom*

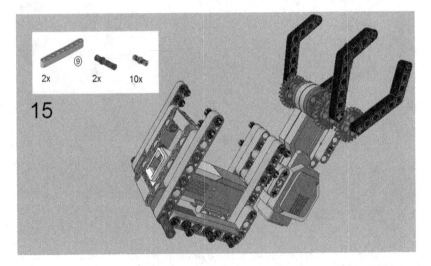

Figure 7-15. *Snap on the 9M beams on both sides, and insert the 3M connector pegs on each side. Insert two connector pegs on each side of the 9M beams, and three connector pegs on each side of the 7M beams*

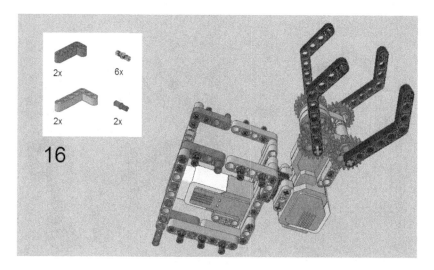

Figure 7-16. *Snap on the 4 x 2 and 5 x 3 beams on the structure. Insert the connector peg/cross-axles, and connector pegs on those angular beams*

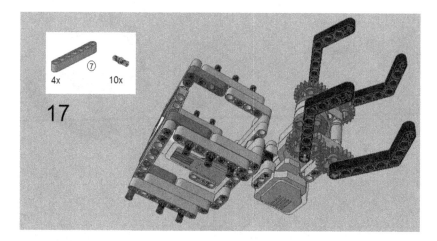

Figure 7-17. *Snap on the 7M beams and the connector pegs on each side as shown*

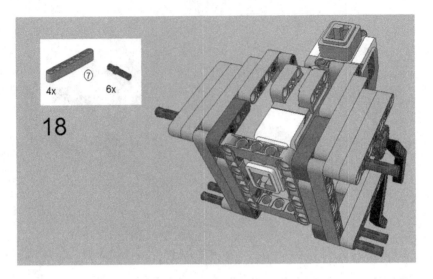

Figure 7-18. *Insert the 7M beams and the 3M connector pegs*

Figure 7-19. *Insert the 3M beams, and then the connector peg and connector peg/cross axles*

The biggest challenge of this is really figuring out how to link together a Large Motor with a Medium Motor so that not only will they link together, but stay linked together strongly. The challenge of building with LEGO MINDSTORMS is making certain that your creation is strong and can withstand multiple uses with minimal adjustments.

You will note that I used a minimum of two connector pegs to lock something in place, and I found this will hold just about anything together. See if you can improve on the construction of the claw below.

If you like, you can attach some cables to the Large and Medium Motors in the claw and try them out using the Motion Control application on the EV3 Brick and saw how it works. You can even try programming them for certain moves if you like.

You might also want to make improvements on the grip of the hand portion of this claw. I used the 4 x 6 beams here, but you can use something of your own design to get a better grip. You might be surprised with what you come up with.

Now that you have your wrist and hand, you will need to create something of an arm for it. The one I created here was quite small, but enough so it can at least lift an object off the ground a little bit. This was easily the most difficult part about constructing this Robot Arm, as it requires a machine to left the Large Motor and Medium Motor, which are already pretty heavy.

In order to create this, for lack of a better term, Elbow, I had to create a bendable joint that would stay bent even if it was still in the air. Just imagine trying to hold the Olympic torch in the air for hours at a time, and you can imagine the strain that would be on your arm. Machines have the advantage of not "tiring out", but they are still vulnerable to strain.

The Elbow Joint that I came up with uses two worm gears on each side, which hold a regular gear in between. As the worm gears turn in opposite directions, this causes the regular gears to turn which can spin an axle. The axle holds quite a load, but the worm gears hold the load in place when they are not spinning.

You will find that this type of construction with the worm gear to be very inspirational when you are trying to get constructions to raise up, like a crane. Since the load that this elbow joint was bearing was so heavy, I decided to use the EV3 Brick as a counterweight, and this forms the controls for this Robot Elbow Base.

Project 7-2: The Robot Elbow Base

I called this a Robot Elbow Base because it is the elbow portion of the arm, which can bend like a real elbow and carry some weight. It is designed to be used with Project 5-1, the claw section, and it will have the EV3 Brick so the entire Robot Arm can be programmed and controlled. Figures 7-20 to 7-40 show how to build it.

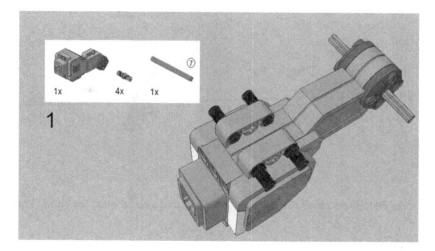

Figure 7-20. *Insert the four connector pegs on the Large Motor as shown. Center the 7M axle on the Large Motor*

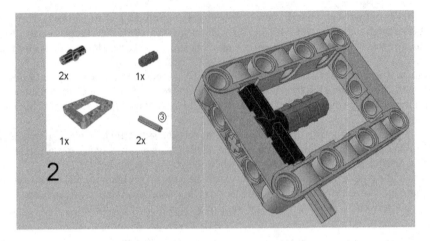

Figure 7-21. *Lock the 180-degree angle elements in with the 3M axle. Insert the 3M axle on one side and place the cross-axle on the other side*

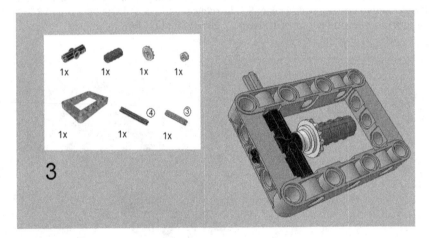

Figure 7-22. *Repeat the first few actions of step 2, but use a 4M axle and insert the half bush and 12 tooth bevel gear*

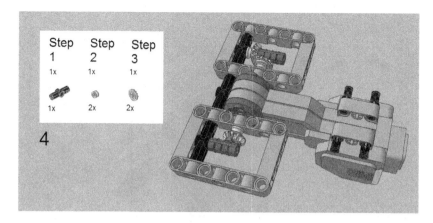

Figure 7-23. *Here is where you combine the three steps into one creation. On the 7M axle on the Large Motor, insert the half bushes and 12 tooth bevel gears on. The gears will mesh on one side as shown, and the 180-degree angle element helps link the beam frames together*

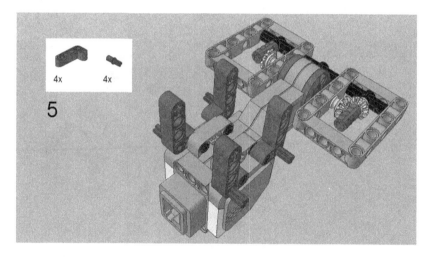

Figure 7-24. *Insert the four 4 x 2 beams on the Large Motor, and the connector peg/cross axles on the corners*

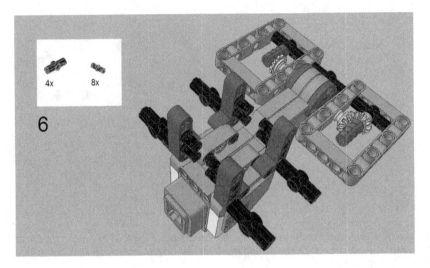

Figure 7-25. *Insert the eight connector pegs on the 4 x 2 Beams as shown, and the 180 angle elements on the connector peg/cross axles*

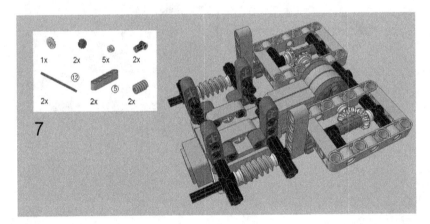

Figure 7-26. *On each side, slide on a 12M axle. In between will be the worm gear, half bushes, 8 tooth gear, and 5M beam. Note how the bevel gear goes in on one side, and how 1M of axle sticks out on one side and 2M on the other*

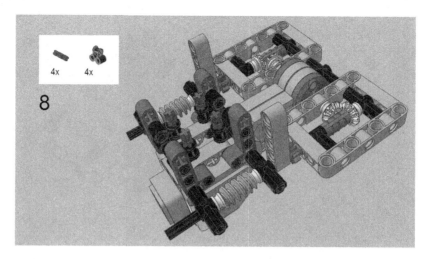

Figure 7-27. *Snap on the 1 x 2 cross blocks on the connector pegs, and the 2M axles halfway in as shown*

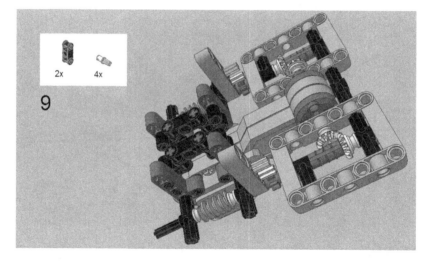

Figure 7-28. *Insert the double cross blocks on the top, and snap in the connector peg cross axles as shown*

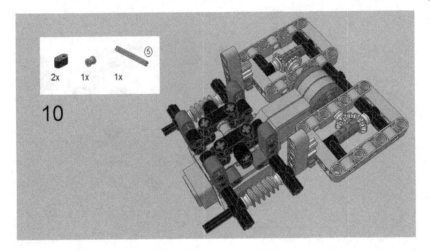

Figure 7-29. *Take the 5M axle and put a bush in the center of the double cross blocks. Secure the 5M axle in place with the cross and hole beams*

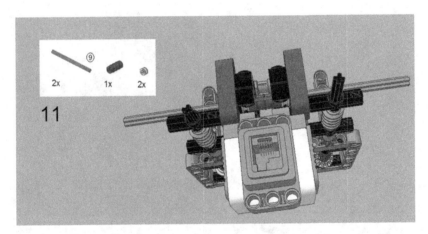

Figure 7-30. *Slide the 9M axles at the bottom of the cross and hole beams, and secure them with the cross-axle extension and half bushes*

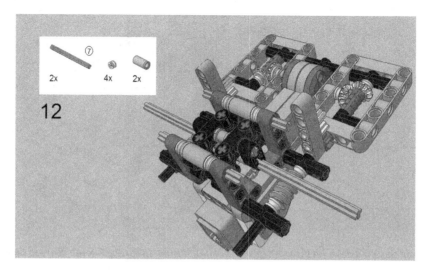

Figure 7-31. *Slide on the 7M axles on the tops of the 4 x 2 beams, making certain that the tubes and bushes are in the proper place*

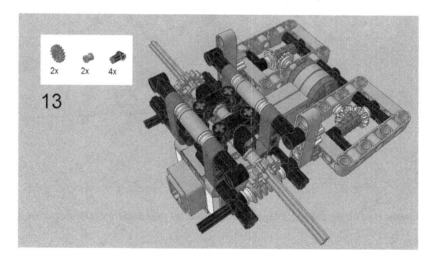

Figure 7-32. *Slide on the bushes on the 9M axles, then slide on the two 16-tooth gears so they mesh with the worm gears. Cap off the 7M axles with the zero degree elements*

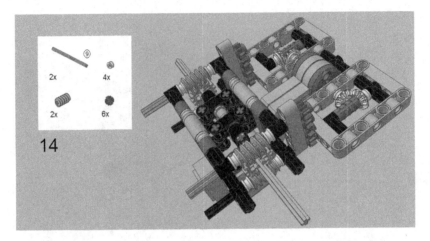

Figure 7-33. Slide on the 9M axles with the worm gears and half bushes. Insert the 8-tooth gears so they mesh

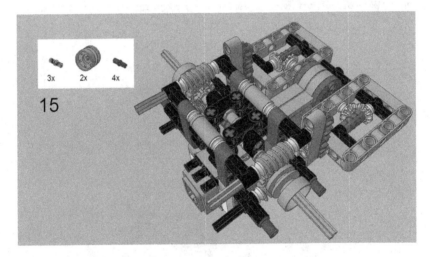

Figure 7-34. Slide on the rims on the 9M axles. Snap on the connector pegs and connector peg/cross axles

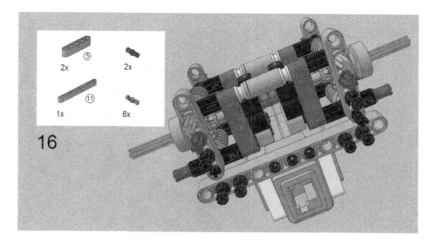

Figure 7-35. *Snap on the 11M beam, and slide on the 5M beams. Snap on the connector pegs and connector peg/cross axles*

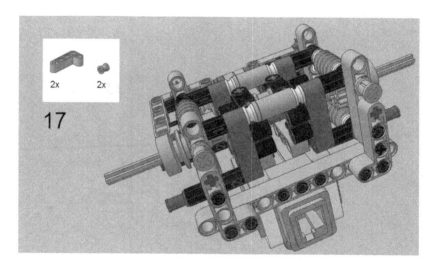

Figure 7-36. *Snap on the 4 x 2 beams as well as the bushes*

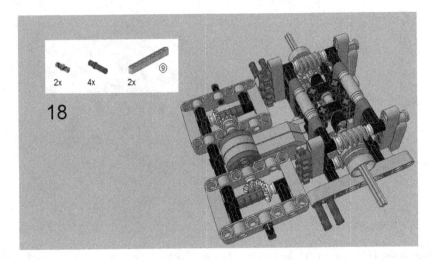

Figure 7-37. *On the sides, snap on the 9M beam, then 3M connector pegs. Insert the connector pegs in the center of the beam frames*

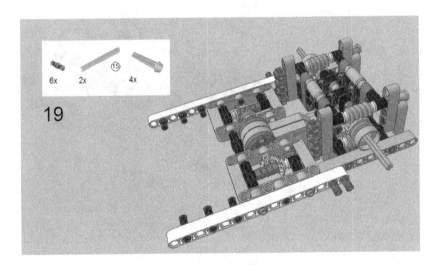

Figure 7-38. *Snap on two 15M beams, along with the connector pegs. Slide in the 3M axle with bump so it secures on the angle element pieces*

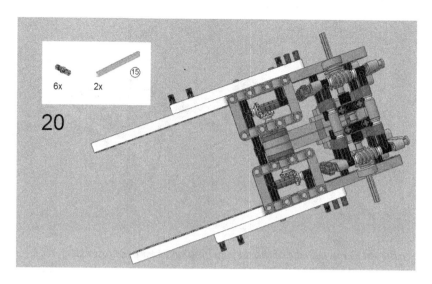

Figure 7-39. *Snap on two more 15M beams, along with the connector pegs*

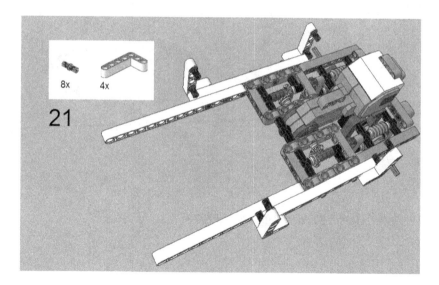

Figure 7-40. *Snap on the 5 x 3 beams, and place connector pegs on them*

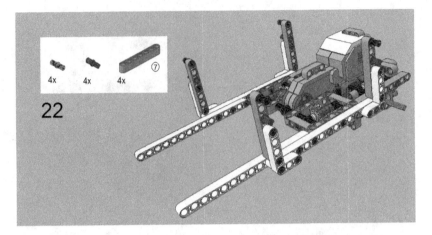

Figure 7-41. Snap on the 7M beams with the connector pegs and connector peg/cross axles

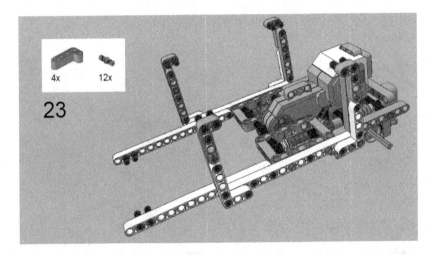

Figure 7-42. Snap on the 4 x 2 beams along with the connector pegs

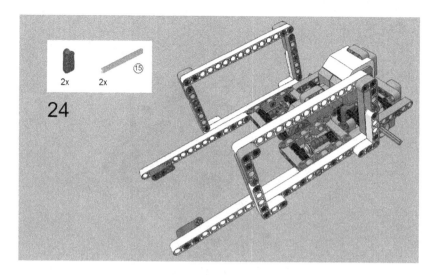

Figure 7-43. *Snap on the 15M beam and the 3M cross blocks*

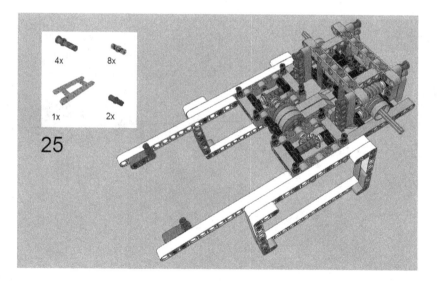

Figure 7-44. *Place the 5 x 11 beam frame on top and lock it into place with the friction snaps. Insert the connector pegs on the beam frames and the connector peg/cross axles on the 3M cross blocks*

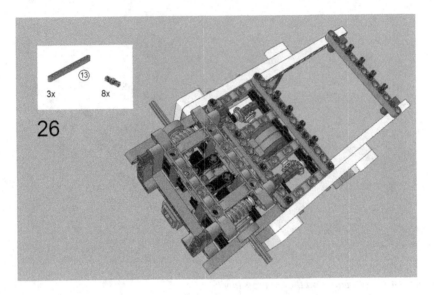

Figure 7-45. Lock the 13M beams into place along with the connector pegs

Figure 7-46. Using the double angle beams, lock the claw and arm attachment to the base as shown

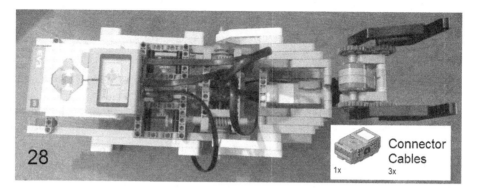

Figure 7-47. *Snap on the EV3 Brick and use the Ports A, B, and D*

Programming the Robotic Elbow

When it comes to working the Robotic Elbow, I highly recommend setting up the Large Motor program. All that is required is to simply set it up so it will turn by degrees, as shown in Figure 7-48.

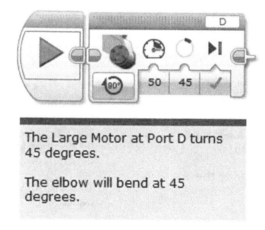

The Large Motor at Port D turns 45 degrees.

The elbow will bend at 45 degrees.

Figure 7-48. *A program to bend the Elbow*

Programming the Robot Wrist

I recommend setting up the Medium Motor so it rotates by rotations. You will note the use of non-whole numbers for the amount of turns. This is because the Medium Motor is programmed to turn the 20Z double bevel gear, which turns the turntable piece. Since these pieces are not the same size, it is necessary to adjust for the proper amount. See Figure 7-49 for a proper example.

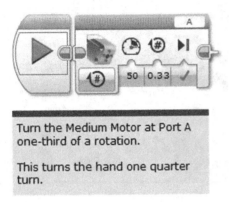 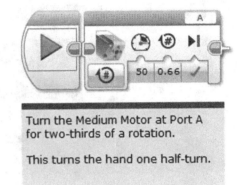

Turn the Medium Motor at Port A one-third of a rotation.

This turns the hand one quarter turn.

Turn the Medium Motor at Port A for two-thirds of a rotation.

This turns the hand one half-turn.

Figure 7-49. *A program for turning the wrist*

Programming the Robotic Hand

Like the Robotic Elbow, I highly recommend setting up a program that can move by degrees. This will insure that you have a good clench. Examples can be seen in Figure 7-50.

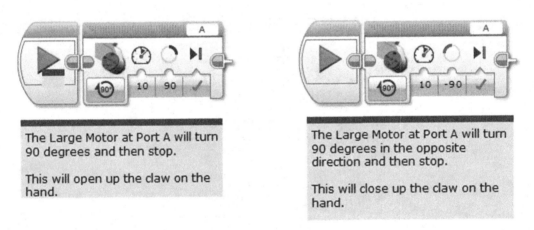

The Large Motor at Port A will turn 90 degrees and then stop.

This will open up the claw on the hand.

The Large Motor at Port A will turn 90 degrees in the opposite direction and then stop.

This will close up the claw on the hand.

Figure 7-50. *A Program for the movement of the Robot Hand*

Summary

What you have seen in this chapter is the instructions of building a robotic arm. The set-up is not too difficult thanks to the application of EV3 motors and programming.

The trickiest setup for the elbow is insuring that it is strong as it bends and can hold the weight that is borne upon it. The instructions that I have provided should do the trick on that.

As for the Wrist, the turntable and Medium Motor are ideal for setup on a similar type of swivel as seen in Chapter 5.

As for the Robotic Arm, the Large Motor with some gears and fingers will insure something with a good grip.

CHAPTER 8

Thinking like a LEGO MINDSTORMS Creator and the Walking Robot

As I have said before, this book is not about giving you some instructions for models, and then giving you the programs that you will need to run them. LEGO is all about creation, and I see little reason to give you things to build when the true joy of LEGO is creating a masterpiece that you can proudly say: "see that, I made that from start to finish." And "I put my blood, sweat, and tears into that." Do you really want to just build something from instructions and show it off saying: "hey, I followed the instructions."

Seriously, if you want to learn to be a real cool LEGO MINDSTORMS creator, you will need to create. I probably could have put this chapter at the beginning of the book, but I decided that a better place would be the end, as it really summarizes with examples on what needs to be done to become a real LEGO MINDSTORMS Creator.

Questions to Ask Before Building

It is difficult to ascertain where true inspiration comes from. Perhaps you might see something and want to build it in the form of LEGO MINDSTORMS.

You can ask yourself a series of questions before you begin to build:

- **What am I building?** As you figure out the purpose of what you are trying to create, you will be better able to put it in some sort of physical form with the LEGO MINDSTORMS bricks.

- **What will it do?** Unless you are satisfied with a static, statue-like form, you will inevitably want to build some creation that will "do" something. You may not be able to build a robotic arm that will be as versatile as a regular human arm, but at least you can program it to move things.

- **How am I going to incorporate the sensors and motors?** As I have stated before, you will want your model to "do" something, and much of that will require the sensors, motors, and possibly adding the EV3 Brick to the construction.

- **What kind of program will I need?** Since the EV3 Brick will be involved, you will need to get the programming blocks involved. You will need to figure out how to get those sensors, Display, sounds, EV3 buttons, and more to do precisely what you want them to do.

Example of the Walking Robot

Let's say you want to make a walking robot. I always found that walking robots were very challenging to build when working with LEGO. I'm sure that if you tried building a walking LEGO creation, you will face some of the same problems that I faced, which starts with just getting the motion of the legs down. Fortunately, EV3 has the capacity to let robots walk with the use of motors.

In case you are interested, the Expansion Set has a model of a walking elephant that uses four legs, and only requires one Large Motor to set them into motion. This is because it uses a set of interlocked gears to make certain that the legs work in sync with each other. Unfortunately, the robot elephant is only capable of one-dimensional motion by walking forward and backward, and is incapable of turning.

In this chapter, I will show you how to make a robot with four legs that is capable of shifting its direction. You might notice that the legs of this robot bear a strong resemblance to one that I did in Chapter 7 of my LEGO Technic Robotics book. I never was able to get that robot to turn very well (at all), but thanks to the power of LEGO MINDSTORMS EV3 programming, one Medium Motor, and two Large Motors, this one can move in many directions across the floor.

This robot is actually three different projects: the Left Leg, the Right Leg, and the Body. You will note that although the Left Leg and Right Leg use the exact same number of parts, they are not the same instructions as they must be mirror images of each other. As for the Body, this is where the EV3 Brick is mounted, along with a turntable for steering. Please also note that Projects 8-1, 8-2, and 8-3 require more parts than are in the Core and Expansion set combined, and will require you to get parts from elsewhere before a completing a four-legged walker.

Project 8-1: The Left Leg

One of the hardest parts about creating a robotic leg that can walk is creating the mechanism for it to take a step. It is really all about assembling a device that can turn, but still be limited by how much it can move. This allows for a walking mechanism that can lift a leg, and yet still remain upright. Figures 8-1 to 8-8 show how to build the left leg.

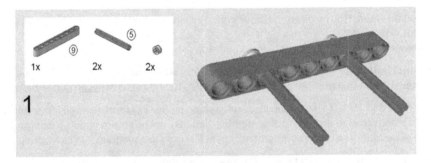

Figure 8-1. *Insert the 5M axles as shown, and cap them off on one side with the half bushes*

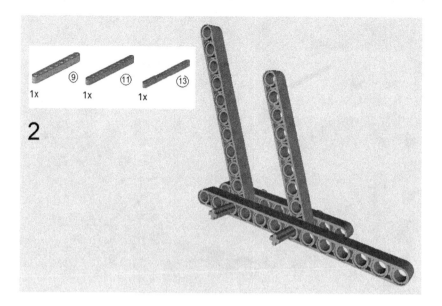

Figure 8-2. *Slide on the 9M beam and 11 beam on the first through-hole on the axles, and slide on the 13M beam*

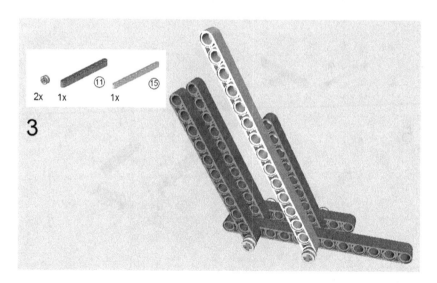

Figure 8-3. *Slide on the 15M beam and 11M beam similar to the last step, and cap off the axles with half bushes*

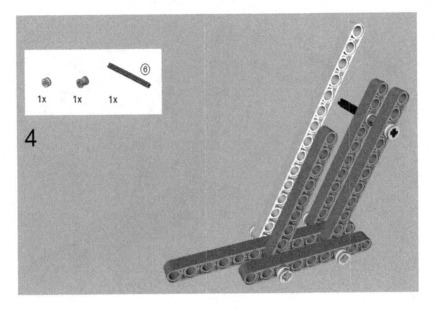

Figure 8-4. *Slide on the 6M axle, placing the bush and half bush as shown*

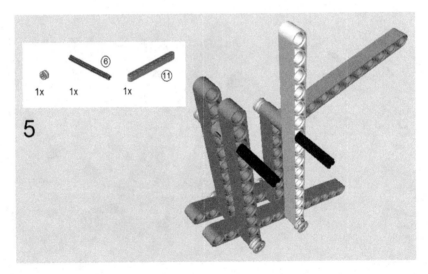

Figure 8-5. *Slide on the 6M axle so it goes through the 11M beam at the end and the 15M beam as shown*

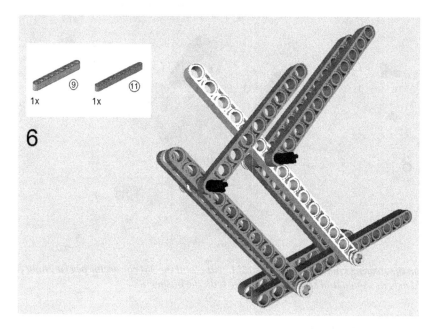

Figure 8-6. *Slide an 11M beam on the 9M and 6M axle as shown*

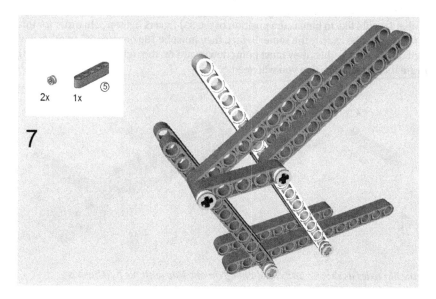

Figure 8-7. *Slide a 5M beam on the 6M axles as shown, and secure it into place with two half bushes*

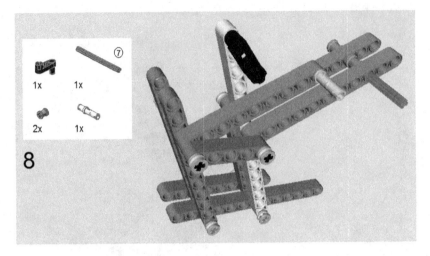

Figure 8-8. Snap on the steering knuckle arm on the 15M beam, and the 3M connector peg (without friction) on the 9M beam. Place the 7M axle as shown and secure it into place with the bushes

Project 8-2: The Right Leg

As you might have guessed, we cannot do a walking robot with a left leg and not have a right leg. You will notice that it uses the exact same pieces, but it is a mirror image of the left leg.

The one thing that I would like to note is the position of the 3M Levers in Step 3. In order for this model to walk, the levers on each side cannot be exactly the same. In fact, they must be 180 degrees off. In other words, if the 3M Levers point upward on the left leg, then they must point downward on the right leg. I will explain why later, but Figures 8-9 to 8-16 are the instructions that you will need.

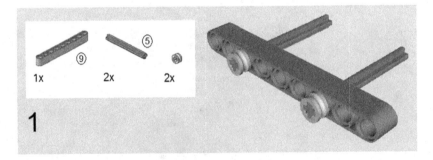

Figure 8-9. Insert the 5M axles as shown, and cap them off on one side with the half bushes

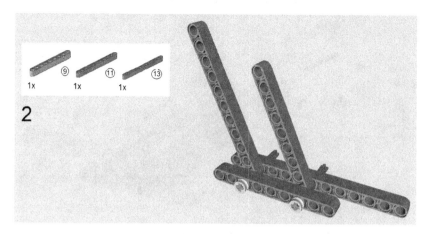

Figure 8-10. *Slide on the 9M beam and 11 beam on the first through-hole on the axles, and slide on the 13M beam*

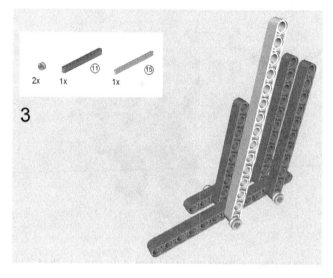

Figure 8-11. *Slide on the 15M beam and 11M beam similar to the last step, and cap off the axles with half bushes*

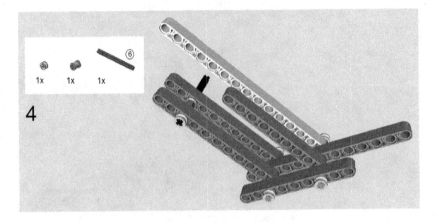

Figure 8-12. *Slide on the 6M axle, placing the bush and half bush as shown*

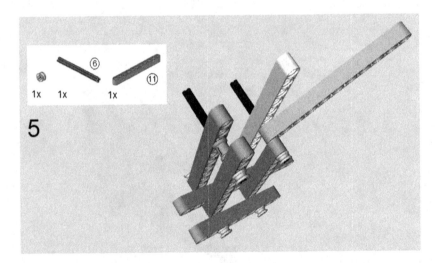

Figure 8-13. *Slide on the 6M axle so it goes through the 11M beam at the end and the 15M beam as shown*

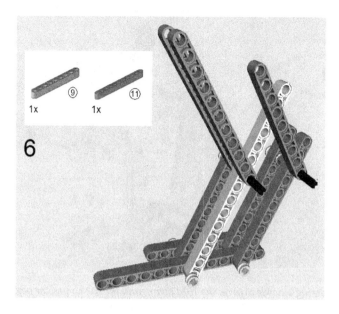

Figure 8-14. *Slide an 11M beam on the 9M and 6M axle as shown*

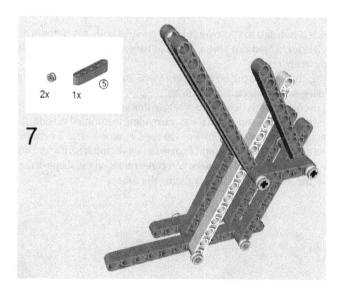

Figure 8-15. *Slide a 5M beam on the 6M axles as shown, and secure it into place with two half bushes*

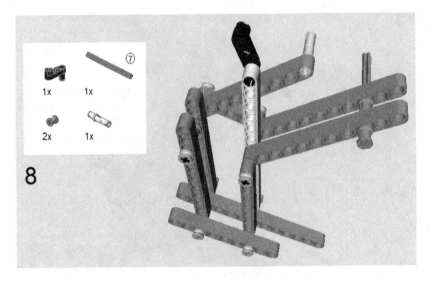

Figure 8-16. *Snap on the steering knuckle arm on the 15M beam, and the 3M connector peg (without friction) on the 9M beam. Place the 7M axle as shown and secure it into place with the bushes*

Project 8-3: The LEGO Robot Body

Now that the legs are created, it is only fair to show you how to create a body to put them on. There really is a lot on this body, as it houses the EV3 Brick, a Medium Motor, and two Large Motors, but they hold the legs on so they are stable, and keep them moving freely.

In case you are wondering, the legs are put on in the last step. You will need four to complete this, so make two copies of the left leg and right leg from Projects 8-1 and 8-2.

Another disclaimer that I need to make is that you may notice that some of the pieces are in colors that are not available in the Core and Expansion sets (this won't be apparent if you are reading the printed version, for example, but all the figures are available to download from apress.com, which allows you to see the colors). This is because this construction requires more than a few pieces than are available in the Core and Expansion sets combined, like the Robot Arm project of the last chapter. I would advise you to ignore the color of the piece and concentrate on the shape of the piece.

Figures 8-17 to 8-42 show the instructions for completing the robot.

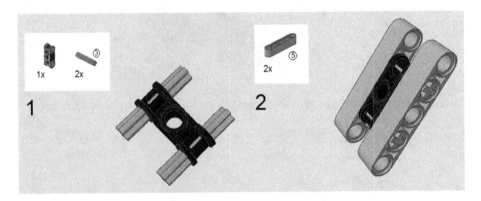

Figure 8-17. *Center the 3M axles on the double cross block as shown. Center the 5M beams on the 3M axles, and they will be secured in place in the next step*

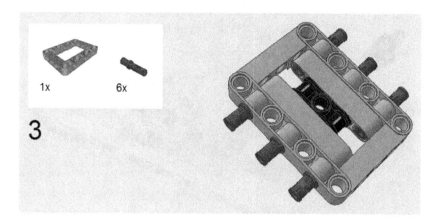

Figure 8-18. *Center the construction from Steps 1 and 2 on the 5 × 7 beam frame, and secure it into place with the six 3M connector pegs*

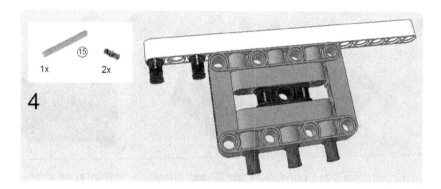

Figure 8-19. *Snap on the 15M beam, and snap on the connector pegs as shown*

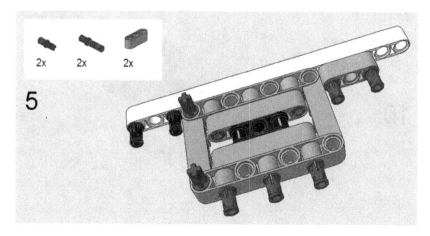

Figure 8-20. *Snap on the connector peg/cross axles on the 5 × 7 beam frame. Center the 3M connector pegs on the edges of the 3M beam, and snap it into place as shown*

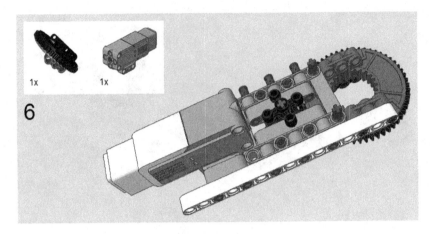

Figure 8-21. *Snap on the large turntable, and the Medium Motor as shown*

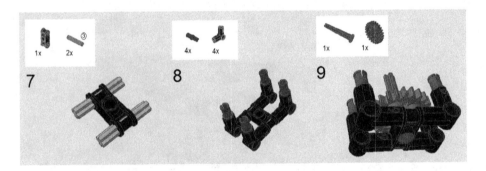

Figure 8-22. *Repeat the steps from Step 1, but slide on four 90-degree angle elements with connector peg/cross axles. Slide on the 4M axle with stop through the center hole, and slide a 24-tooth gear on it*

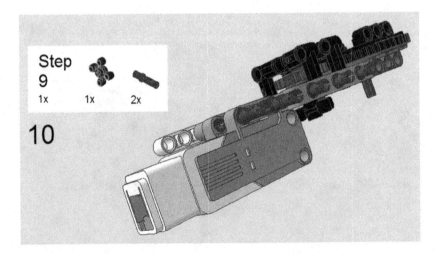

Figure 8-23. *Snap on the creation from Steps 7-9 underneath the 5 × 7 beam frame and secure it with the 4M axle with stop with the angular wheel on top. Insert two 3M connector pegs on the Medium Motor*

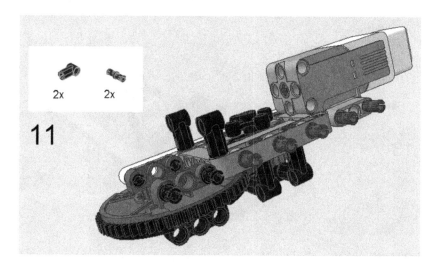

Figure 8-24. *Slide on the zero degree elements on the connector peg/cross axles, and snap on the connector pegs on the turntable*

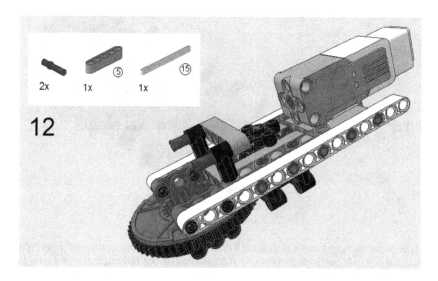

Figure 8-25. *Center the 3M connector pegs on the zero degree elements. Snap on the 5M beam and 15M beam as shown*

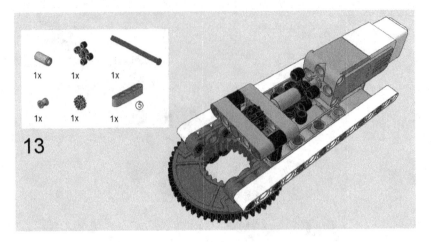

Figure 8-26. *On the 8M axle with stop, place the 5M beam, tube, bush, 12 tooth bevel gear, and angular wheel so it is inserted in the Medium Motor*

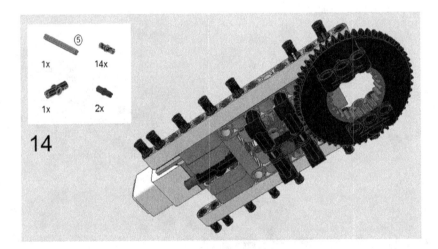

Figure 8-27. *Insert the connector peg/cross axles on each end of the 180 angle elements, and insert it into the 5 × 7 beam frame as shown. Push the 5M axle (not seen in figure) so it is centered on the 180 angle element, and then snap in the connector pegs. Insert seven connector pegs on each side as shown*

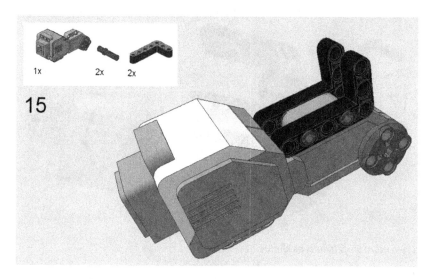

Figure 8-28. *Center the 3M connector pegs on the Large Motor*

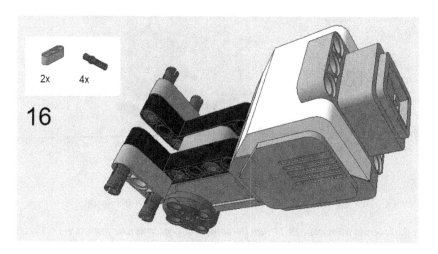

Figure 8-29. *Use the 3M connector pegs and 3M beams on each side*

Figure 8-30. *Insert two more 5 × 3 beams as shown*

Figure 8-31. *Insert the creation from steps 15-17 into the connector peg/cross axle from step 14. This isn't exactly a stable connection, but it will be secured in the next step*

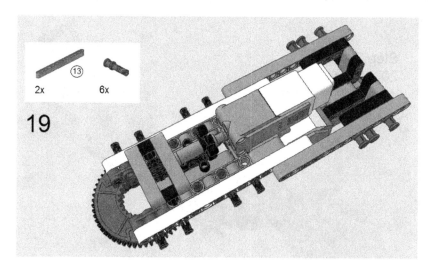

Figure 8-32. *Snap on a 13M beam on each side, and secure it into place with three friction snaps on each side*

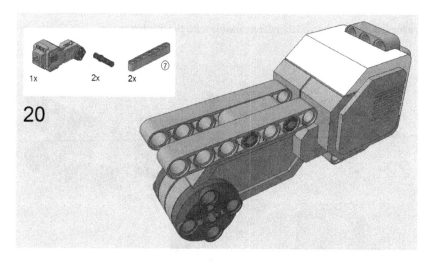

Figure 8-33. *Center the 3M connector pegs on the Large Motor, and snap on a 7M beam on each side*

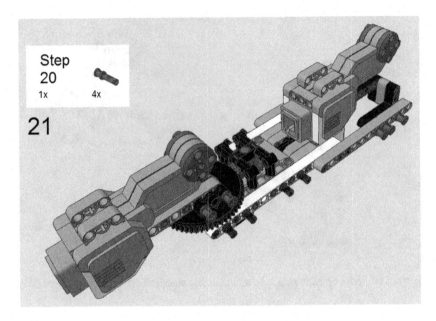

Figure 8-34. *Secure the creation from step 20 to the turntable with the friction snaps*

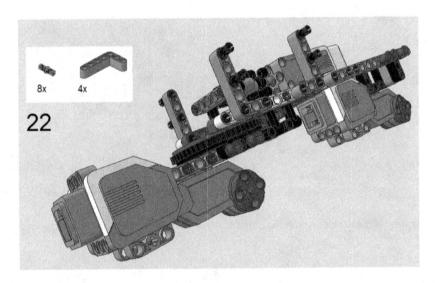

Figure 8-35. *Snap on two 5 × 3 beams on connector pegs on the sides, and put connector pegs on the 5 × 3 beams as shown*

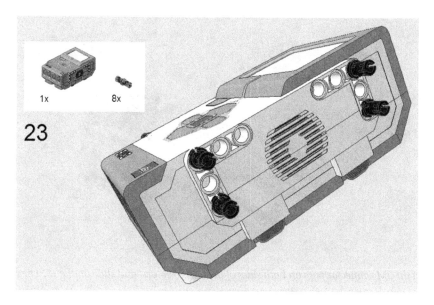

Figure 8-36. *Place four connector pegs on each side of the EV3 Brick as shown*

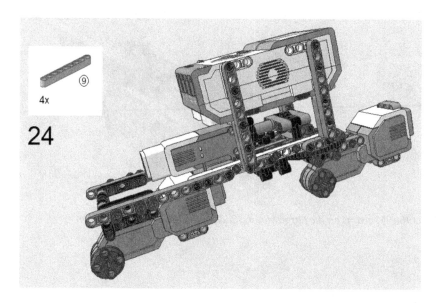

Figure 8-37. *Using the 9M beams, secure the EV3 Brick from the last step to the rest of the creation*

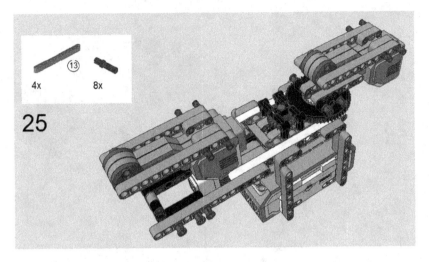

Figure 8-38. *Insert the 3M connector pegs on both sides of the Large Motors, and slide on the 13M beams*

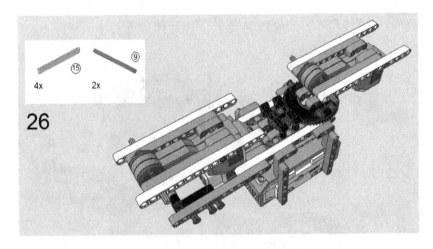

Figure 8-39. *Center the 9M beams on the Large Motors. Slide on the 15M beams as shown*

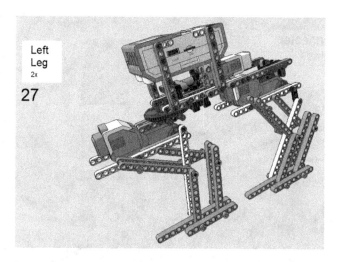

Figure 8-40. *Insert two left legs (Project 8-1) on the left side. Note the position of the steering knuckle arms*

Figure 8-41. *Insert two right legs (Project 8-2) on the right side. Note the position of the steering knuckle arms*

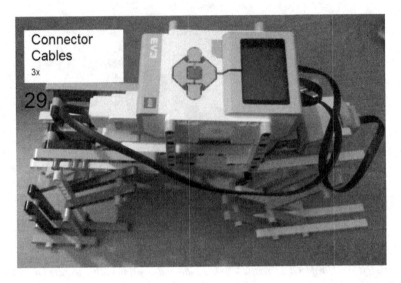

Figure 8-42. *Use connector cables to connect to the motors. Connect the Medium Motor to Port A, the front Large Motor to Port B, and the back Large Motor to Port C*

■ **Note** Just to make sure, remember that there needs to be a difference between the left and right leg. That is, the 3M levers in Steps 3 of both instructions have to be 180 degrees opposite. So if the 3M lever on the left front leg is pointing straight down, then the 3M levers on the left back leg must be pointing up. Manually adjust these legs if they are not correct.

Programming the Walking Robot

Now that your four-legged robot is built, it is time to get it up and walking. You will find that walking it forward is simple and only requires the Tank programming block, but you need to make certain to begin walking when the Levers are 180 degrees off on each side, as stated in the Note above. Figure 8-43 shows examples of what you can do with Adjust by Seconds, by Degrees, and by Rotations. I highly recommend that both B and C have the exact number of rotations, or you might get some weird walking results.

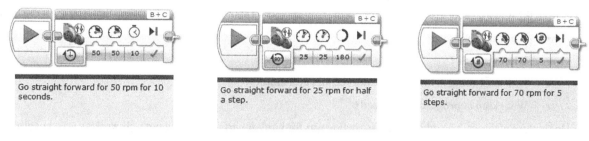

Figure 8-43. *A program for forward motion on the walking robot*

Of course, you are definitely going to want your walking vehicle to turn. You will notice that the turntable gives this ability to effectively swivel the front legs, and this gives the walker the ability to turn. I know that I have usually given very detailed instructions for programming, but now I am going to give you a crude program and let you fill in the details (see Figure 8-44).

Figure 8-44. *A program for how to make the walking robot turn*

You can see that the first programming block simply commands the two Large Motors to go forward, which ensures that the feet are moving forward. The second programming block commands them to stop. The third commands a turn for 90 degrees, and then stop. At the Fourth, only the Large Motor at Port B goes for five seconds, which is enough to start it turning. The fifth turns the front legs back 90 degrees, which straightens out the legs completely. Then the sixth commands the legs to go forward again, in a new direction.

You will notice that I did not specify how many actual degrees it will turn; I'm sure you have realized that the front legs won't turn at a right angle, as it cannot turn that far. As with all the projects, you will want to play around with it so you can get it down exactly. This means a lot of trial and error, and possibly trial by error. Eventually, you can program paths for it to follow and let it roam.

In fact, I highly recommend programming situations with the brick buttons or all other facets of the programming blocks. For example, the Gyro Sensor could be used on the front in order to calibrate a precise turn. Still, this takes a little trial by error to make this precise, and eventually you will find the right combination to produce the same results over and over again.

Summary and Final Words

Constructing a walking robot creation is a complicated undertaking, but the LEGO MINDSTORMS makes it easier. The key is creating legs that can move and yet somehow not topple the construction over. The legs that I have provided in this chapter will work well if you construct them properly.

In addition to constructing the walking creation, it is also important to program it properly for forward movement, as well as turning. It is possible to program to roam all across the floor.

I used the walking robot as an example of the four questions one should ask before building, that is:

- **What am I building?**

- **What will it do?**

- **How am I going to incorporate the sensors and motors?**

- **What kind of program will I need?**

In the case of the walking robot, the construction was the hardest part. It required not only working legs, but also a way of motorizing them. The construction had to be made solid so that these motors and the EV3 Brick were held together without any danger of coming apart. The four legs had to bear the weight, and the steering mechanism had to be flexible but also strong. I guarantee that constructing any LEGO MINDSTORMS creation will be the hardest step, not to mention positioning the sensors and motors to be just in the right places.

Yes, creating a LEGO MINDSTORMS creation is all about building and then building it again. You have to go for stability as well as versatility. In other words, you have to build it strong and build it to work at the same time.

In addition to building the construction, you also will have to program it, which can often be as hard as the physical building process. Like building, this involves programming something, and then programming it again to insure that your creation does exactly what you say it will do.

Therefore, I give one last piece of advice in two parts: Keep creating, and keep trying.

I know that I have already talked about the importance of creativity, and want to let you know that it is something that the world needs more of. There are way too many LEGO builders who just imitate a set of instructions, and that is a good way to learn. The point of learning is to do something different, and not just follow in the footsteps of those who have gone before you. This is why you should challenge yourself to make LEGO MINDSTORMS creations that no one else has ever made.

Once you get that idea, the chances are that you won't get it right the first time. You may have to build it, build it again, then re-design it, and repeat the process until you get it right. Even when you do get it right, you should build it again to make it even better.

As I said at the beginning of this book, I have no idea who is actually reading this. Perhaps you are not yet an adult, or you could be a senior citizen. Either way, I would give my two-part advice. Use the creative instinct that you have to make creations that are as lifelike as EV3 programming will allow them to be.

Index

Get the eBook for only $10!

Now you can take the weightless companion with you anywhere, anytime. Your purchase of this book entitles you to 3 electronic versions for only $10.

This Apress title will prove so indispensible that you'll want to carry it with you everywhere, which is why we are offering the eBook in 3 formats for only $10 if you have already purchased the print book.

Convenient and fully searchable, the PDF version enables you to easily find and copy code—or perform examples by quickly toggling between instructions and applications. The MOBI format is ideal for your Kindle, while the ePUB can be utilized on a variety of mobile devices.

Go to www.apress.com/promo/tendollars to purchase your companion eBook.